The Gift of Sublimation

The Gift of Sublimation

A Psychoanalytic Study of Multiple Masculinities

Nathan Carlin

and

Donald Capps

CASCADE *Books* · Eugene, Oregon

THE GIFT OF SUBLIMATION
A Psychoanalytic Study of Multiple Masculinities

Cascade Publications
An Imprint of Wipf and Stock Publishers
199 W. 8th Ave., Suite 3
Eugene, OR 97401

www.wipfandstock.com

ISBN 13: 978-1-4982-0301-2

Cataloguing-in-Publication Data

Carlin, Nathan.

    The gift of sublimation : a psychoanalytic study of multiple masculinities / Nathan Carlin and Donald Capps.

    xvi + 196 p. ; 23 cm. Includes bibliographical references.

    ISBN 13: 978-1-4982-0301-2

    1. Sublimation (Psychology). 2. Sublimation—Study and teaching. 3. James I, King of England (1566–1625). 4. Masturbation—Moral and ethical aspects—History. 5. Male homosexuality—Religious aspects—Christianity. I. Capps, Donald. II. Title.

BF175.5 S92 C100 2015

06/23/2015

Portions of chapters 1–6 are taken from the following articles: Donald Capps and Nathan Carlin, "Sigmund Freud and James Putnam: Friendship as a Form of Sublimation," *Pastoral Psychology* 59 (2010) 265–86; Donald Capps and Nathan Carlin, "The Homosexual Tendencies of King James: Should This Matter to Bible Readers Today?" *Pastoral Psychology* 55 (2007) 667–99; Donald Capps and Nathan Carlin, "Methuselah and Company: A Case of Male Envy of Female Longevity," *Pastoral Psychology* 58 (2009) 107–126; Donald Capps, "From Masturbation to Homosexuality: A Case of Displaced Moral Disapproval," *Pastoral Psychology* 51 (2003) 249–72; Donald Capps and Nathan Carlin, "The 'Religiously Mediated Change' of 11 Gay Men: A Case of Unexceptional Sublimation," *Pastoral Psychology* 57 (2008) 125–46; and Nathan Carlin, "God's Gender Confusion: Some Polymorphously Perverse Pastoral Theology," *Pastoral Psychology* 59 (2010) 109–24. Permission to reprint these portions is granted by Springer via the Copyright Clearance Center.

The sublimation of instinct is an especially conspicuous feature of cultural development; it is what makes it possible for higher psychical activities—scientific, artistic, or ideological—to play such an important part in civilized life, and one gains the most if one can sufficiently heighten the yield of pleasure from the sources of psychical and intellectual work.

—SIGMUND FREUD,
FROM *CIVILIZATION AND ITS DISCONTENT*

Contents

Acknowledgments

WE WOULD LIKE TO thank the editorial staff at Cascade Books and Wipf and Stock Publishers, especially Matthew Wimer, assistant managing editor, and K. C. Hanson, editor-in-chief. And we would like to thank Jeremy Funk for copyediting and Calvin Jaffarian for typesetting. We also would like to thank the marketing team—especially James Stock, marketing director. The two of us have published a number of books with Wipf and Stock Publishers, and, with each project, it has been a real pleasure working with the press. We are especially grateful for the press's commitment to publishing books in psychology of religion that are psychoanalytically oriented.

Portions of this book have been revised from previous publications in *Pastoral Psychology*. We would like to thank Springer for granting us permission to reprint this material via the Copyright Clearance Center.

In *The Interpretation of Dreams*, Sigmund Freud writes, "It seems a bad thing and detrimental to the creative work of the mind if Reason makes too close an examination of the ideas as they come pouring in—at the very gateway, as it were."[1] It is a rare thing to experience freedom in academic life. Sometimes this is because of the critical voices of others, and other times this is because of one's own inner critical voices. But we have attempted to embrace this advice from Freud both in our own individual work and in our collaborations together; this book is an expression of our generous exchanging of ideas, which we have experienced as liberating.

---

1. Freud, *The Interpretation of Dreams*, 103.

Introduction

IN THIS BOOK WE focus on one of Sigmund Freud's ideas—the idea of *sublimation*. We believe that this was one of his most important ideas, but it is rarely referred to in the books on psychoanalysis written for seminary students, pastors, pastoral counselors, or chaplains. As we will see in chapter 1, it was an idea that caught the attention of members of the audience who came to hear Freud lecture at Clark University in Worcester, Massachusetts, in 1909. In fact, some of them embraced psychoanalytic ways of thinking largely because of this idea.

In his own writings, Freud gave a great deal of attention to the role that sublimation plays in the work of artists.[1] Our emphasis here is on the role of sublimation in the lives of men, especially in their relationships with other men, but also with women. This means, as the subtitle indicates, that this book is a study of masculinity—specifically, a study of multiple masculinities. Masculinity studies, as a cognate of women's studies, can be seen as a subfield of gender studies. Our use of the term "multiple masculinities" implies that there is no single masculinity that is normative, and that conceptions of masculinity are not uniform across time periods or cultures, or even within a given society.[2] In this book, we assume such a point-of-view because it is descriptively accurate and we support its moral implications. However, we need to point out that this

1. For example, Freud, *Leonardo da Vinci and a Memory of His Childhood*; and Freud, "Moses of Michelangelo."

2. See Connell, *Masculinities*.

book is not an exhaustive or representative study of all the possible varieties of masculinities, as if such a task could be accomplished in a single book. We do not explore, for example, race, ethnicity, or economic class in relation to masculinity. The material included in this book has been influenced by two factors: (1) the debates surrounding homosexuality in Christian churches over the past several decades (debates concerning the morality of homosexual acts, for example, and debates regarding homosexuality and interpreting the Bible); and (2) issues relating to gender, especially the fact that women live longer than men do, and the religious significance of this fact. We believe that this gender difference has not received the attention it deserves in gender studies and in religious studies.

Over the past decade, we have coauthored three books and twelve articles, and it has seemed almost effortless.[3] We like to tell ourselves that this is because we, in our writing together, regress to what Erik H. Erikson has called "the play age," or roughly the age of three to five years old.[4] When one observes the play of children at this age, one notices that they typically engage in making things and performing scenes (i.e., playacting), and sometimes they work alone and other times they work together. When they do not feel as though they are under the watchful and critical eye of the teacher or another classmate, there is an air of contentment among them, and a quiet sense of intimacy pervades the classroom. This is the feeling that we have experienced in our writing together.

We noted above that religious sublimation is the psychoanalytic concept that has had a major part to play in our exploration of both the relationship between religion and sexuality and the relationship between religion and gender. Sublimation is a psychoanalytic term, and, in this regard, we know that psychoanalysis, the dream child of Freud, raises various red flags for potential readers, especially readers who have been informed that Freud was hostile toward religion. We believe, however, that this book presents a different Freud, and that it does so precisely because it focuses on his concept of sublimation. This concept will be explained and illustrated in much greater detail in the following chapters, but, in essence, it refers to the process of sexual desires considered unacceptable or unworthy becoming redirected toward what are considered acceptable and worthy interests and aspirations.[5]

---

3. The previous books are Capps and Carlin, *Living in Limbo*; and Carlin and Capps, *100 Years of Happiness*.

4. Erikson, *Toys and Reasons*, 98–103.

5. A significant text in this regard is Gay, *Freud on Sublimation*.

Chapter 1 provides an introduction to the concept of sublimation. It focuses on Freud's own writings on sublimation and places particular emphasis on what he said about sublimation in his lectures at Clark University in Worcester, Massachusetts, and on his subsequent correspondence with James Jackson Putnam, a Boston neurologist and therapist who was deeply influenced, both professionally and personally, by Freud's idea of sublimation. We suggest in this chapter that the friendship that developed between the two men was itself an illustration of the gift of sublimation.

Chapter 2 makes use of recent scholarship that has focused on the homosexual tendencies of King James, who commissioned the translation of the King James Bible. We suggest that the related pacifist tendencies of King James provided a scholarly model for male cooperation that was inherently superior to the martial model of male enterprise advocated by his opponents. Thus, we applaud King James for his religious sublimation of male aggression.

Chapter 3 focuses on sublimation and gender by means of the biblical story of Methuselah. On the basis of empirical evidence that women live longer than men because they bear children and engage in maternal activities toward their offspring, we argue that the exaggerated ages of men in the Bible are a case of male envy of women's longevity, and we propose that these feelings of envy may be sublimated through their own assumption of maternal roles toward infants and children. Thus, chapters 1, 2, and 3 make the case for a more *relational* understanding of masculinity than is typically the case in writings and pronouncements on men and manhood. It is noteworthy in this connection that the dictionary defines *masculine* as "having qualities regarded as characteristic of men and boys, such as strength, vigor, boldness, etc.; manly; virile."[6]

Chapters 4 and 5 focus on aspects of the sexual revolution of the 1960s and subsequent decades that have particular relevance to American religious culture, to which we and (we assume) the majority of our readers belong. Chapter 4 focuses on religious and philosophical expressions of the moral disapproval of masturbation, a disapproval that was supported in the nineteenth and early twentieth centuries by the medical community, which attributed many physical, emotional, and mental problems to masturbation. We suggest that the decline in moral disapproval of masturbation in the 1960s has been redirected toward homosexuality and, as

---

6. Agnes, *Webster's New World College Dictionary*, 883.

a result, homosexuality has been subjected to greater moral disapproval over the past several decades than in earlier decades.

This chapter sets the stage for chapter 5, which centers on the efforts of a church community to covert men with a homosexual orientation to a heterosexual orientation. We conclude that the sublimation of sexual desires that some of the men experienced as a result of these efforts is a case of *unexceptional* sublimation, which is to say that their adoption of a heterosexual masculinity—however significant it may have been for them personally—is not the major achievement that its promoters have made it out to be.

Chapter 6 proposes the way forward and takes into account the fact that the authors identify themselves as pastoral psychologists (more on this below). Thus, it playfully—and seriously—deals with contemporary discussions of religion, gender, and sexuality by suggesting that the God of the Bible is gender confused and has made some rather poor decisions in the midst of this confusion. If God were able to accept a wider range of masculinities and sexualities, he/she would be much better off, and so would the Christian men who relate to the Bible and its portrayal of the divine Being. We have every reason to believe that God has, in fact, accepted a wider range of masculinities and sexualities. As was said of the most godly man in human history, "he [has gone] ahead of [us] into Galilee" (Matt 28:7–10).[7]

As our title and subtitle indicate, this book is a psychoanalytic exploration because of its emphasis on sublimation. But the book also reflects the fact that we, as we noted, consider ourselves to be pastoral psychologists. We think of pastoral psychology as being similar to psychology of religion in that both typically ask the same questions and use similar methods of inquiry, but pastoral psychology implies an element of faith or belief and thus an affirmative though not uncritical stance toward religion. The qualifying word *pastoral* also implies that the ultimate objective of pastoral psychology is to be genuinely helpful to those who read and reflect on what it has to say. For example, in an article on male body image and intimacy, Nathan Carlin discusses the fact that friendship tends to be a part of homosexual identity in a way that is usually not the case for most heterosexual men.[8] He cites Andrew Sullivan's suggestion that heterosexual men's fear of intimacy is intrinsically connected to

7. See Capps and Carlin, *Living in Limbo*, 40–42.

8. Carlin, "From Grace *Alone* to *Grace* Alone."

a fear of homosexuality, and that this fear has "too often denied straight men the bonds they need to sustain themselves through life's difficulties," meaning that "when they socialize, they too often demand the chaperone of sports or work to avoid the appearance of being gay. Or they need to congregate in groups that tend to diminish the quiet intimacy that all of us need."[9] We would simply want to add that, in addition to the need for quiet intimacy, men—gay, straight, or otherwise—also have a need for thoughtful community, and both needs take us back to the play age and to the scene of small boys playing together in a nonthreatening environment. This was the spirit in which we wrote the chapters of this book; it also is the spirit in which we hope our readers will engage what we have written here.

9. Sullivan, *Love Undetectable*, 234–35.

PART I

The Liberating Effects
of Sublimation

––––––––––– 1 –––––––––––

Freud's Idea of Sublimation

Introduction

IN HIS SHORT GLOSSARY of Freudian ideas and concepts Nick Rennison defines *sublimation* in this way:

> Sublimation—the unconscious mental process by which instinctual, socially unacceptable energy or libido is transferred to a non-instinctual, socially acceptable activity, e.g., Freud believed that the sublimation of unsatisfied libido was behind the creation of great art and literature.[1]

Rennison describes *libido* in this way:

> Libido—in psychoanalytic theory, the sexual drive and energy which is directed towards individuals and objects in the outside world. Neurotic and other psychiatric illnesses are often the result of libido that is inappropriately directed.[2]

In this chapter we will present Freud's concept of sublimation, focusing on his presentation of the concept in several of his writings, including

1. Rennison, *Freud & Psychoanalysis*, 89.
2. Ibid., 87.

Five Lectures on Psychoanalysis, which he delivered at Clark University in Worcester, Massachusetts, in 1909.[3]

The Concept of Sublimation

Freud spoke about sublimation in his *Introductory Lectures on Psycho-Analysis,* which he presented in two successive winter terms at the University of Vienna (1915 and 1916). In the first lecture he commented on the fact that psychoanalysis has been criticized for asserting that instinctual impulses that must be described as sexual, in both the wider and narrower sense of the word, play an extremely large role in the causation of neuroses. But, Freud noted, psychoanalysis has emphasized that these same sexual impulses also make contributions "to the highest cultural, artistic and social creations of the human spirit."[4]

Freud also notes that the second assertion has been subject to even greater criticism than the first, and suggests that the reason for this is that psychoanalysis holds that civilization has been created under the pressure of the exigencies of life at the cost of the instincts. Moreover, psychoanalysts believe that, because civilization is constantly being re-created, "each individual who makes a fresh entry into human society repeats this sacrifice of instinctual satisfaction for the benefit of the whole community."[5] While various instinctual forces are subject to this sacrifice, among them the sexual impulses play an important role. In this process, "they are sublimated—that is to say, they are diverted from their sexual aims and directed to others that are socially higher and no longer sexual."[6]

The problem is that this arrangement is unstable. The sexual instincts are "imperfectly tamed," and so in every individual who is supposed to join in the work of civilization there is the risk that his or her sexual instincts may refuse to be put to that use. From the perspective of society, no greater threat to its civilization could arise than if the sexual instincts were to be liberated and returned to their original aims, and for this reason society "does not wish to be reminded of this precarious portion of its foundations."[7] So, because psychoanalysis points out that this

---

3. Freud, *Five Lectures on Psycho-Analysis.*

4. Freud, *Introductory Lectures on Psycho-Analysis,* 26.

5. Ibid., 27.

6. Ibid.

7. Ibid.

process is going on all the time and that every individual is subject to it, psychoanalysis is subjected to a great deal of antipathy.

Freud returns to the topic of sublimation in his twenty-third lecture on the paths to the formation of neurotic symptoms. At the very end of the lecture, he cites the case of the artist who, typically an introvert, has a natural tendency toward neurosis. The artist is possessed by powerful instinctual needs, including desires for honor, power, wealth, fame, and sex, but he is not able to achieve these satisfactions. So he turns away from reality to the life of fantasy and transfers all his libido to the wishful constructions of his fantasies. This path could lead to neurosis. But if his constitution includes a "strong capacity for sublimation," this could enable him to shape some particular material until it has become a faithful image of his fantasy and yield him a great deal of pleasure. The artist also makes it possible for others to derive a similar pleasure that outweighs the fact that their own instinctual desires have been repressed and are no longer accessible to them. Freud concludes the lecture with the observation that when this occurs the artist earns the gratitude and admiration of others and thereby achieves *through* his fantasy what he had originally achieved only *in* his fantasy—that is, through sublimation he subsequently achieves honor, power, wealth, fame, and sex.[8]

In *Group Psychology and the Analysis of the Ego*, originally published in 1921, Freud makes a brief reference to sublimation that has bearing on the fact that some sublimations are religious in nature. His observation occurs in the postscript. He notes that a psychology that will not or cannot penetrate the depths of what is repressed considers affectionate emotional ties to be the expression of forces that have no sexual aims in spite of the fact that they are actually derived from such aims. In contrast, psychoanalysis recognizes that these affectionate emotional ties have been diverted from their original sexual aims. Freud confesses that it is difficult to describe this diversion of aims, but we know that the instincts

8. Ibid., 467–68. Later, in his lecture on transference, Freud comments briefly on the role that sublimation may play in the relationship between the analyst and the patient, and notes that it relates to the patient's wish to be loved by the analyst. He suggests that some women "succeed in sublimating this transference" of feelings onto the doctor and "in molding it till it achieves a kind of viability" whereas other women continue to express these transference-related feelings in their "rude, original, and for the most part, impossible form" (ibid., 550). In his following lecture on analytic therapy, Freud indicates that, through interpretation, which transforms what is unconscious into what is conscious, the ego becomes more conciliatory toward the libido and allows it to be expressed in a sublimated form.

preserve some of their original sexual aims. Thus, "an affectionate devotee, even a friend or an admirer, desires the physical proximity and the sight of the person who is now loved only in the 'Pauline' sense."[9]

Freud suggests that we may recognize in this diversion of aim the "beginning of the *sublimation* of the sexual instincts," or, if we choose, we may wish to "fix the limits of sublimation at some more distant point."[10] He implies here that there is some flexibility in the very idea or concept of sublimation, that some may think of it as occurring at the point when the original sexual aim is relinquished while others may want to reserve the term *sublimation* for a later stage in the process (i.e., when something of discernible social value is realized or achieved). In either case, what is noteworthy here is that Freud refers to love in the "Pauline" sense, that is, a form of expression of love that is spiritual in nature. He wants to suggest that such spiritual expressions of love have their origins in sexual desires that have undergone repression.[11]

In light of his observation in *Introductory Lectures on Psycho-Analysis* that this diversion of sexual aims is often unstable, it is interesting that Freud goes on to cite an example provided by his friend Oskar Pfister, a Swiss pastor who became an early convert to psychoanalytic ways of thinking, in Pfister's book titled *Frömmigkeit des Graften von Zinzendorf*: "of how easily even an intense religious tie can revert to ardent sexual excitement."[12] On the other hand, Freud points out that it is also very

9. Freud, *Group Psychology and the Analysis of the Ego*, 91.

10. Ibid. (italics original).

11. We are reminded here of cases in which pastors have used the word *love* in a spiritual sense, only to have it construed as having sexual connotations. See Capps, *Giving Counsel*, 235. Freud's suggestion that spiritual expressions of love have their origins in sexual desires that have undergone repression suggests that there are grounds for such construals, however implausible this may seem.

12. Freud, *Group Psychology and the Analysis of the Ego*, 92. Pfister's best-known book is *Christianity and Fear*. Freud returns later in the postscript to his earlier discussion (in chapter 5) of the church and the army (in which he suggested that both are "artificial groups" in the sense that "an external force is employed to prevent them from disintegrating and to check alterations in their structure" [*Group Psychology*, 32]). He notes that the Roman Catholic Church had "the best of motives for recommending its followers to remain unmarried and for imposing celibacy upon its priests; but falling in love has often driven even priests to leave the Church" [ibid., 94–95]. Freud adds that, in the same way, love for women by men "breaks through the group ties of race, of national divisions, and of the social class system, and it thus produces important effects as a factor in civilization," and that "homosexual love is far more compatible with group ties, even when it takes the shape of uninhibited sexual impulses—a remarkable fact, the explanation of which might carry us far" [ibid., 95].

usual for sexual impulses, "short-lived in themselves, to be transformed into a lasting and purely affectionate tie; and the consolidation of a passionate love marriage rests to a large extent upon this process."[13]

If Freud emphasizes in *Group Psychology and the Analysis of the Ego* the sublimation of instinctual desires in the form of affectionate emotional ties, in *Civilization and Its Discontents*, originally published in 1930, he focuses on the sublimation of instinctual desires in the form of work. He acknowledges that work is often experienced as drudgery and that we do not look upon it as a source of pleasure. In fact, we tend to think of pleasures as experiences that occur only when we are not working. Yet, he cites the technique of shifting instinctual aims "in such a way that they cannot come up against the frustrations from the external world," and here "sublimation of the instincts lends its assistance."[14] What this involves is heightening the yield of pleasure from the sources of physical and intellectual work. Freud thinks in this regard of "an artist's joy in creating, in giving his fantasies body, or a scientist's in solving problems or discovering truths," and notes that although we may not be able to account fully for this sense of pleasure, it seems "finer and higher" than the pleasures derived from "the sating of crude and primary instinctual impulses."[15]

In a footnote, he suggests that no other technique for the conduct of life "attaches the individual so firmly to reality as laying emphasis on work," for one's work at least gives one "a secure place in a portion of reality, in the human community."[16] Freud adds that professional activity "is a source of special satisfaction if it is a freely chosen one—if, that is to say, by means of sublimation, it makes possible the use of existing inclinations, of persisting or constitutionally reinforced instinctual impulses."[17] Unfortunately, work is not highly prized as a path of happiness, and few of us strive after it as we do other possibilities of satisfaction. In fact, "the great majority of people only work under the stress of necessity, and this natural human aversion to work raises most difficult social problems."[18]

---

13. Ibid.

14. Freud, *Civilization and Its Discontents*, 29.

15. Ibid., 30.

16. Ibid.

17. Ibid.

18. Ibid.

Nevertheless, it is noteworthy that Freud considers work to be a sublimation of sexual impulses that are otherwise socially unacceptable. Given the examples of sublimation he offers in *Group Psychology and the Analysis of the Ego* and in *Civilization and Its Discontents*, it is also noteworthy that when he was asked what he thought a normal person should be able to do well, he replied "to love and to work."[19]

Finally, as his allusion to "Pauline" love suggests, some sublimations have religious associations and meanings. This is not surprising, for religion, after all, is an expression of civilization itself. It is also deeply implicated in other expressions of civilization, such as the ones that Freud himself discusses in the writings we have considered here (i.e., art and the sociopolitical order). It is especially noteworthy in this case that in *Moses and Monotheism*, which was published after his death (in 1939), Freud suggests that "the special peculiarities of a monotheistic religion borrowed by Egypt" shaped the character of the Jewish people "through the disdaining of magic and mysticism and encouraging them to progress in spirituality and sublimation."[20]

Because most scholars tend to believe that Freud was irreligious, they have overlooked the fact that he recognized that sublimations may take a religious form. This does not mean, of course, that he would endorse all religious sublimations, or that we should do so. In fact, in Freud's case history of a Russian patient of his, Sergei Pankejeff, he notes that when he was a young boy Sergei's inappropriate sexual instincts were sublimated through the efforts of his mother and his nurse, who introduced him to the sacred stories of the Christian religion. As Freud puts it, "Religion did its work for this hard-pressed child—by the combination which it afforded the believer of satisfaction, of sublimation, of diversion from sensual processes to purely spiritual ones, and of access to social relationships."[21]

However, in Freud's view, the sublimation *was* successful for Sergei Pankejeff in the educational sense, but it was ineffectual as far as Sergei's obsessional neurosis was concerned. Moreover, "a lasting disadvantage" resulted from the fact that the sublimation process "had led to a victory for the faith of piety over the rebelliousness of critical research."[22] Sup-

---

19. See Erikson, *Identity: Youth and Crisis*, 136.

20. Freud, *Moses and Monotheism*, 108–9.

21. Freud, *History of an Infantile Neurosis*, 115.

22. Ibid., 70.

porting this conclusion was the fact that Sergei's "intellectual activity remained seriously impaired," for "he developed no zeal for learning."[23] Freud also notes that Pankejeff's homosexual feelings toward his father were repressed through his identification with Christ and the divine Father, and that this kept the sexual impulse directed toward its original aim "and withdrew it from all the sublimations to which it is susceptible in other circumstances."[24] It was only when this impulse was liberated through psychoanalysis years later that it could be redirected toward other social interests.

Having surveyed various writings of Freud's on sublimation, we would now like to turn to his *Five Lectures on Psycho-Analysis*. As we noted above, these lectures were delivered in 1909 at Clark University in Worcester, Massachusetts.

Freud's Visit to America

Accompanied by Carl G. Jung and Sandor Ferenczi, Freud made a "historic expedition" to America in 1909.[25] Freud was fifty-three years old when the three colleagues made the trip; Jung was thirty-four; and Ferenczi was thirty-five. The occasion was the twentieth anniversary of the founding of Clark University. At the insistence of G. Stanley Hall, its first president, Clark University was established as a graduate school designed for the training of scientists, scholars, and teachers, and for twelve years it had remained an exclusively graduate-level institution. However, when its founder, Jonas Clark, died, an undergraduate college was added because he had explicitly provided for it in his will and designated that it not be under Hall's administration.[26]

Hall, a psychologist, was deeply invested in the study of children and had recently published his two-volume work on adolescence.[27] Previously, he had written articles on moral and religious education.[28] Later

---

23. Ibid.

24. Ibid.

25. Rosenzweig, *Historic Expedition to America*.

26. Ibid., 19.

27. Hall, *Adolescence*.

28. Hall, "Moral and Religious Training of Children"; Hall, "Religious Content of the Child-Mind"; and Hall, "Some Fundamental Principles of Sunday School and Bible Teaching."

he wrote a book on Jesus.[29] Hall had formulated a plan for a Children's Institute at Clark University, and his invitation to Freud to participate in the twentieth-anniversary celebration was part of an attempt to enlist Freud in furthering his aims in establishing the Children's Institute. As Saul Rosenzweig points out, "He saw Freud as a developmental psychologist whose views on early childhood, including sexuality and the unconscious, were crucial for understanding the child below the surface of everyday observation."[30] Freud declined Hall's first invitation on the grounds that he could not afford to lose three weeks of private practice. He accepted the second invitation when Hall nearly doubled the honorarium intended to cover travel expenses, indicated that Freud would receive an honorary degree, and stated that the conference would be moved from July to September, which would not interfere with Freud's private practice. Rosenzweig suggests that Jung was invited to replace a previously invited lecturer on pedagogy and that Freud had played a role in arranging for his invitation.[31]

Twenty-nine lecturers participated in the conference (eight of whom were in the behavioral sciences), and all were awarded honorary degrees. Freud delivered five lectures, and Jung delivered three. Freud invited Ferenczi to accompany him to the United States, but he did not present any lectures. William James, the Harvard professor in philosophy and psychology and author of *The Varieties of Religious Experience*,[32] arrived in Worcester on Thursday afternoon. He attended Jung's lecture (which was on word association) and Freud's lecture (which was on the interpretation of dreams) on Friday morning. Later that day, James invited Freud to walk with him to the Union Depot, where James would take the train for Boston. In his autobiographical study, Freud describes what happened:

> I shall never forget one little scene that occurred as we were on a walk together. He stopped suddenly, handed me a bag he was carrying and asked me to walk on, saying that he would catch me up as soon as he had got through an attack of angina pectoris which was just coming on. He died of that disease a year later;

29. Hall, *Jesus, the Christ, in the Light of Psychology*.

30. Rosenzweig, *Historic Expedition to America*, 23.

31. Ibid., 36–37.

32. James, *Varieties of Religious Experience*.

and I have always wished that I might be as fearless as he was in the face of approaching death.[33]

Although Freud took James's self-diagnosis at face value, Rosenzweig suggests that James may have suffered a brief lapse of consciousness (*petit mal*) prompted by the fact that Freud had lectured on dreams, for James had mentioned having had several lapses in consciousness in recent months, one of which had to do with dreams.[34] In any event, James wrote in a letter to a friend that he had gone to the conference "in order to see what Freud was like," and added that he hoped "Freud and his pupils will push their ideas to their utmost limits, so that we may learn what they are," for "they can't fail to throw light on human nature."[35] On the other hand, the impression that Freud made on James personally was that of "a man obsessed with fixed ideas"; and "I can make nothing in my own case with his dream theories, and obviously 'symbolism' is a most dangerous method."[36]

Another significant person who attended the conference was James Jackson Putnam. Like Freud's, his medical training was in neurology and he was one of the country's foremost pioneers in the Boston psychotherapeutic movement. He was also noted for his communal activism: he worked with charities and led campaigns against the use of neurologically damaging substances in common building materials.[37] Putnam's book *Human Motives*, published in 1915, contains chapters on the psychoanalytic movement and its educational value.[38] This is what Freud wrote about him in his autobiographical study:

> We also met James J. Putnam there, the Harvard neurologist, who in spite of his age [he was sixty-two years old] was an enthusiastic supporter of psychoanalysis and threw the whole weight of a personality that was universally respected into the defense of the cultural value of analysis and the purity of its aims. He was an estimable man, in whom, as a reaction against a predisposition to obsessional neurosis, an ethical bias predominated; and the only thing in him that we would regret was his inclination to

33. Freud, *Autobiographical Study*, 99.

34. Rosenzweig, *Historic Expedition to America*, 177; James, "Suggestion about Mysticism."

35. Rosenzweig, *Historic Expedition to America*, 174.

36. Ibid.

37. Prochnik, *Putnam Camp*, 6.

38. Putnam, *Human Motives*, 67–133.

attach psychoanalysis to a particular philosophical system and to make it the servant of moral aims.[39]

Putnam invited Freud, Jung, and Ferenczi to a three-day sojourn at his camp in the Adirondacks following the conference. The camp had been purchased in 1876 by Putnam and his brother Charles, William James, and Henry Bowditch, a physiology professor at Harvard.

In his book on Putnam's camp, George Prochnik provides a full account of this three-day sojourn and of Putnam's work in behalf of psychoanalysis in America. He emphasizes that Putnam was profoundly impressed by Freud's presentation of the idea of sublimation in his fifth and closing lecture, and imagines that Putnam may well have steered the conversation toward this topic during the sojourn at Putnam Camp.[40] In any event, the subject of sublimation was a very prominent feature of their correspondence over the next several years (1909–1916). We will turn to this correspondence later in the chapter. But here we would simply note that when Freud learned of Putnam's death in 1918, he said that Putnam "was a pillar of psychoanalysis in his country" and added that, due to the war which had recently ended, he had received no news from America the past two years and now, he lamented, the news was that he had lost "dear old Putnam."[41]

Freud's Presentation of His Concept of Sublimation

Because his lectures were presented extemporaneously in German, Freud wrote them out after his return to Vienna, largely at the instigation of G. Stanley Hall, who was planning to have them translated for publication in the *American Journal of Psychology*, of which he was founder and editor. He wanted to devote a single issue to Freud. In the course of writing the lectures, Freud made extensive changes, moving large amounts of material from one lecture to another. However, the general theme of the lectures was "On Psychoanalysis" and the topics of the individual lectures

39. Freud, *Autobiographical Study*, 98–99.

40. Prochnik, *Putnam Camp*, 37.

41. Prochnik, *Putnam Camp*, 375. Another early supporter of Freud was Isador H. Coriat, a psychiatrist in Boston. After Putnam's death he was the only practicing psychoanalyst in Boston. His views on sublimation as a goal of psychoanalysis were very similar to Freud's. He wrote two books on psychoanalysis, *What is Psychoanalysis?* and *Repressed Emotions* (see Capps and Carlin, "Sublimation and Symbolization").

are as follows: (1) Beginnings: Breuer and the treatment of hysteria; (2) Methods of therapy: resistance and repression; (3) Free association and determinism; humor and slips; the interpretation of dreams; (4) Sexuality in normal development and in neurosis; and (5) Transference, sublimation, and culture.[42]

In the fifth lecture, Freud began by alluding to the topic of the previous lecture, in which he had discussed "infantile sexuality and the tracing back of neurotic symptoms to erotic instinctual components."[43] He went on:

> The deeper you penetrate into the pathogenesis of nervous illness, the more you will find revealed the connection between the neuroses and other productions of the human mind, including the most valuable. You will be taught that we humans, with the high standards of our civilization and under the pressure of our internal repressions, find reality unsatisfying quite generally, and for that reason entertain a life of fantasy in which we like to make up for the insufficiencies of reality by the production of wish-fulfillments.[44]

Freud notes that the "energetic and successful man is one who succeeds by his efforts in turning his wishful fantasies into reality," but where this effort fails "as a result of the resistances of the external world and of the subject's own weakness, he begins to turn away from reality and withdraws into his more satisfying world of fantasy, the content of which is transformed into symptoms should he fall ill."[45]

However, in certain favorable circumstances "it remains possible for him to find another path leading from these fantasies to reality, instead

42. Rosenzweig, *Historic Expedition to America*, 393. Regarding the first lecture, at the time Breuer and Freud collaborated on their book *Studies on Hysteria*, published in 1893, Breuer (1842–1925) had a large practice in Vienna and a reputation as a man of scientific attainments, while Freud (1856–1939) was just qualifying as a doctor. However, the two men had been friends for some years. See Breuer and Freud, *Studies on Hysteria*. As for lectures 3 and 4, as noted earlier, William James's attendance at the fourth lecture prompted him to make comments about Freud's views on dream interpretation. In the published lectures, Freud moved this material to the third lecture. This relocation also explains why James had nothing to say about Freud's views on sexuality.

43. Freud, *Five Lectures on Psycho-Analysis*, 54.

44. Ibid., 55.

45. Ibid.

of becoming permanently estranged from it by regressing to infancy."[46] For example:

> If a person who is at loggerheads with reality possesses an *artistic gift* (a thing that is still a psychological mystery to us), he can transform his fantasies into artistic creations instead of into symptoms. In this manner he can escape the doom of neurosis and by this roundabout path regain his contact with reality.[47]

By this "roundabout path" one regains one's relation to reality. But "If there is persistent rebellion against the real world and if this precious gift is absent or insufficient, it is almost inevitable that the libido, keeping to the sources of the fantasies, will follow the path of regression, and will revive infantile wishes and end in neurosis."[48] Freud adds that today "neurosis takes the place of monasteries which used to be the refuge of all whom life had disappointed or who felt too weak to face it."[49]

Freud then notes that the chief result of psychoanalytic investigation of neurotics is that "neuroses have no psychic content that is peculiar to them and that might not equally be found in healthy persons."[50] Thus, whether the "struggle between the conflicting forces ends in health, in neurosis, or in a countervailing superiority of achievement "depends on *quantitative* considerations, on the relative strength of the conflicting forces."[51]

This conclusion leads to a discussion of the role that transference plays in the psychoanalysis of a neurotic patient. Freud introduces the notion of transference because it proves the power of the sexual drive in neuroses. Transference, he explains, occurs when the patient "directs toward the physician a degree of affectionate feeling (mingled, often enough, with hostility) which is based on no real relation between them and which—as is shown by every detail of its emergence—can only be traced back to old wishful fantasies of the patient's which have become unconscious."[52] Only by reexperiencing these feelings in the therapeutic relationship does the patient become convinced of the existence and the

---

46. Ibid.
47. Ibid., 55–56. Here Freud cites Otto Rank's *Der Künstler*.
48. Ibid., 56.
49. Ibid.
50. Ibid.
51. Ibid.
52. Ibid., 56–57.

power of these unconscious sexual impulses. It is also important to note that the analytic process itself does not create this transference (transference arises spontaneously in all human relationships), and what makes the psychoanalytic process different is that it reveals this transference "to consciousness and gains control of it in order to guide psychical processes towards the desired goal."[53]

A brief discussion of the allegation that psychoanalysis does more harm than good follows. Freud addresses the concern that the patient's "cultural acquisitions" will be destroyed by the release of his repressed impulses. This concern, he argues, fails to take account "of what our experiences have taught us with certainty—namely that the mental and somatic power of a wishful impulse, when once its repression has failed, is far stronger if it is unconscious than if it is conscious, so that to make it conscious can only be to weaken it."[54] He adds, "An unconscious wish cannot be influenced and is independent of all opposing tendencies, whereas a conscious one can be inhibited by everything that is similarly conscious and stands in opposition to it. Psychoanalytic work, therefore, provides a better substitute for unsuccessful repression precisely by serving the interests of the highest and most valued endeavors."[55]

The Fate of Liberated Unconscious Wishes

This declaration brings Freud to the issue of sublimation, the concluding topic of the lecture and of the whole lecture series on psychoanalysis. He introduces the topic of sublimation by asking two related questions: "What, then, becomes of the unconscious wishes which have been set free by psycho-analysis?" And, "Along what paths do we succeed in making them harmless to the subject's life?"[56] He suggests that there are "several such paths" that these unconscious wishes, now freed by psychoanalysis, may take:

> The most frequent outcome is that, while the work is actually going on, these wishes are destroyed by the rational mental activity of the better impulses that are opposed to them. *Repression* is replaced by a *condemning judgment* carried out along the best

53. Ibid., 57.
54. Ibid., 59.
55. Ibid.
56. Ibid.

lines. That is possible because what we have to get rid of is to a great extent only the consequences arising from earlier stages of the ego's development.[57]

In the past, the patient was able only to repress "the unserviceable instinct because he himself was at that time imperfectly organized and feeble." But now, "in his present maturity and strength, he will perhaps be able to master what is hostile to him with complete success.[58]

A second outcome of the work of psychoanalysis is that it becomes possible for the unconscious instincts that have been uncovered by psychoanalysis to be "employed for the useful purposes which they would have found earlier if development had not been interrupted."[59] Freud explains,

> For the extirpation of the infantile wishful impulses is by no means the ideal aim of development. Owing to their repressions, neurotics have sacrificed many sources of mental energy whose contributions would have been of great value in the formation of their character and in the activity of life. We know of a far more expedient process of development, called "*sublimation*," in which the energy of the infantile wishful impulses is not cut off but remains ready for use—the unserviceable aim of the various impulses being replaced by one that is higher, and perhaps no longer sexual.[60]

Freud adds that it is the components of the *sexual* instincts that are especially accessible to "this kind of sublimation, for exchanging their sexual aim for another one which is comparatively remote and socially valuable."[61] In fact, "it is probably that we owe our highest cultural successes to the contributions of energy made in this way to our mental functions. Premature repression makes the sublimation of the repressed instinct impossible; when the repression is lifted, the path to sublimation becomes free once more."[62]

There is, however, a third possible outcome of the work of psychoanalysis. Freud explains,

57. Ibid.
58. Ibid., 59–60.
59. Ibid., 60.
60. Ibid. (italics original).
61. Ibid.
62. Ibid.

A certain portion of the repressed libidinal impulses has a claim to direct satisfaction and ought to find it in life. Our civilized standards make life too difficult for the majority of human organizations. Those standards consequently encourage the retreat from reality and the generating of neuroses, without achieving any surplus of cultural gain by this excess of sexual repression. We ought not to exalt ourselves so high as completely to neglect what was originally animal in our nature. Nor should we forget that the satisfaction of the individual's happiness cannot be erased from among the aims of our civilization.[63]

Thus, we need to view the second outcome of psychoanalysis—that of *sublimation*—with a degree of caution:

The plasticity of the components of sexuality, shown by their capacity for sublimation, may indeed offer a great temptation to strive for still greater cultural achievements by still further sublimation. But, just as we do not count on our machines converting more than a certain fraction of the heat consumed into useful mechanical work, we ought not to seek to alienate the whole amount of the energy of the sexual instinct from its proper ends. We cannot succeed in doing so; and if the restriction upon sexuality were to be carried too far it would inevitably bring with it all the evils of soil-exhaustion.[64]

Noting that his audience may regard this warning as an exaggeration, he "ventures on an indirect picture of my conviction" by relating an old story and leaving to them to make use of it as they choose. He continues:

German literature is familiar with a little town called Schilda, to whose inhabitants clever tricks of every possible sort are attributed. The citizens of Schilda, so we are told, possessed a horse with whose feats of strength they were highly pleased and against which they had only one objection—that it consumed such a large quantity of expensive oats. They determined to break it of this bad habit very gently by reducing its ration by a few stalks every day, till they had accustomed it to complete abstinence. For a time things went excellently: the horse was weaned to the point of eating only one stalk a day, and on the succeeding day it was at length to work without any oats at all. On the morning of

63. Ibid., 60–61.
64. Ibid., 61.

that day the spiteful animal was found dead; and the citizens of Schilda could not make out what it had died of.[65]

Freud comments: "We should be inclined to think that the horse was starved and that no work at all could be expected of an animal without a certain modicum of oats."[66] And with this observation he concluded his lecture, thanking his audience "for your invitation and for the attention with which you have listened to me."[67] Thus, his last official words to his American audience were ones that cautioned against the temptation "to strive for still greater cultural achievements by still further sublimation."[68]

Sublimation and Psychoanalytic Method

As we noted earlier, Freud and Putnam corresponded on a regular basis over the next seven years. In the first of these letters (dated November 17, 1909) Putnam began by stating that Freud's "visit to America was of deep significance to me," and then went on to say that although he had begun to use psychoanalytic methods in his therapeutic work, he felt that the "psychoanalytic method needs to be supplemented by methods which seek to hold up before the patient some goal toward which he [or she] may strive." [69] For example,

> I am now treating a lady of much intelligence—a school-teach-er—who is a great sufferer from morbid self-consciousness and blushing. I am making good headway and tracing out the origin of these symptoms, but find that I have also to meet the difficulty that she has lost all interest in life and living. The current theories of the universe do not bring her any satisfaction, her work bores her, and she wishes only to "get out." I feel that it ought to be possible for us to work up ways of dealing systematically with such a state of mind as this. Perhaps you would say and perhaps it is true, that a complete psychoanalysis accomplishes this result by discovering the causes for the state of general discouragement but if that is so I should like to see that side of the matter developed more fully.[70]

65. Ibid., 61–62.
66. Ibid., 62.
67. Ibid.
68. Ibid.
69. Hale, *James Jackson Putnam and Psychoanalysis*, 87.
70. Ibid.

In his response (dated December 5, 1909) Freud wrote that he thought Putnam's "complaint that we are not able to compensate our neurotic patients for giving up their illness is quite justified."[71] On the other hand,

> It seems to me that this is not the fault of therapy but rather of social institutions. What would you have us do when a woman complains about her thwarted life; when, with youth gone, she notices that she has been deprived of the joy of loving for merely conventional reasons? She is quite right, and we stand helpless before her, for we cannot make her young again. But the recognition of our therapeutic limitations reinforces our determination to change other social factors so that men and women shall no longer be forced into hopeless situations.[72]

Freud goes on to suggest that our "therapeutic impotence" indicates the need for the prevention of the neuroses, but, in any case, "Where the conditions are not so hopeless sublimation creates new goals as soon as the repressions are lifted."[73] Thus, Freud responded to Putnam's view that psychoanalytic method needs to be supplemented by methods that seek to hold up before the patient "some goal toward which he may strive" with the observation that the sublimation itself will create its own goals.

As their correspondence continued, a central theme emerged: Whenever Putnam proposed that the sublimation of sexual instincts should be an integral part of psychoanalytic treatment, Freud would express his own refusal to take this step, preferring instead to limit psychoanalysis to overcoming the repression of sexual instincts and leaving patients to develop their own sublimations.[74]

71. Ibid., 90.

72. Ibid., 90–91.

73. Ibid., 91.

74. In *Freud and the Americans,* Nathan Hale notes, "As Freud argued, one might initiate sublimation by conscious choice, but the process itself worked spontaneously and unconsciously. Moreover, it was concerned chiefly with the childhood partial sexual drives rather than adult genital sexuality. Many people were seizing on sublimation as the only 'respectable' side of psychoanalysis, and saddling 'neurotics, perverts, criminals and social failures' with 'all too heavy reconstruction programs,' according to Monroe A. Meyer, a New York psychoanalyst who had worked with Freud. He thought that his countrymen delighted in sublimation because of their zeal for aspiring to 'dizzy, puritanical heights" (341; quotations are from Meyer's review of Ernest Jones, *Papers on Psychoanalysis,* 266–67). Hale goes on to note Freud's insistence that "patients would discover their own modes of sublimation," and that, in this, Freud "exceeded the American faith in human capabilities" (341).

Friendship as a Form of Sublimation

Another topic that emerged in their correspondence was the matter of religion. At one point Freud said that it "would be a great delight to me to discuss religion with you since you are both tolerant and enlightened," and suggested that they might have the chance to do so at the next psychoanalytic congress (as Putnam had indicated his intention to attend). Freud added, however, that he is afraid that religion may be only "a pious wish-fulfillment," that a "'Just God' and 'kindly Nature' are only the noblest sublimations of our parental complexes, and our infantile helplessness is the ultimate root of religion."[75] Thus, he suggests that religious ideas may offer a valuable sublimation, but essentially because the ultimate root of religion is our infantile helplessness.

A related issue concerned Putnam's view that sexual instincts, now no longer repressed, may be put into the service of higher ethical purposes. As their discussion of this issue continued, it became clear that Freud was comfortable with the view that sublimations may be moral, but resisted Putnam's view that they may be expressive of higher ethical purposes, such as communal responsibility, friendship, and love. That these ethical principles exist was not under dispute, for Freud knew full well that there are many persons—including philosophers and theologians—who have presented and promoted such principles. What he questioned was the claim that these principles are appropriately called sublimations. After all, Putnam had not provided any solid evidence that these ethical principles derive from the *un*-repression of sexual instincts. In fact, Freud contended that we do not know enough about human psychology to be able to say with any degree of certainty where these ethical principles originate. Here, again, religion was implicated in these differences of view, for in the course of their correspondence, Freud made several allusions to the fact that he was "irreligious," while Putnam wanted Freud to recognize that his commitment to truth was a form of "religion," and because it was, this should have enabled Freud to view Putnam's emphasis on our community obligations and ethical aspirations more positively.

In this regard, Putnam played a role similar to that of Oskar Pfister, the Swiss pastor who, as we noted above, embraced psychoanalysis. Like Putnam, Pfister did not take Freud's claims to be irreligious at face value. In fact, he once asserted that, among his friends, there is no "better Christian" than Sigmund Freud. This declaration prompted Freud to

75. Hale, *James Jackson Putnam and Psychoanalysis*, 97.

reply that he was more than content simply to know himself as Pfister's friend.[76] This response to Pfister, although obviously said in jest, points to what we consider one of Putnam's most important insights, namely, that friendship itself may be viewed as a form of sublimation. To explore this insight, we turn to Putnam's letter (dated September 30, 1911) in which he discussed his own self-analysis and included a detailed interpretation of a dream of his.[77]

The dream account follows a description of an event that had occurred when the family was at the Hague on their way to Paris. His sixteen-year-old daughter had experienced an attack that he feared was epileptic in nature. It occurred in the morning when she was dressing, and at a time when her menstruation was expected. He does not describe the attack, but notes that over the past year she had been experiencing frequent but very slight momentary "jerkings" or "shakings" but without any alterations of consciousness. Recalling their earlier conversation about the difficulty of distinguishing epilepsy from hysteria, Putnam asks for Freud's advice as to whether he should arrange for her to be psychoanalyzed, although he believes that the usual signs of a marked hysteria are absent, and that except for the physical symptoms of jerkings and shakings, she seems to be healthy and normal.

The dream occurred the night before he left the conference at Weimar. It was a picture, but the symbolism seemed fairly clear. A simple drawing appears alongside his verbal account of the dream:

> It appears that (as in an earlier dream) I was driving, and (perhaps) in a similar wagon to the one I described to you as a "dog-cart." I was near the top of a hill. At first I was on the road indicated by the dotted line F.G., which wound down the hill in a generous curve. At once however I became aware of leaving this (safe?) road and driving across the grass, which was short, as if intending to make a "short cut" in the general direction of E. At first all went well but very soon I became aware of two facts; first, that the hill was getting steep; next, that at E. it was marshy and that I could see several irregular spots or holes containing water, which reflected the blue of the afternoon sky.[78]

---

76. Gay, *Freud*, 191–92.

77. Hale, *James Jackson Putnam and Psychoanalysis*, 125–29.

78. Ibid., 126. We have made slight editorial changes in this and the following quotations (for example, providing English translations of German words).

Putnam makes an association between the blue of the afternoon sky and an earlier dream, which he had related to Freud previously, in which he saw a brilliant blue or yellowish stone hanging from the neck of a young girl, and notes that his daughter, the same daughter who was experiencing unusual jerkings and shakings, had recently purchased a bluish emerald pendant. His account of the dream continues:

> I then tried to stop the horse but my pulling on the reins seemed to make no impression on him whatever. He plodded steadily on without seeming to notice my pull or perhaps the latter was like the efforts which patients with hysterical paralysis make, when they apparently use great effort but bring nothing to pass. Then I woke up.[79]

Following this description of the dream itself, Putnam relates his "general interpretation" of it:

> The horse stands for my instinctual drive (sexual, mainly) which I would wish to regulate but cannot check. My "driving alone" and leaving the safer road, yet feeling anxious on account of the steepness of the hill and the boggy ground below (in which I imagined I should get overturned) indicates my wish to be independent, yet points also to the fact that I am rather dependent on my brother and on my wife, both of whom I associate in my mind with "driving," especially in the above mentioned "dog-cart." Possibly this feeling about my wife and my brother (dependence, yet "protest," and sometimes irritation—really, at myself) may refer both to father and mother or homosexual vs. heterosexual. The holes containing water may have a sexual meaning, as I seemed to be going into them, yet dreading the fact.[80]

To clarify the suggestion that the holes containing water may have a sexual meaning, he continues:

> I should say, in this connection, that my sexual relations with my wife have been rather infrequent for many years, of late years exceedingly infrequent, and that I have "dreaded" them—partly because I believed that many of my friends did not continue such relations at my age [he is sixty-four years old], but mainly because although the first effect was one of great relief from a very unpleasant state of tension yet for a number of days

79. Ibid., 127.
80. Ibid.

afterwards I always felt exhausted, sleepy, depressed, etc. At the time of the meeting at Weimar I had had no such relations for a good many months, but the "tension" was I think coming on, partly as a result of the fact that I was expecting to meet my wife after a two weeks absence, partly as a "reaction" from the intellectual excitement of the congress. I did not sleep more than one or two hours that last night at Weimar and although I was not aware of any sexual excitement yet it may have been present "in the unconscious."[81]

Putnam concludes his general interpretation of the dream by noting that "it is certainly true that the sexual drive *has* always been like a horse that I could not satisfactorily drive or restrain, though I have never been, in any sense, a 'pervert,' and never experienced the exhaustion after sexual intercourse until a good many years after being first married."[82]

He goes on in the letter to relate a fantasy of his adolescence, one in which he longed for a married life and home of his own and pictured himself sitting before an open fire in an otherwise unlit room, with wife and young children playing about and receiving the usual caresses and attentions. He notes that in his vision the children were more prominent than the wife. He recognizes that this was a rather common picture of domestic happiness, one that he supposes was idealized somewhat from personal memories, but "possibly referring to a close feeling for my mother and father."[83] Then he adds,

> Affection, readiness to be caressed, narcissism, "protest," autoeroticism, homosexuality, heterosexuality—all played large parts in my early life, as also a sense of inferiority ("too small sexual organs," etc.) and desire for recognition as an escape from inferiority. I think I have also tried, as I imagine many others have, to compensate for assumed internal lacks, by external aids—things that I could *buy*, influential friends, etc.[84]

Putnam adds that he has been fond of courageous people but timid himself and "not at harmony with myself."[85] In addition, he has been "ill at ease with others," but far less so since his marriage.

81. Ibid.
82. Ibid.
83. Ibid., 128.
84. Ibid.
85. Ibid.

In his response (dated October 5, 1911), Freud noted that Putnam describes himself as "a very bad character," but Freud added that "a far worse man would be uncovered were I to lay myself bare in an analysis as you have done," and furthermore, Freud wrote, "you overlook the fact that your sincerity itself indicates greatness of soul."[86] He then proceeded to answer Putnam's questions "to the best of my ability." With regard to his daughter, Freud suggests that "the most probable diagnosis is nine to one in favor of hysteria rather than epilepsy."[87] This being the case, he can simply disregard the symptoms if no others appear and the attack is not repeated. If, however, it seems to be progressive, "an analysis is surely indicated, and, I hope, would show you the advantage of this form of therapy in the case of someone dear to you."[88] He added that he would, of course, keep this confidential.

As for Putnam's dream, Freud replies that his interpretation seems entirely correct, but that there may be one additional interpretation:

> The safe road you followed might refer to the therapy you had used before; the new route which soon proves to be so disagreeable, is psychoanalysis, of which you seem to be very much afraid. You are much too frightened by your fantasies, and do not seem to wish to believe that they cannot possibly be transformed into reality. As soon as you give up that fear, you will learn more about your fantasies, find them interesting and experience relief.[89]

In other words, Putnam is not in any danger of acting on his fantasies.

As for Putnam's adolescent fantasy, Freud notes he cannot say much about it "because you described the underlying motives so hastily and piled up everything disagreeable."[90] What he *can* say is that his friend should not attribute too much importance to Alfred Adler's concepts of organ inferiority, protest, and the desire to dominate because "these are superficial, secondary and most often conscious" and "do not touch the real forces at work."[91] Freud thinks that, on the whole, Putnam is

---

86. Ibid., 129.

87. Ibid.

88. Ibid. See also Capps, "Teenage Girls in Rural New York."

89. Hale, *James Jackson Putnam and Psychoanalysis*, 130.

90. Ibid.

91. Ibid.

suffering from a too early and too strongly repressed sadism expressed in over-goodness and self-torture. Behind the fantasy of a happy family life, you would discover the normal repressed fantasies of rich sexual fulfillment. It is the influence of these fantasies which causes the sense of physical dissatisfaction with one's wife. These are symptoms of aging, which I am beginning to experience myself, as I told you in Zurich.[92]

Thus, Freud reacted to Putnam's allusions to his organ inferiority but did not respond in any direct way to his sexual confusion during adolescence (as suggested in Putnam's allusion to his autoeroticism and homosexuality), nor did Freud comment on Putnam's observation that he has tried to compensate for "assumed internal lacks" by external aids, such as trying to *buy* his friendships. Also, Freud did not have anything to say about Putnam's suggestion that in his ideal domestic scene, the children had a more prominent place than the wife, or his observation that he became more at ease with others after he became married. These thoughts, together with his disclaimer to being a "pervert," suggest that, as an adolescent, Putnam was struggling with his homosexual desires that perhaps played a role in his feeling ill at ease with others. His marriage, therefore, reinforced his heterosexuality, as it enabled him to relate to other men from the safety of his marital state.

However, the dream, together with his adolescent fantasy, suggest that Putnam's homosexual desires have been reactivated by the very fact that he has spent the past couple of weeks with other men, and he now dreads the prospect of meeting his wife after two weeks' absence and the likelihood that their reunion will involve sexual relations. On the other hand, it is noteworthy that Putnam characterizes the "excitement" of the Congress as "intellectual," as this suggests that his homosexual desires are, in fact, sublimated ones. This being so, Freud is correct in his reassurances that Putnam need not be frightened by his fantasies because they cannot possibly be transformed into reality. These fantasies, at any rate, have been successfully sublimated over the years.

What remain repressed, however, are his sadistic desires, a repression manifested in his overgoodness and self-torture. Freud seems to have in mind, here, Putnam's sexual feelings relating to his wife, as he relates this repressed sadism to his fantasy of a happy family life behind which lies "the normal repressed fantasies of rich sexual fulfillment."[93] If these

92. Ibid.
93. Ibid.

fantasies were no longer repressed but allowed to be fully entertained, Putnam would no longer feel "the sense of physical dissatisfaction" with his wife. This too would constitute a significant sublimation.

But we are primarily concerned here with Putnam's view that friendship may be a form of sublimation. In this regard, it is noteworthy that in his account of his adolescent fantasy, he indicates he felt that, in order to compensate for "assumed internal lacks," he needed to *buy* his friendships. Putnam assumed, in other words, that others would not agree to be his friend merely for his own sake. There had to be something in it of extrinsic value for them. This is, in fact, a continuing theme in his correspondence with Freud, for both men recognize that Putnam can be of great service to Freud in creating a hospitable climate for psychoanalysis in America; and, conversely, Freud continued to arrange for Putnam's articles to be published in the *Zentralblatt fur Psychoanalyse* and in *Imago* (the journal for the application of psychoanalysis to the humanities and social sciences, which Freud himself edited).[94]

On the other hand, Freud's allusion to "the symptoms of aging" as a possible explanation for Putnam's "sense of physical dissatisfaction" with his wife, and to the fact that he had mentioned his own struggles in this regard to Putnam when they were in Zurich, indicates that their friendship went far beyond these extrinsic values. Their correspondence indicates that they could confide in one another, as when Freud would complain to Putnam about the untrustworthy members of the psychoanalytic movement, and Putnam revealed his struggles with what he called the feeling of not being "at harmony with myself." In addition, there is the simple fact that in their correspondence from November 17, 1909, to June 2, 1914, Putnam addressed Freud as either "Professor" or "Dr. Freud," and Freud addressed Putnam as "Colleague." Then, on June 19, 1914, Freud addressed Putnam as "Friend and Colleague."[95] Putnam addressed Freud as "Dr. Freud" and "Professor" in two subsequent letters, but then in a letter dated February 22, 1915, he addressed Freud as "Friend," and drew a picture of two hands clasping one another. Freud responded by addressing Putnam simply as "Friend," and said that his "handclasp across the wide ocean made me very glad" and added, "Let me assure you that even the postal disruptions of this war will not estrange us." Freud went on to

94. See Hale, *Freud and the Americans.*
95. Hale, *James Jackson Putnam and Psychoanalysis,* 175.

note, however, that at times "the idea that there is a censor paralyzes the desire to write."[96]

In all subsequent letters except one (a brief letter from Putnam addressed to Freud as "Professor," in which he apologized for misrepresenting Freud's relationship to Josef Breuer in his book *Human Motives*), both men addressed one another as "Friend." In many of these letters, they expressed frustration over the fact that they could not assume that their letters were arriving at their intended destinations due to the war. We believe that this very frustration was itself a sign of their friendship, and thus further confirmation of Putnam's view that friendship is a form of sublimation.

Conclusion

Freud's essay "Thoughts for the Times on War and Death" was published at the very time that the two men were commenting on the role the war was playing in frustrating their desire to communicate with each other. In a lengthy letter dated August 13, 1915, which he decided not to send, Putnam suggested that Carl Jung's attitude toward Freud should not be "laid at the door of religion itself, any more than the behavior of soldiers, as you yourself pointed in your paper on the war, ought to be laid to the failure of sublimation."[97] He added,

> You said, very truly, that we ought not so much to feel disappointed at the apparent downfall of civilization in war, but ought, instead, to recognize that we had overrated the amount of civilization which had actually been present.[98]

Freud, however, had also argued that the very "pressure of civilization" is "shown in malformations of character, and in the perpetual readiness of the inhibited instincts to break through to gratification at any suitable opportunity," and, therefore, "anyone thus compelled to act continually in the sense of precepts which are not the expression of instinctual inclinations, is living, psychologically speaking, beyond his means, and might

96. Freud's reference to a censor is noteworthy in light of the fact that psychoanalysis is itself a method intended to overcome the censorship of desires, especially sexual desires, which are considered by the patient to be morally inappropriate and personally demeaning.

97. Hale, *James Jackson Putnam and Psychoanalysis*, 195.

98. Ibid.

objectively be designated a hypocrite, whether this difference be clearly known to him or not."[99]

This observation about living beyond our psychic means brings us back to Freud's story about the efforts of the citizens of Schilda to break the horse of his "bad habit" of eating a large amount of expensive oats. At first, the project of weaning him off his instinctual desires worked, but eventually the fact that he was living beyond his psychic means caught up with him and with the people who relied on him to do the work they expected of him.[100] And Freud's observation also brings us back to Putnam's dream about his effort to keep the horse he was driving from leaving the safe road and taking off into the marshy grass, and to Freud's reassurances that Putnam can trust the horse and the place to which the horse is taking him.[101] Thus, the lifting of sexual repression need not be feared, but neither is it necessary to force upon ourselves—and on others—sublimations that are excessively demanding and high-minded. The correspondence between Putnam and Freud expresses a sublimation that takes the form of friendship, and neither man feels any particular need to elevate this particular friendship into some sort of ethical ideal. That this sublimation occurred in the rather ordinary process of an exchange of letters from 1909 to 1916 supports Freud's point that sublimation need not be made a conscious or explicit goal of psychoanalysis. It also supports Putnam's view that sublimation often takes a "communal" form, in this case, a handclasp across the sea. The very fact that the two men do not seem to be especially aware that their correspondence has become an instance of sublimation over the years supports Freud's view that it is usually best to allow sublimation to create its own goals.

What lessons may we learn from the fact that the sublimation—in the form of friendship—that these two men experienced occurred largely through correspondence? The obvious lesson is that they did not need to be in each other's physical presence to experience a close relationship to one another.[102] In fact, it may well have been the case that if they had been

99. Freud, "Thoughts for the Times upon War and Death," 217.

100. Freud, *Five Lectures on Psycho-Analysis*, 61–62.

101. Hale, *James Jackson Putnam and Psychoanalysis*, 126, 130.

102. In his article on male body image and intimacy titled "From Grace *Alone* to Grace *Alone*," Nathan Carlin discusses male friendships and cites Philip Culbertson's identification of types of friendships among men today. These types include friendships of convenience, special-interest friendships, historical friendships, crossroad friendships, cross-generational friendships, and close friendships (Carlin, "From

in each other's physical presence to a much greater degree they may have found reasons to distance themselves from one another. A less obvious lesson is that their friendship was largely based on the intellectual stimulation they received from one another. Although each made references to their personal lives, their correspondence was largely professional in nature. In fact, the sublimation that occurred between the two men was a direct consequence of their ongoing discussions and reflections on the very subject of sublimation. We doubt very much that it would have occurred if their correspondence had focused instead on their personal friendship. Sometimes, perhaps especially for men, such matters are better left unsaid.

Grace *Alone*," 287). Culbertson defines "close friendships" as "involving revealing aspects of our private self—our feelings and thoughts, our wishes and fears and fantasies and dreams" (Culbertson, *Counseling Men*, 79). The friendship between Freud and Putnam was a close one even though—or perhaps because—it occurred primarily through correspondence.

2

King James and the
Sublimation of Aggression

Introduction

IN THIS CHAPTER, WE focus on the fact that one of King James's first acts after becoming king of England was to commission the translation of the Bible. While his role in the commissioning of this translation is noteworthy in itself, there are two specific reasons why we have chosen to discuss it in this book. One is the fact that James's contemporaries believed that he had strong homosexual tendencies. The other is the fact that the organizational structure for the process of translation was patterned after the organizational structure of the military, though its purposes were peaceful. We believe, therefore, that the translation of the Bible was an expression of religious sublimation—in this case, the sublimation of aggressions that have their origins in the sexual wishes and desires of early childhood.

To present this argument, we will first discuss how the King James Version of the Bible came to be. Then we will present a brief account of King James's personal history, followed by an account of his homoerotic relationships, with particular emphasis on his relationship to Robert Carr. These accounts will provide the context for our consideration of what these relationships meant to his own contemporaries (especially in light of the charge that he was effeminate and that his effeminacy was responsible for his pacifism). Finally, we will present our argument that his enlightened understanding of male companionship was itself a form of religious sublimation and that this expression of religious sublimation played a central role in the commissioning of the translation of the Bible.

The King James Version: How It Came to Be

In his book on the King James Version of the Bible, Alister McGrath tells an engaging story of how the King James Bible came to be, and of its enormous effects on British language and culture.[1] We will limit our discussion here to what prompted King James to commission a new translation of the English Bible.

Even if they have not had any direct experience with the King James Version of the Bible, most Christians know about it, and they assume that it was the first translation of the Bible into the English language. However, William Tyndale's translation of the New Testament into English was published at Worms, Germany, in 1526, and was smuggled into England seventy-five years before the Authorized Version (popularly known as the King James Version) was first printed, in 1611.[2] In the meantime, a translation of the whole Bible was published in 1560. It came to be known as the Geneva Bible because the translating was done in Geneva, Switzerland. It was largely the work of William Whittingham, who was assisted by Anthony Gilby and Thomas Sampson.[3] The New Testament was based on Tyndale's English translation, with some significant modifications, while the Old Testament was entirely new.

The Geneva Bible found its way into England and was very popular.[4] A product of Puritanism, it was more than a translation of the Bible because it offered additional detailed comments on critical verses. Many of these commentaries were set alongside Old Testament passages that told of the evil and corruption of the kings of Israel and emphasized the obligation of God-fearing people to disobey the commands of the king when these commands are in conflict with the will of God.[5] Not surprisingly, King James developed a strong personal dislike for the Geneva Bible, as

1. McGrath, *In the Beginning*.
2. Ibid., 73.
3. Ibid., 114.
4. Ibid., 78.
5. Ibid., 143.

did the bishops of the Church of England, and supplanting the Geneva Bible with one of their own was to their mutual advantage.

The Hampton Court Conference convened in mid-January 1604, and was presided over by King James.[6] The Puritan leaders who attended the conference hoped that it would authorize the Geneva Bible for use in churches and public worship, thus reversing earlier prohibitions introduced by Archbishop Whitgift. Although King James had no interest in authorizing the Geneva Bible, he had been recently installed as the king of England (having already served as king of Scotland from 1567, a year after he was born), and he wanted to be seen as conciliatory toward the English Puritans. However, none of the items on the Puritan leaders' agenda appealed to him or to the bishops, and it appeared that the conference would result in the endorsement of something very like the status quo. This would have pleased the bishops but alienated the Puritans.

Then, however, John Reynolds, the leader of the Puritan delegation, surprised the conferees by proposing a new Bible translation.[7] Having perceived that the Puritan demand for recognition of the Geneva Bible as the only Bible authorized to be read in the churches would go down to defeat, he evidently believed that his proposal, if adopted, would open the way for a number of translations to be authorized for use in public worship, including the Geneva Bible. When Bishop Bancroft, the leader of the Anglican delegation, expressed his opposition to this proposal, King James saw his opening:

> Here was a major concession he could make without causing any pressing difficulties to anyone. A translation of this magnitude took time, so he was not committing himself to anything with major short-term implications. The longer the translation took, the better. It would postpone religious controversy to an indeterminate point in the future. He concurred immediately with the suggestion.[8]

James directed the "best-learned in both universities"—Oxford and Cambridge—to begin work on a new translation of the Bible. Their work was to be reviewed by the bishops, then presented to the Privy Council, and finally ratified by royal authority so that, as King James put it, "the

---

6. Ibid., 156.

7. Ibid., 161.

8. Ibid., 161–62.

whole church would be bound by it, and none other."[9] It would contain no marginal notes and would be used in all the churches of England only during public worship. Bishop Bancroft now became a vigorous supporter of the idea of a new translation because the stipulations that were adopted preserved the vested interests of the Church of England against Roman Catholics on the one hand and Puritans on the other.[10] Furthermore, Bancroft was able to secure for himself a leading role in selecting the translators and in limiting their freedom. His support for the project would also win the king's favor at the very time that Archbishop Whitgift, who was in poor health, would need to be replaced. Bancroft's diligence in supporting the new translation paid off; he became the new archbishop in October 1604.[11]

King James directed that the Bible would be divided into six sections, with roughly the same number of men allocated to the translation of each section.[12] Each group would consist of nine men, making a total of fifty-four men overall. Although fewer than fifty-four men have been identified as having worked on the six-year project, this may have been due to the early deaths of several. Some of the groups completed their work in 1608, others in 1609, and still others in 1610. Twelve delegates selected from the six groups then convened and listened as the draft translations were read orally. This procedure was adopted because "the King James Bible was designed to be read publicly in church, and there is no doubt that the translators gave careful consideration to ensuring that the translation could be understood by those *to whom it was read*, rather than just those who read it."[13] However, only a few changes resulted from this procedure. The final draft was delivered to the printer in 1611 (the precise date is unknown).

Given that the Puritans continued to mistrust the new translation (in part because it included the deuterocanonical books), King James's hope that the Authorized Version would become the Bible of the whole English populace was not fulfilled. The Geneva Bible remained the Bible of the Puritans, while the King James Bible was the Bible of the Anglican

9. Ibid., 163.

10. Ibid., 164.

11. Ibid., 165.

12. Ibid., 178.

13. Ibid., 187 (italics original).

establishment.[14] Many who settled the American colonies had one book only—the Bible—and "the evidence suggests that the first English Bible to be brought to the New World was the Geneva Bible. Not only had this been available longer, but it was the translation of choice for the Puritans, who valued its extensive annotations."[15] However, in 1782 the U. S. Congress approved the efforts of Robert Aitkin (an immigrant from Scotland to Philadelphia in 1769 who quickly established himself as a printer and publisher) to print an American Bible. The translation he used was the King James Version (with the deuterocanonical books omitted). McGrath notes that Aitkin's "activities had ensured that the King James Bible—despite its British establishment pedigree—would be the translation of choice of the United States," and "even in the closing decades of the twentieth century American Christianity continued its love affair with this translation."[16] He adds,

> As rival translations—such as the Revised Standard Version—began to gain the upper hand in the period immediately following the Second World War, a staunch defense of the integrity of the King James Bible was mounted by its supporters in the United States. It was argued that the King James Bible was more accurate as a translation, was based on a more reliable text than its rivals, and used somber and sober language appropriate to such a dignified topic. A series of popular polemical works argued that the King James Bible alone represented the authentic "Word of God"; all other versions involved distortions, additions, or other changes detrimental to the reliability of the text. Although these views are typical of a decided minority of conservative American Protestants, they remain an important witness to the continued respect and admiration in which the King James Bible is widely held.[17]

McGrath does not discuss King James personally in any great detail, but he does make a brief allusion to his homosexual tendencies. In noting that the commissioning of the new translation of the Bible "was one of the first positive acts of the new king of England,"[18] he indicates that James was under severe criticism from almost the very beginning

14. Ibid., 280.
15. Ibid., 293.
16. Ibid., 299.
17. Ibid.
18. Ibid., 171.

of his English reign. McGrath mentions in this regard a spectacular performance of Ben Jonson's *The Masque of Blackness*, "which caused consternation and scandal, partly on account of its extravagance,"[19] and then alludes to James's homosexual tendencies:

> Further concerns were expressed over the king's increasingly obvious homosexual tendencies, which led to certain royal favorites being granted favors that were the subject of much comment and envy. Robert Carr, some twenty years younger than James, was one such favorite: he became the earl of Somerset in 1613. Although James fondled and kissed his favorites in what was widely regarded as a lecherous manner in public, the court was prepared to believe that his private behavior was somewhat more restrained.[20]

McGrath's allusion to King James's "homosexual tendencies" is quite brief. But David M. Bergeron and Michael B. Young provide excellent biographical material relating to James's "homosexual tendencies" and how these tendencies were understood and interpreted by James's own contemporaries.[21] To place the issue of James's homosexual tendencies in context, it will be useful to provide a brief account of King James's personal history, centering especially on the fact that he was separated from his mother when barely a year old, had no contact whatsoever with his father, and had a very troubled marriage.

King James's Personal History

James was born in Edinburgh, Scotland, on June 19, 1566. He was the son of Mary Queen of Scots. That he was born at all was something of a miracle because, as Bergeron portrays the situation, just a few months earlier, in March, "Mary watched in horror as her husband, Lord Darnley, and other conspirators in a struggle for power killed her secretary, David Riccio, in the Palace of Holyroodhouse. They threatened her, Darnley holding her arms, and apparently hoped to induce a miscarriage. From that horrifying experience Mary lost whatever shred of respect she still had for her husband; she seemed all the more determined to give birth

19. Ibid., 170.

20. Ibid., 170–71.

21. Bergeron, *Royal Family, Royal Lovers*; Young, *King James and the History of Homosexuality*.

to her child successfully."[22] Young adds: "Although Riccio was dead, the rumor survived that he was the father of Mary's child. Born three months later, on 19 June 1566, James would always be sensitive about this false and painful rumor concerning his legitimacy."[23]

The suspicion that her child was the son of her Italian secretary may simply have served as the pretext for the murder of Riccio, and Darnley's attempt to cause Mary to miscarry may indicate that he genuinely believed that Riccio was the father of the child. In any event, Darnley initially denied that he was James's father, but Mary forced him to acknowledge his paternity. He did not attend James's baptism, however, which was conducted according to Catholic rites.[24] The following year, Darnley, who was already suffering from syphilis, which would have been fatal in that era, died in an explosion: "His death, or murder, to be precise, had Mary's tacit approval. She was now free to pursue her new passion: the earl of Bothwell. Indeed, in a Protestant ceremony in May, they were married. But the moral and political consequences of this marriage forced both of them into separate exile. In fact, the Scottish lords required Mary to abdicate the throne in favor of her infant son. She fled from Scotland, never to see her son again."[25]

His Mother's Execution

On July 29, 1567, Mary's thirteen-month-old child became King James VI of Scotland. In his early years, James was in the custody of the earl of Mar and his family, who moved into Stirling Castle, and, as Bergeron notes, "the earl's family was as close as James would come to understanding family life."[26] On August 3, 1586, Mary was arrested for plotting to kill Queen Elizabeth of England. James, then twenty years old, sent emissaries to intervene in behalf of his convicted mother, "but he also sent conflicting signals, letting Elizabeth and her government understand that there would be no severe repercussions should Mary be executed."[27] Citing letters that James and Mary wrote each other during this time,

22. Bergeron, *Royal Family, Royal Lovers*, 19.

23. Young, *King James and the History of Homosexuality*, 8.

24. Bergeron, *Royal Family, Royal Lovers*, 21.

25. Ibid.

26. Ibid.

27. Ibid., 42.

Bergeron notes that James asserted to his mother that he had been constant in his efforts to secure her freedom—"I pray you not to take me to be a chameleon"—while Mary called him "a liar and a double dealer."[28]

Mary was executed on February 8, 1587. While some of James's supporters recommended that he avenge her death, and he himself talked as if he would, Bergeron notes that "James had no intention of avenging his mother's death; he had truly come to desire it."[29] Thus, even as his mother had tacitly approved the murder of his father so James tacitly supported the execution of his mother. Her death, however, continued to weigh on James's mind: "With Mary dead and his path thereby eased toward the English throne, James nevertheless remained troubled by her execution and his part in it. His reaction all the way through 1612 suggests that he could not readily assuage his guilt about her. No longer a force in his personal and political life, she lingered in his psychological life as he attempted in several ways to revise history to suit the image of himself as a dutiful son."[30]

His access to the English throne was based on the fact that his cousin, Queen Elizabeth, did not have a male heir, and this placed him directly in line for the English title. Now that his mother was safely out of the way, James began to refer to Elizabeth as his "mother," and, as Bergeron points out,

> In many ways Elizabeth functioned as surrogate family for one who knew neither father nor mother, brother nor sister. We remind ourselves that James's image of the queen came as the product of discourse—letters exchanged, messages sent. Having never met his cousin, James created an image of her, rather as he had of his own mother, through documents that came to him— the raw materials that fed his imagination. In a 1586 document in which Elizabeth assured James of an annual pension and of his potential claim to the English throne, she also used familial terms, claiming to have had "a special and motherlye cair over our said darrest brother and cousing ever since his byrthe, respecting him as our owne sone." When James made the political decision to abandon Mary's idea of Association [in which she and James would share the rule of Scotland] and to embrace the alliance with England, he essentially accepted the mother-substitute in preference to his natural mother. This accounts

28. Ibid., 43.

29. Ibid., 44.

30. Ibid., 45.

at least in part for his silence concerning his mother's trial and execution.[31]

Although Elizabeth was, for James, a mother-substitute, this did not preclude the possibility in his own mind that she might also become his wife. In August 1586, the very month that his mother had been charged with treason and was awaiting trial, he made an offer of marriage to Elizabeth (who was thirty-three years his senior) on the grounds that it might be of benefit to the realm. He admitted to the man to whom he later confided this information, however, that she showed no inclination to accept his offer. As Bergeron points out, "No event more clearly reflects James's calculated abandonment of his natural mother and his attempt to ingratiate himself further with Elizabeth. Since James never met Elizabeth, he seemed to have trouble deciding whether she was his sister, mother, or possible wife. She existed as a political reality but otherwise as an idealized figment of his imagination."[32]

His Marriage to Princess Anne

A new chapter began in James's life two years after Mary's death. In 1589, when he was twenty-three-years old, he married Princess Anne of Denmark. As he readied himself to sail to Denmark to claim Anne as his bride, he wrote a letter to the people of Scotland in which he explained his apparent delay in getting married: "The reasons were that I was alone, without father or mother, brother or sister, king of this realm and heir apparent of England."[33] As Bergeron suggests, he was implicitly acknowledging that "he did not truly know what a family was. Cut off from routine family involvement, James, though surrounded by much noise, some adulation, and occasional threats, lived in a kind of silent world, untouched by a love that may occur in family bonds."[34] Then, presaging the unhappiness of James's marriage to Anne, Bergeron adds, "Small wonder that he had such difficulty in understanding what it meant to be a husband and a father. He looked at the canvas of familial experience, and it stared back in unrelieved whiteness."[35]

31. Ibid., 47–48.
32. Ibid., 48.
33. Ibid., 3.
34. Ibid.
35. Ibid.

James may also have been engaging here in a sort of equivocation, using his lack of family experience as a cover for his lack of sexual interest in women. As Michael B. Young points out, pressures were mounting for James to marry: "Up to this point he had shown no interest in women. As one observer reported, he 'never regardes the company of any woman, not so muche as in any dalliance.' James himself wrote, 'God is my witness I could have abstained longer.'"[36] Young also notes that, in the letter James wrote to the people of Scotland, he observed that, as King of Scotland and heir apparent to the throne of England, he needed heirs of his own to strengthen his position. He went on to acknowledge that his lack of heirs had "bred disdain," that "I was generally found fault with by all men for the delaying so long of my marriage," and that people had even begun to suspect "my inability as if I were a barren stock."[37]

James's trip to claim the fourteen-year-old Anne as his bride was their first meeting together. Bergeron indicates that he became convinced that he was in love with her on the basis of her picture and reports of her beauty.[38] After an attempt to get Anne to Scotland was stymied by violent seas, James sailed to Norway and made his way to Oslo, where Anne awaited him. They were married in Oslo on November 23, 1589, and then traveled to Denmark for another wedding ceremony according to Lutheran rites. They returned together to Scotland on May 1, 1590.

Anne, being attractive and kind, was an instant success in Scotland and became quickly endeared.[39] But, as Bergeron puts it, "feasting in Copenhagen and pageants in Edinburgh do not a marriage make," and "the early flush of romantic enthusiasm" soon faded.[40] Anne "found herself far removed from the warmth of her own family," and her husband, "rather uncouth of manner and given to lecturing her, often seemed indifferent to her needs and intent on controlling her."[41] In 1593, Anne became pregnant, and the impending birth of their first child, Prince Henry, spurred new joy. But over the next several years of their marriage, James and Anne "bickered" over the destiny of their children. She "wanted to

36. Young, *King James and the History of Homosexuality*, 14.

37. Ibid.

38. Bergeron, *Royal Family, Royal Lovers*, 50.

39. Ibid., 52.

40. Ibid., 53.

41. Ibid.

fulfill her maternal instincts and nurture her own children" while he "had other ideas; he wanted to be sure that he controlled the royal children."[42]

Shortly after Prince Henry's birth on February 19, 1594, James decided to place his son in the custody of the earl of Mar, the same man who had cared for James during his own infancy and childhood. Anne resisted this plan and fought to regain custody of her son. The two of them battled throughout 1595 and well into 1596. In Bergeron's view, each had a solid case: Anne wanted to be a mother to her child, and James wanted to offer maximum protection for his son, the heir to the Scottish throne.[43] But they were unable to work out a compromise and, to the lasting resentment of his young wife, his will prevailed. On August 19, 1596, Anne gave birth to another child, whom James named Elizabeth, "thereby tightening his grasp on the succession to the English throne."[44] In 1598 another daughter, named Margaret, was born, but she lived only two years. On November 19, 1600, Anne gave birth to a second son, who was named Charles. A contemporary noted at the time that James made it clear to Anne that given his dislike for her at the time, he also disliked this newborn son and felt that he should be baptized with little fanfare. Anne wanted to postpone the baptism until spring, when her brother, King Christian IV of Denmark, could attend, but plans for a December baptism proceeded, and Anne refused to attend it. Charles was sent to live in the household of Alexander Seton, Lord Fyvie. In January 1602, a third son, Robert, was born, but he died four months later. Given the genuine sorrow of the royal couple over this loss, arrangements were made for their son Henry to come for several days to comfort his mother, "a poignant moment that James at least allowed."[45]

He Becomes King of England

One year after the death of Robert, Queen Elizabeth died, and on March 26, 1603, James received the news that he had been chosen king of England. On April 5, James left for England alone, with the intention that his family would come later. Anne was pregnant again. With her husband on the road to London, Anne tried once again to gain custody of

---

42. Ibid.
43. Ibid., 56.
44. Ibid., 59.
45. Ibid., 61.

nine-year-old Prince Henry, basing her renewed effort on a letter from Henry in which he expressed regret over his father's absence and his desire that his mother would fill the void he felt in his life. When she was rebuffed by the Earl of Mar, she suffered a miscarriage. Receiving the news of her miscarriage, James relented and allowed Anne and Henry to travel together to England. Bergeron suggests that James and Anne had "reached an understanding of one another. We certainly cannot call it romantic; at best we can note a sense of accommodation that begins to govern their relationship."[46]

When James assumed the throne in 1603, one of his first acts was "to confront the issue of his long-dead mother."[47] In August he had a rich pall of velvet hung over her grave in Peterborough Cathedral. Noting that virtually every modern interpreter "has seen this action as the beginning of some kind of expiation," Bergeron mentions two additional steps that James took in "confronting his mother's death."[48] In 1605 Anne gave birth to a daughter, and James named her Mary, in honor of his mother. This meant that the first royal child born on English soil in over eighty years bore the name of the executed queen of Scotland. Then he ordered the construction of an elaborate tomb for his mother in Westminster Abbey. On October 8, 1612, her body moved in solemn procession through London to its final resting place. Bergeron comments: "James had finally put to rest his mother and the guilt that he bore about her fate. His mother became memorialized in a tomb—a tangible sign of James's stilled conscience. This burial in a magnificent tomb also completed James's fiction of himself as dutiful son, a fiction ironically set into motion by her death, as if her death liberated him not only politically but also imaginatively."[49]

In light of the fact that James's effort to expiate his guilt over his mother's death began when he assumed the throne of England in 1603, we believe that it was more than coincidental that his commissioning of the new translation of the Bible occurred at the very time that he was "confronting" his mother's death. In its own way, the Bible translation that was to bear his name was part of this expiation process. We will return to this suggestion later.

46. Ibid., 62.
47. Ibid., 73.
48. Ibid.
49. Ibid., 74.

In 1606 Anne was pregnant again, and on June 22 she gave birth to another daughter, named Sophia, in honor of Anne's mother. The baby lived only a few hours and died on the day of her birth. Bergeron comments: "After seven births and three miscarriages, there would be no more children. Anne did not try to console James or herself, as she had after the death of Robert, that they would soon have another child. A gulf of silence that already existed between husband and wife would widen. After Sophia's birth and death, Anne sank into a desperate depression."[50] The following year their daughter Mary died, and she was buried near her sister Sophia without a funeral. When she died, James continued with his plans to go hunting. Bergeron notes that one biographer interpreted James's reaction to his daughter's death as a case of "psychic numbing."[51] Even so, to Bergeron, the episode is disturbing:

> An obvious insensitivity on the part of both Anne and James strongly suggests that something had been happening to parental and familial sensibilities: an indifference that diminished human feelings had begun to take hold. James's hunting and continuing to live his indulgent life in the immediate aftermath of Mary's death, her almost anonymous burial, and Anne's remoteness speak tellingly about the royal family, one no longer held tightly together by emotional bonds. In the pounding of hooves, the barking of dogs, the scurrying of pursued animals in the chase, we may hear a silent disregard of parental demands.[52]

While not discounting these interpretations, we would also conjecture that the anonymous burial of Mary was due, in no small measure, to the fact that she was James's mother's namesake. It is conceivable that he considered her death to be the price—the final expiation—he was to pay for his failure to intervene in his mother's behalf twenty years earlier. Given his knowledge of the Bible that was to bear his own name, he was surely aware of the prophet Nathan's reproof of King David and of his assurance that David himself would not die but "the child also *that* is born unto you shall surely die" (2 Sam 12:14, KJV). James could commission a Bible that excluded commentary relating the guilty behaviors of the kings of Israel to the actions of the English monarchy, but he could not silence his own conscience which would attest to his guilt by association.

50. Ibid., 81.

51. Ibid., 83.

52. Ibid.

Familial Difficulties and Death

The year 1610 marked the sixteen-year-old Henry's investiture as Prince of Wales. As heir apparent to the throne, he was very popular with the citizenry, so much so that his father manifested signs of jealousy, though Henry seems to have been careful not to offend his father. It also fell to Henry, as the eldest son, to attempt to mediate between his quarreling parents. From 1610 to 1612 James was actively involved in securing a marriage partner for Henry, and although Henry indicated that he was in no hurry to marry, he wished "'to see my Father a grandfather.'"[53] Various potential matches—Spanish, Italian, and French—were proposed, but, for one reason or another, they did not materialize. In late October 1612, however, King James's privy council approved a match between Prince Henry and Maria, the third daughter of the duke of Savoy, and the very same day Henry took ill. Henry died, possibly of typhoid fever, on November 5.

While each parent visited Henry during his illness, they went to separate residences as the fateful time drew near, and James did not go to console Anne after receiving the news of his eldest son's death.[54] Neither parent attended Henry's funeral. While Henry's death was due to physical causes, the fact that it occurred when marriage negotiations were being made on his behalf may have contributed to his vulnerability to illness. In a letter to his father shortly before he took to his bed, Henry expressed his desire that his father resolve the marriage issue, indicating that he was determined "my part to play, which is to be in love with any of them."[55]

With Henry's death, Princess Elizabeth became an increasingly important member of the royal family, due, in no small measure, to the fact that she was named after Queen Elizabeth. When she married Frederick, Elector Palatine of Germany, three months after Henry's death, James anticipated the prospect of becoming a grandfather. But seven years later, her marriage to Frederick was to become a major political problem for James when Spanish forces invaded the Palatinate, forcing Frederick and Elizabeth to flee for safety to the Hague in the Netherlands. Elizabeth pleaded with her father to commit English troops to the restoration of Frederick's rightful claim to the Palatinate and Bohemia, but James refused to intervene, on the grounds that Frederick had gone against his

---

53. Ibid., 105.
54. Ibid., 109.
55. Ibid., 106.

father-in-law's advice by supporting a Bohemian insurrection against Ferdinand, the emperor of the Holy Roman Empire, and in accepting the Bohemians' election of him as their new king. In James's view, Frederick had dug his own grave, and it was neither the duty nor the prerogative of the king of England to come to his assistance. Frederick and Elizabeth, having lost their kingdoms in Europe, did not seek refuge in England because James would not allow it. He feared that Elizabeth would use her popularity with the people to stir their passions, rousing the Puritans and others who were opposed to Spain. Jealousy, however, was also a factor, as Elizabeth's "presence would have deflected attention from his reign, and James did not like royal competition for attention."[56]

Queen Anne became ill in January 1619, and a contemporary noted that James did not visit her at Hampton Court.[57] Nor was he at her bedside when she died on March 2, 1619. Typically, the funerals of members of the royal family took place about a month after the death, but Anne's funeral was delayed because James and the court were engaged in an unseemly search for money to pay for a funeral. A court insider noted that there was talk of melting the Queen's golden plate and making coins from it, and of selling her jewels for "good value."[58] About ten weeks after her death, a funeral finally took place. Prince Charles, who would succeed to the throne when his father died six years later, attended the funeral, but James did not. James wrote a letter to Anne's brother, King Christian IV of Denmark, on the day of her death, praising her "felicity of departure" and expressing the hope that he might "conclude the brief drama of this life" in a similar spirit.[59] He was not, however, there to observe her "departure," suggesting that he was writing for public consumption. As Bergeron points out, "Certainly James's assertion of Anne's saint-like departure did not square with the facts; only under pressure of the bishops did she prepare herself for death. As in other letters that James wrote to his brother-in-law, he did not hesitate to create a fiction of familial love, to put the best face on events."[60]

Six years later, in early March 1625, James himself became ill and died on March 27. Nine thousand persons attended the royal funeral

56. Ibid., 151.
57. Ibid., 139.
58. Ibid., 162.
59. Ibid., 141.
60. Ibid.

which, ironically, was probably the only funeral that King James ever attended. Bergeron observes: "The world now imposed its ceremonies and fictions on the king. Bishop John Williams preached the funeral sermon, itself lasting over two hours. [John] Chamberlain [a court insider] concluded, 'In summe all was performed with great magnificence, but the order was very confused and disorderly.' Magnificent but disorderly—what an apt image of and commentary on James himself, his government, and his personal life."[61] For Bergeron, it is most telling that the bishop's two-hour sermon contained "not a word about James's relationship with or love for his family."[62] Bergeron concludes that James had been unable to "reconcile his political responsibilities with familial demands," and that this man "who had known neither father nor mother, brother nor sister, never fully comprehended the role of parent or husband, torn by conflicting and irreconcilable desires."[63]

King James's Homoerotic Attraction to Robert Carr

Bergeron's suggestion that King James was torn by "conflicting and irreconcilable desires" might seem a commonplace where political leaders are concerned, as we often hear of a political leader's conflict between the desire for political influence and the desire to be a good family man. But the "irreconcilable desires" in James's case have much more to do with his desire for loving relationships with other men, despite the political and familial costs involved.

In the foregoing account of James's family history, we have not discussed a major theme of Bergeron's *Royal Family, Royal Lovers*—namely, the fact that his homoerotic relationships with men played a significant role in the mistrust and eventual emotional distance between James and Anne. Neither have we considered the theme, emphasized by Bergeron and Young, of the enormous political costs to James himself of these relationships.

As Bergeron shows in *Royal Family, Royal Lovers* and further explores in *King James and Letters of Homoerotic Desire*,[64] the three major male relationships in James's life were with Esmé Stuart, Duke of Lennox;

---

61. Ibid., 186.
62. Ibid.
63. Ibid.
64. Bergeron, *King James & Letters of Homoerotic Desire*.

Robert Carr, Earl of Somerset; and George Villiers, Duke of Buckingham. His relationship with Stuart occurred from 1579 to 1583 when James was between thirteen and seventeen years old. His relationship with Carr took place from 1607 to 1615, in the early years of his reign as king of England, when James was between forty-one and forty-nine years old. His relationship with Villiers began in 1616, when James was fifty years old, and continued to James's death in 1625 at the age of fifty-nine. James was attracted to other men in the course of his adult life, but these were the most lasting friendships, the ones that, individually and collectively, support historians' recognition of James's lifelong need for sexual intimacy with other men.

A thorough consideration of all three relationships would make for a much too lengthy chapter. Therefore, we have chosen to focus our attention on James's relationship with Carr for several reasons: this was his first significant homosexual relationship after he assumed the throne of England; it had the greatest negative impact on his relations with Anne and his children; and it occurred during the period that the Bible he had commissioned was translated and produced.

In *Royal Family, Royal Lovers,* Bergeron discusses the impact of James's male relationships on his relationship with Queen Anne. His first significant male relationship, with Esmé Stuart, occurred before his marriage to Anne, but his second relationship, with Robert Carr, began in 1607, eighteen years after he married the fourteen-year-old Danish princess. This relationship continued to 1615, when James's attentions turned to George Villiers. According to Bergeron, James's relationship with Carr began at the point in James and Anne's marriage when there was not much of a relationship left—"only personal accommodation and separate little kingdoms within the kingdom."[65] Bergeron cites historian William McElwee's observation that the deaths of their daughters Sophia in 1606 and Mary in 1607 "seem to have damaged the relationship between James and Anne irreparably."[66] McElwee also notes that James "had lost the affections of his son Henry and his daughter Elizabeth by 1607 and that Charles was still too young to fill James's need to spoil and pamper his children."[67] Thus, Carr was more the consequence than the primary cause of the emotional distance that had come to prevail in the

---

65. Bergeron, *Royal Family, Royal Lovers,* 90.

66. Ibid., 90–91; see McElwee, *Wisest Fool in Christendom,* 169.

67. Ibid., 91.

royal family. Nonetheless, as Bergeron points out, James's involvement with Carr was "a source of continuing tension within the royal family, especially with Anne and Henry"—a tension that was "not only a question of personal behavior," for "Carr's rise to power had dangerous political implications."[68]

Carr, a Scot, had come to England with James in 1603 as a lowly page in the royal household. Sometime thereafter he was dismissed from this service; Bergeron does not indicate the cause of his dismissal. He went to France, "where he gained some level of sophistication,"[69] then returned to England. Court intriguers had noticed King James's attraction to Philip Herbert at James's coronation as King of England in 1603 when Herbert had come forward to pay homage to the king and kissed James on the cheek. This was scandalous in itself, but what shocked the onlookers even more was that the king "merely laughed and lightly tapped him on the cheek."[70] Young believes that James, who appointed Herbert the earl of Montgomery, probably had sexual relations with him.[71]

Carr's Rise to Political Influence

An accident in 1607 brought Carr to James's attention. Carr fell from his horse during a tilt attended by James, and James wanted to determine if the young man had been seriously injured. Bergeron notes that James "took one look at Carr, and apparently became immediately smitten with him."[72] James soon installed Carr as gentleman of the bedchamber, a position that placed him in James's personal company, and made him available to James's sexual advances. McGrath suggests that "the court was prepared to believe that [James's] private behavior was somewhat more restrained" than his public behavior,[73] but there were many who were prepared to believe the opposite. A contemporary observed, for example, that James's public behavior of kissing and leaning his head against Carr's shoulders and neck "prompted many to imagine some things done in

68. Ibid.

69. Ibid., 87.

70. Ibid., 73. An intriguer is a person who engages in plotting and machinations, usually for personal gain.

71. Young, *King James and the History of Homosexuality*, 147.

72. Bergeron, *Royal Family, Royal Lovers*, 87.

73. McGrath, *In the Beginning*, 171.

the tyring-house, that exceed my expressions not lesse than they do my experience."[74] As these "things" were unmentionable, today's reader is left to guess at what these contemporaries imagined was going on between James and Carr in the royal bedchamber. Whatever they imagined, it certainly exceeded the intimacies in which they engaged in full public view.

Meanwhile, Carr steadily gained power in the king's court. By 1611 he had become Viscount Rochester and by 1613 Earl of Somerset. Bergeron notes the effect of Carr's rise to power on the royal family: "James lavished attention and affection on Carr in ways that his own family seldom experienced from him. Carr's prominence continued to dominate the next period of James's life in England until his [Carr's] downfall. Surely Anne saw the danger in Carr's rise to power and the way in which James's fixation moved family members a little farther out of his view, to the outer edges of a growing silence."[75] However, Carr's (now Somerset's) political career began to unravel when he decided in 1613 to marry "the treacherous and wily Frances Howard, at the time married to the earl of Essex."[76] Aware of Somerset's desire to marry her, Howard began divorce proceedings against her husband that summer, contending that he was impotent and that the marriage had never been consummated. James intervened in Somerset's behalf by arranging for a commission to rule on the divorce, and when the original panel seemed reluctant to rule in favor of divorce, he added two more bishops to the panel who assured him beforehand that they would vote the way he wanted them to vote. By a vote of 7–5, the commission reached a favorable decision. Bergeron comments: "Whatever one may think about James's method of securing justice, justice ironically prevailed because the earl of Essex and his wife both genuinely wanted a divorce, just not on each other's terms."[77]

However, Young takes a more critical view. He notes that a "panel of women who physically examined Lady Essex certified that she was a virgin, though contemporaries found this hard to believe."[78] He cites Essex's biographer's observation that the earl "would find it difficult indeed to forget the humiliating divorce," and that he bore a grudge for the rest of

---

74. Bergeron, *Royal Family, Royal Lovers,* 87.

75. Ibid., 87–88.

76. Ibid., 127.

77. Ibid.

78. Young, *King James and the History of Homosexuality,* 30.

his life, seeking some way to "avenge himself."[79] His chance to "vindicate his name and demonstrate his manhood" came many years later when he was chosen to lead the parliamentary forces in the civil war against Charles I, James's son. Unfortunately, according to Young, he proved a disappointment because, when Charles chased him into Cornwall to the town of Lostwithiel, he fled.[80] Father of seven children, James could not be accused, as Essex had been, of sexual impotence, but due to his affections for other men he was accused of being less than a man. We will return to the issue of James's contemporaries' association of homosexuality and unmanliness.

James's Approval of Carr's Marriage

Somerset and Howard were married on December 26, 1613, and James and Anne attended the wedding. The festivities concluded with a play by Thomas Campion titled *The Description of a Maske*, which included a song with the following lines: "Let us now sing of Love's delight, / For he alone is Lord to-night; / Some friendship between man and man prefer, / But I th' affection between man and wife. / What good can be in life, / Whereof no fruites appeare?" Bergeron comments: "One wonders if James sensed any special topicality in the song."[81] Even if he did not—after all, he was noted for his tendency to get drunk at festive occasions—the song's significance lies in its contention that affection between "man and wife" is superior to male friendship because it issues in progeny. James, of course, was aware that his political power derived to a great extent from the fact that he had produced sons who could succeed him. We may assume, therefore, that as a practical matter he shared the point of view this song expressed. On the other hand, his letters to Esmé Stuart, Robert Carr, and George Villiers are powerful testimony to his belief that, as a matter of the heart, nothing can compare to the love that is shared between "man and man."[82]

Over the next several months Somerset's political career began to crumble. Court intriguers who resented his arrogance, petulance, and insolence began devising means to topple him and to put Villiers in his

---

79. Ibid., 115; see Snow, *Essex the Rebel*, 70.
80. Young, *King James and the History of Homosexuality*, 115.
81. Bergeron, *Royal Family, Royal Lovers*, 128.
82. Bergeron, *King James & Letters of Homoerotic Desire*.

place. Meanwhile, James simply grew weary of him. In Bergeron's view, Somerset committed the unpardonable sin of ignoring James and of assuming prerogatives without first securing the king's consent.[83] Although James aided Somerset's marriage, he probably resented the fact that he had lost out to Howard in the battle for Somerset's affections.

Their Fractured Relationship

James "tried to repair a fractured relationship" in a lengthy and deeply emotional letter in early 1615, accusing Somerset of mistreating him and taking advantage of his loyalty and support. He concluded the letter with the suggestion that it now lay in Somerset's power to restore the relationship between them.[84] While much of the letter focused on how Somerset had misled him about court factions and opinions, James also mentioned Somerset's sudden outbursts and sullen behavior toward him, and Somerset's having on various occasions withdrawn "yourself from lying in my chamber, notwithstanding my many hundred times earnest soliciting you to the contrary."[85] As Bergeron notes, "Clearly James alluded to sexual favors being denied him."[86] Young agrees:

> What purpose did James have for "many hundred times earnestly soliciting" Somerset to lie in his chamber if it was not for sex? What did James want from Somerset that could not have been obtained elsewhere without requiring "lying in my chamber"? Diehard deniers of James's sexual relations with other men could argue that these words show that Somerset refused to go to bed with James. But then they would have to admit that "many hundred times" that is what James was asking him to do. It seems more reasonable to infer that Somerset initially won favor by pleasing James sexually but later, probably after his marriage to Frances Howard, withdrew from physical relations. "Withdrawing," in fact, was the word James used.[87]

Young goes on to cite the memoirs of the French ambassador, who noted that at the outset Somerset "submitted entirely to the whims of his

---

83. Bergeson, *Royal Family, Royal Lovers*, 128.

84. Ibid., 129–30.

85. Ibid., 129.

86. Ibid.

87. Young, *King James and the History of Homosexuality*, 43.

master, and he appeared to have no other passion than to second all his desires." Later, however, Somerset became arrogant and "rejected with rudeness the caresses of the king."[88] To Young, it is noteworthy that James did not consider it unreasonable to solicit Somerset to lie with him—nor did he seem to feel any shame, embarrassment, or personal blame for having done so.

When James wrote this letter, he was unaware of the involvement of Somerset's wife in the plot to murder Sir Thomas Overbury, who had had a very close relationship with Somerset before Somerset's marriage to Howard.[89] Aware of the two men's relationship, James had Overbury confined to the Tower when he refused James's offer of an ambassadorial position abroad—an offer that was probably intended by James to remove Overbury as a rival for Somerset's affections. However, Howard had arranged for Overbury's death by poisoning prior to her marriage to Somerset. Since Overbury died on September 15, 1613, she knew of her guilt as she went to her wedding in late December. However, it wasn't until October 1615, two years later, that it became publicly known that Overbury's death was due to poisoning, and both Somerset and his wife were placed under house arrest. The exact nature of Somerset's own involvement was unclear, but he surely knew after the fact—if not before—of his wife's involvement in Overbury's murder.

James was profoundly shocked when he heard the news, and appointed a commission to investigate the charges against Somerset and his wife. According to Bergeron: "These startling events dispelled whatever remaining hopes James had for repairing his relationship with Somerset. He now sought to put a safe distance between himself and his favorite, having correctly sensed the potential danger."[90] When Somerset realized that James would leave him to the workings of the judicial system, he made "ugly" threats against the king. As Bergeron notes, "A few of James's letters to Somerset would have proven embarrassing for the king."[91] But James, convinced of Somerset's guilt, stood his ground. In May 1616 Somerset and his wife stood trial. She pleaded guilty, while Somerset claimed his innocence.

---

88. Quoted in ibid.
89. Bergeron, *Royal Family, Royal Lovers*, 131.
90. Ibid.
91. Ibid., 132.

However, after a daylong trial, the assembled lords found him guilty as well. James commuted their death sentence, but they were confined to the Tower until 1622 when they gained their release and moved to the country. On October 7, 1624, James granted Somerset, but not his wife, a pardon. Bergeron concludes that, in 1615, "James had watched an essential part of his world crumble when he encountered the disaffection of the man whom he had loved for eight years, the man who, James wrote, had enjoyed his 'own infinite privacy' with James. The king had much time to contemplate and remember, to feel the frustrated desires and lack of reconciliation, to endure the silence that spanned the distance between the palace and the Tower."[92]

Bergeron does not discuss Howard's motivations for arranging the death of Overbury before her marriage to Somerset, but it is reasonable to assume that she wanted to ensure that her husband would be faithful to her, even as James had desired that Somerset would be faithful to him. She would certainly have been aware that Overbury's "crime"—his refusing an ambassadorial position—was hardly grounds for lifelong imprisonment. Thus, by having Overbury poisoned and by swearing to secrecy those responsible so that Overbury's death was represented as due to natural causes, Howard hoped to eliminate the threat that Overbury would likely have posed to her marital relationship with Somerset.

Young points out that even before Somerset's fall from grace, James had begun to turn his affections toward Villiers, who managed to catch James's eye when opponents of Somerset succeeded in having him appointed cup-bearer, which brought him into regular contact with the king.[93] Somerset had bitterly protested Villiers's appointment, but to no avail. In Young's view, the fact that Queen Anne asked James to promote Villiers to the post of groom of the bedchamber indicates the accommodation that she had worked out with her husband: "As George Abbot, the Archbishop of Canterbury, and the leader of the Villiers forces, explained, 'James had a fashion, that he would never admit any to nearness about himself but such an one as the Queen should commend unto him.'"[94] In this way, she had a voice in the selection, and if she should complain about it later, James could say that she had no grounds for complaint because, as the Archbishop put it, "you were the party that commended

92. Ibid.

93. Young, *King James and the History of Homosexuality*, 31.

94. Ibid., 32.

him unto me."[95] Young believes that Queen Anne reluctantly agreed to help the archbishop and his allies in their promotion of Villiers because of her intense dislike for Somerset. However, Bergeron notes that Anne's support of Villiers thereby "sealed the enlarging gap that existed between royal husband and wife," and, therefore,

> Some sense of hopelessness must have governed Anne's action, a recognition that she had lost James's genuine interest years ago. Anne may have seen herself as merely playing a role, participating in James's fiction while fully understanding the reality. Perhaps she held some vestige of hope that her action would endear her to James, a hope nevertheless unsupported by facts. By seeming to be instrumental in Villiers's advancement, Anne temporarily exercised a kind of political power. Any or all of these ideas might have prompted her action.[96]

In any event, essentially the same pattern that took place in the case of Somerset transpired here as well. Going further than his wife's recommendation that Villiers be appointed a groom of the bedchamber, James made him a gentleman of the bedchamber, and from there Villiers rose inexorably through the ranks of the peerage (viscount in 1616, earl in 1617, marquis in 1619), achieving the exalted status of Duke of Buckingham in 1623.[97] Just twenty-two years old when James met him in 1614, Villiers had become one of the most powerful men in England by the age of thirty-one. As evidence that James, like Anne, was capable of accommodation, Villiers's marriage in 1620 had all the formal support and none of the sense of betrayal that accompanied Somerset's marriage to Howard. In fact, James seems to have found in the family of the Earl of Buckingham that family of which he had been deprived as an only son growing up without parents. As Young puts it,

> It is touching to see how happily he involved himself in Buckingham's family, constantly sending gifts, visiting Kate [Buckingham's wife] when she was sick, making a special fuss over little Mall [their daughter Mary]. At the end of his life, James behaved more solicitously towards Buckingham's family than he had previously towards his own. And having never shown

95. Ibid.

96. Bergeron, *Royal Family, Royal Lovers*, 138.

97. Young, *King James and the History of Homosexuality*, 32.

much interest in the company of women, he now delighted in the company of Buckingham's mother, wife and daughter.[98]

However, Young goes on to discuss the disastrous consequences of Buckingham's turn to foreign affairs in conjunction with James's son, Charles, and the role that the two young men played in maneuvering England into the Thirty Years' War (a war that began in 1618 between German Catholics and Protestants but that eventually involved several European nations). In 1628, just three years after James's death in 1625, Buckingham was stabbed to death "by a disgruntled sailor who was applauded by a nation groaning under the strains of a costly, inglorious war."[99]

Was King James a Sodomist?

Thus far, McGrath's phrase "homosexual tendencies" has served in this chapter as a general descriptor for James's relationships with Esmé Stuart, Robert Carr, and George Villiers. Yet, as anyone knows who reads even cursorily in the enormous literature on human sexuality that has been produced over the past few decades, the very word *homosexual* is a contested, debatable term, especially when applied to earlier historical periods. It is often pointed out that because the word *homosexual* did not appear until the last decades of the nineteenth century—the precise dating is often debated as well—it is anachronistic to use it, for example, in reference to King James, who lived at the end of the sixteenth century and at the beginning of the seventeenth. Indeed, as Young points out, "Some scholars believe that the whole mental construct of homosexuality, like the word itself, is of relatively recent origin," and one school of thought locates the "invention of homosexuality" at the very end of the seventeenth century while others postpone it till the eighteenth or nineteenth century.[100] In either view, James and his contemporaries had no concept or understanding of homosexuality per se. In Young's view, it is true that James and his contemporaries did not have a concept of a homosexual as distinct from a heterosexual, so for this reason Young chooses not to refer to James as a homosexual.[101] On the other hand, although it is probably correct to say that homosexuality is the invention of the modern

98. Ibid., 33.

99. Ibid., 34.

100. Ibid., 3.

101. Ibid.

world, Young believes that these more modern ways of thinking about homosexuality were already underway in James's time. Therefore, if premodern ways of thinking were still predominant in James's era, "they existed alongside other ways that would eventually come to be thought of as modern."[102]

A specific illustration of the coexistence of premodern and modern ways of thinking rests in the fact that the premodern concept of sodomy was seldom invoked in contemporary references to James's behavior. In fact, James himself wrote a vigorous condemnation of sodomy in *Basilikon Doran* (which means "royal gift"), a book he wrote to instruct Prince Henry on how to be a good king.[103] Was he being hypocritical, condemning sodomy if others committed it, but not if he engaged in it himself? Young thinks the answer is more complex, namely, that "James could have been perfectly earnest in condemning sodomy while simultaneously engaging in what we today call homosexual behavior. When James invited Somerset into his bed or succeeded in getting Buckingham into bed, there is no reason to believe that he recognized what he was doing as that 'detestable, and abominable sin, amongst Christians not to be named.'"[104]

Young is quoting here a statement by Sir Edward Coke, the famous jurist of the period, who explained in his *Institutes* that sodomy is "a detestable, and abominable sin, amongst Christians not to be named, committed by carnal knowledge against the ordinance of the Creator, and order of nature."[105] Legally, it was classified as a felony, and anyone convicted of it was subject to execution. The severity of the punishment, however, meant that even if it could not be named, it needed to be defined, and it was Coke's view that it was necessary to prove that penetration had occurred in order to establish a case of sodomy:

> In his own words, there had to be ejaculation or *emissio seminis*, but also "there must be *penetratio*, that is, *res in re*." For Coke, therefore (if we set aside bestiality), sodomy meant two men having anal intercourse to the point of ejaculation. This legal definition was exceedingly narrow. It specified only one sex act between men, anal intercourse, and excluded all other genital sex acts—masturbation, oral sex, and intracrural or

102. Ibid., 4.
103. Ibid., 49.
104. Ibid.
105. Ibid., 48–49.

intrafemoral intercourse. Men rubbing their bodies together or mutually masturbating were not committing sodomy.[106]

In Young's view, it is a "good question" whether James in fact committed sodomy, as this depends on what, precisely, he did when he went to bed with his favorites. Young therefore asks whether it may be possible to get beyond the euphemism—"went to bed"—and be more specific about what James and his favorites actually did in bed. He concludes, "There is only one possible clue, and it suggests masturbation."[107] This clue, he suggests, occurs in a letter from Villiers. As Young notes, Villiers (or Buckingham) and James enjoyed double meanings and wordplay in their letters, and Buckingham may therefore have had a double meaning in mind when he wrote the following thanks to James for appointing him a duke: "'There is this difference betwixt that noble hand and heart, one may surfeit by the one, but not by the other, and sooner by yours than his own.'" Young adds: "Whether or not these specific words refer to masturbation, it is entirely possible that James and his favorites refrained from anal intercourse. And if they did not engage in anal intercourse, it is arguable that they did not engage in sodomy."[108]

Young acknowledges that we cannot know whether James made the same distinction in his mind that Sir Edward Coke had made on legal grounds: "He was a notorious hypocrite where swearing and drinking were concerned; he could simply have been the same where sodomy was concerned. Or he could simply have felt that, as an absolute monarch, the normal rules did not apply to him. But if he refrained from anal intercourse, there is no necessary reason why the accusation of sodomy should even have crossed his mind."[109] So Young concludes that we cannot know for certain whether James engaged in sex (other than masturbation) with Carr and Villiers. But what we *do* know is that his relations with his favorites raised suspicions in the public at large. As Young points out,

> These people had no way of knowing precisely what James and
> his favorites did in bed, and in any case there is no reason to

106. Ibid., 49.

107. Ibid., 71.

108. Ibid., 49.

109. Ibid., 50. It is worth noting that if James could claim that the normal rules did not apply to him, the men with whom he had sex could not have made the same claim. Conceivably, this fact played a role in Carr's and Villiers's withdrawal of their affection for James and their decision to seek marriage.

think that they drew the fine distinctions that lawyers such as Coke did. It is true that there were very few legal prosecutions against sodomy in early Stuart England, and it may be true that there was "tacit acceptance" of sex between males in many households and schools. But people did take notice of James and his favorites.[110]

Young cites the diary entry of Sir Simonds D'Ewes in 1622 in which he tells about how he and a good friend had discussed the sin of sodomy and how frequently it occurred in London. He noted that if God did not provide "some wonderful blessing against it, wee could not but expect some horrible punishment for it; especially it being as wee had probable cause to feare, a sinne in the prince [i.e. James]."[111]

The Charge of Effeminacy and James's Pacifism

As Coke's statement about sodomy indicates, sodomy was considered a terrible sin and a serious crime. If James was invulnerable to charges of sodomy, however, this did not mean that his "homosexual tendencies" were without serious political costs. In fact, from a political point of view, he was especially vulnerable to what would seem to have been a much lesser crime than sodomy, and his vulnerability in this regard led him to accede to pressure to reverse his longstanding commitment to peace in the final years of his reign. This was the charge of effeminacy.

While the word *effeminate* was sometimes used in James's day to imply that a man was excessively attracted to women, Young states that in a great many more cases it described a male who assumed the "female"— that is, the passive or receptive—role.[112] This could certainly occur in marital relationships between husbands and wives, but it was believed to be the particular consequence of relations between older and younger men. Antitheatrical tracts condemned the practice of boys dressing as women on stage, on grounds that the direct consequence of such behavior is sexual inversion, leading ultimately to sodomy.

Also, a persistent criticism of James by his political opponents, but one that reached a crescendo in the 1620s, was that "he allowed blatantly effeminate favorites who were his known lovers to dominate his court,"

110. Ibid.

111. Ibid., 50; see Bourcier, *The Diary of Sir Simonds D'Ewes*, 92–93.

112. Young, *King James and the History of Homosexuality*, 71.

and these attacks made a direct association between his attraction to effeminate men and his pacifism, that is, his great reluctance to commit the
nation to war.[113] Young acknowledges that we cannot know for certain
how much this association of effeminacy and pacifism was "rhetorical
pose" and how much was "genuine alarm," but what we can know "is that
these authors already defined effeminacy as we do and linked it to male
homosexuality. More importantly, unless they had the bizarre intention
of writing works that would be unintelligible to their readers, they must
have assumed that the public thought in the same terms."[114]

Young discusses the associations made at the time between the
qualities of effeminacy and passivity, on the one hand, and sexual behavior between two males, on the other. Such associations have direct
relevance to James's relationships with Esmé Stuart, Robert Carr, and
George Villiers. Young cites in this connection Michael Rocke's study of
Renaissance Florence in which Rocke

> showed that a great many Florentine males during the 1440s
> passed through three stages of sexual activity: as adolescents
> they were "passive" or "receptive" partners of older men, as
> young men they became the "active" or "dominant" partners in
> such relationships, and around the age of thirty they married
> and more or less stopped having sex with other males. It would
> have been rare, therefore, for homosexual relationships to in-
> volve two adult men. Instead, relationships typically involved
> adults and younger males.[115]

Young notes a growing body of opinion that sexual relations "between
active men and passive adolescents" were typical of all Europe until about
1700, and that, while there is no evidence of homosexual relations occurring in England on the scale found in Florence, when they did occur, they
followed this age-differentiated pattern.

How does this age-differentiated pattern relate to King James?
Young acknowledges that James does not fit the Florentine pattern for
two reasons: (1) he married earlier, and (2) he continued to have male
lovers during his marriage.[116] But marriage was vitally important to him
because of his political need to produce heirs. For Young, the more sig-

---

113. Ibid., 72.
114. Ibid.
115. Ibid., 149; see Rocke, *Forbidden Friendships*.
116. Young, *King James and the History of Homosexuality*, 72.

nificant fact, therefore, is that, in concert with the Florentine pattern, James's relationships with his major favorites were age differentiated: James was thirteen when Esmé Stuart was approximately thirty-seven; he was forty-one when he became infatuated with Robert Carr, who was about twenty; and he was forty-eight when he first had sexual relations with George Villiers, who was about twenty-three. Young points out that, unlike the relationship between Stuart and James, James's relationships with Carr and Villiers were not, strictly speaking, pederastic, as both were young adults rather than boys: "But Carr and Buckingham [Villiers] were barely adults, and James was twice their age. These were certainly age-differentiated relationships. If we take twenty years as the distance between generations, they even qualify as trans-generational relationships."[117]

Young also notes that neither Carr nor Villiers experienced the second stage in the Florentine pattern. Instead, both moved from the first to the third. Indeed, "Somerset apparently made this passage [from stage 1 to stage 3] all too well to suit James, since he stopped going to bed with him sometime after marrying Frances Howard."[118] This may suggest that, in our terms today, James was more homosexual in his sexual orientation than either Carr or Villiers. In any event, in terms of the active and passive roles, James was the only one of the three men who experienced both, and in his reign as king of England, he clearly took the active role.

For Young, this raises an interesting question: If effeminacy was associated with passivity, we would expect that Carr and Villiers would be subject to the charge of effeminacy, as indeed they were. In fact, they had the physical appearance that invited the effeminacy label, as they were young, smooth-skinned, beardless, and androgynous looking, which made them attractive to James. But if James took the active role, would this not have immunized him against the effeminacy charge? This, however, was not the case, for, as Young points out, "the stigma of effeminacy was also attached to James himself."[119] Young therefore wonders

> how much the doubts about his manliness arose from his relations with effeminate favorites and how much from his pacific foreign policy. He appeared to be ruled by his feelings or ruled by his favorites. In both these respects, he looked like the passive

117. Ibid., 150.
118. Ibid.
119. Ibid., 154–55.

or subordinate partner, but it was his passivity in foreign affairs that his critics found most irksome . . . They scolded, implored and exhorted him to take action. His passivity called his manhood into question and made him more susceptible to charges of effeminacy. If he had been a more martial figure, the effeminacy of his favorites might not have rubbed off on him.[120]

When James was newly installed as king of England in 1604, the French ambassador commented on his "extraordinary weakness" and "unmeasured love of peace," and judged that James "will on no provocation, commence a war, but will endeavor to maintain peace, even by bad, foolish, and disgraceful means."[121] Young suggests that James's "aversion to war was probably a natural product of his insecure and violent childhood."[122] He adds that James's deeply personal letter to Somerset in 1615 also seems to suggest that even though James assumed the active role in his sexual solicitations, he was still the passive one in the sense that his partners recognized that he was more emotionally needy than they.

The Charge of Pacifism and Bible Translation

The foregoing discussion of the charge that James was effeminate may not seem to have any relevance to the issue with which we are concerned here, namely, the relationship between James's "homosexual tendencies" and his commissioning of the English translation of the Bible. To be sure, McGrath suggests that the commissioning came at a time when James was being criticized for his "increasingly obvious homosexual tendencies," and McGrath goes on to note that the "commissioning of the new translation of the Bible was one of the first positive acts of the new king of England."[123] McGrath implies that the commissioning of the Bible translation would have offset, to some degree, the complaints that James was engaging in overt homosexual behavior at court. If the populace did not like his behavior at court, they would certainly applaud his interest in the Bible.

However, the foregoing discussion of the effeminacy charge against James suggests that the relationship between James's homosexual tendencies and his commissioning of a new translation of the Bible was more

120. Ibid., 155.
121. Ibid., 78.
122. Ibid.
123. McGrath, *In the Beginning*, 170–71.

complex. Complexity arises because a major sign of James's effeminacy in the eyes of his critics was the fact that he considered himself an intellectual—a man of the pen, not of the sword. As Young points out, "James was a scholar, an intellectual, who thought that true manliness required reflection, not impulsive violence."[124] In this regard, Young notes James's efforts to suppress dueling,[125] and Bergeron notes that when James signed a peace treaty with Spain in 1604 (the same year that he commissioned the new translation of the Bible), he adopted the motto *Beati Pacifici*, a reference to the Beatitude "Blessed are the peacemakers: for they shall be called the children of God" (Matt 5:9, KJV).[126]

Many of his subjects had a very different view, and some wrote tracts that were highly critical of James on this very point. One tract writer, Thomas Scott, compared James to the lazy sluggard in the book of Proverbs (Prov 26:13–16) and cited as evidence the king's attraction to sensual pleasures (coded language for his homosexual tendencies?) and the fact that the king prided himself on his book learning.[127] As Young puts it, "Scott wanted a real man of action, not an effete intellectual."[128] Another polemicist, John Reynolds, noted that Philip of Spain "loves King James his Gowne & Pen, yet no way feares his sword," since "hee never yet knew the way to draw it."[129] Reynolds complained that the other nations have no reason to fear the English because "the element and delight of their King is bookes, not battailes, the pen, not the Pike."[130] The pen is mightier than the sword? Not according to Reynolds. Furthermore, Englishmen would command more respect "if they wore worse cloathes, and had better hearts and swords, and if they were more martiall and lesse effeminate."[131]

---

124. Young, *King James and the History of Homosexuality*, 78.

125. Ibid., 86.

126. Bergeron, *Royal Family, Royal Lovers*, 78.

127. Young, *King James and the History of Homosexuality*, 92. These verses portray the sluggard in a rather negative light, but James could have suggested to Scott that he might want to ponder the next verse: "Like somebody who takes a passing dog by the ears is one who meddles in the quarrel of another" (Prov 26:17). James could have argued that this proverb had informed his international policy and, more specifically, his refusal to commit England to involvement in a war between two other nations. There are other ways to play the role of peacemaker.

128. Ibid.

129. Quoted in ibid., 93.

130. Quoted in ibid.

131. Quoted in ibid.

Young cites another tract by an anonymous author, which circulated around London in 1622. This tract "came dangerously close to accusing James of sodomy. It also made a pointed issue of his manliness. What the anonymous author of this tract wanted, in effect, was for James to remake or refashion himself. Whereas James prided himself on being a man of letters and a peacemaker, this author wanted him to become precisely the opposite. He told James that he could obtain 'with the sword, [that] which you have so often in vaine desired with your pen.'"[132] Thus, in the polemical tracts of the times, there is a strong association between effeminacy and the intellectual life.

The fact that one of James's first acts as King of England was to commission a translation of the Bible was not, therefore, the singularly positive act that McGrath makes it out to be. McGrath is certainly right to point out that "the New Bible would be a rallying point for a Protestant English nation" over and against Roman Catholicism, "which was enjoying a newfound strength and stability on the European mainland."[133] But when it became clear that James had no desire to engage England in battle against Spain or in behalf of German Protestants against Catholic Protestants, the new Bible was less a "rallying point" and more a further sign of James's—and hence, England's—effeminacy. As McGrath himself concludes: "By the time of its [the Bible's] final appearance in 1611, James's popularity had waned substantially. People began to long for the good old days of Queen Elizabeth, with whom James was regularly compared—unfavorably."[134] As Young points out, one of the unfavorable comparisons between James and Elizabeth was that "Elizabeth had been more of a man than James was."[135]

The Sublimation of Male Aggression

We are now prepared to examine the issue with which this chapter has been concerned, namely, the relationship between James's "homosexual tendencies" and his commissioning a new English translation of the Bible. Our argument is twofold. First, we believe that in commissioning this translation, James, in effect, created a model of male cooperative

132. Ibid., 90.

133. McGrath, *In the Beginning*, 171.

134. Ibid.

135. Young, *King James and the History of Homosexuality*, 90.

enterprise that was no less manly than the martial model advocated by his critics. This cooperative model had biblical warrant, the very beatitude that James was fond of quoting and that he took as the motto for his own kingship: "Blessed are the peacemakers, for they shall be called the children of God" (Matt 5:9, KJV).

For a man whose mother left him as a thirteen-month-old baby, and a man who had no contact whatsoever with his father, a beatitude that suggests that peacemaking is the way to become a child of God would seem to have had deep psychological resonance. As we noted, the model that he proposed for the translation was that the entire text of the Bible would be divided into six sections and that each "company" would be composed of the same number of men.[136] McGrath's term, "company," suggests a military analogy. (A company is defined in military terms as a small body of troops normally composed of two or more platoons and a headquarters.) King James would be the commander-in-chief, with the bishops assigned the task of working out the campaign strategy. The translation companies appear to have set almost immediately to work, but the initial progress was slow—so slow, in fact, that "some accused the translators of laziness."[137] Ironically, or fittingly, this was the same charge that Thomas Scott made against King James when he compared him with the lazy sluggard in the book of Proverbs.

Nevertheless, the translators carried out their commission. Significantly for our argument here, they used the military analogy in their preface (which is generally omitted from modern versions of the King James Bible, due to its length). Heading the list of several metaphors was this: "[The Bible] is not only an armor, but also a whole armory of weapons, both offensive and defensive; whereby we may save ourselves and put the enemy to flight."[138] The translators also pointed out that God is "the Author" of the "original," that "the inditer" (the one who dictated it) is "the holy spirit, not the wit of the Apostles or Prophets," and that "the Penmen" (those who wrote it down) "were sanctified from the womb, and endued with a principal portion of God's spirit."[139]

The sword is mightier than the pen? Not to the company of men who translated the King James Bible. In effect, the Bible that bore his

---

136. McGrath, *In the Beginning*, 178.

137. Ibid., 182.

138. Ibid., 190.

139. Ibid.

name was James's answer to the anonymous tract writer who said that he could achieve with the sword what he had been unable to achieve through the pen. James could not have accomplished this alone any more than a general can wage battle without troops, and in a remarkable gesture of goodwill, the translators made clear "that they were building on honorable foundations laid by others."[140] At the same time, they hoped that their own work would be appreciated: "As nothing is begun and perfected at the same time, and the later thoughts are thought to be the wiser: so, if we, building upon their foundation that went before us, and being holpen by their labours, do endeavor to make that better which they left so good; no man, we are sure, hath cause to mislike us; they, we persuade ourselves, if they were alive would thank us."[141] This is very similar to the rhetoric of military men who carry on the struggle to its ultimate conclusion so that their predecessors will not have died in vain. Thus, the company of translators created by James's commissioning of a new English Bible was itself a dramatic refutation of contemporary criticism of the effeminate or effete scholar as exemplified by James himself.

The translation of the Bible may thus be viewed as a religious sublimation of male aggression, the aggression exploited by those who believe that the highest expression of manliness is the ability to wage war, or, as Young puts it, to engage in "impulsive violence."[142] It is noteworthy in this regard that King James is undoubtedly the most often referred to king in English history, and the sole reason for this is that he commissioned the translation of the Bible.

We believe that the commissioning of the translation was also a way for James to sublimate his own aggressions traceable to his early childhood and to the violence that occurred in his parents' relationship. This aggression was evident in his role in the execution of his own mother—a role instigated, in part, by his desire to win the favor of Queen Elizabeth, who became, for a time, a surrogate mother. We have seen that it was in 1603 that he had a rich pall of velvet hung over her grave in Peterborough Cathedral, that in 1605 he named his newborn royal daughter Mary in honor of his mother, and that during the same phase of his kingship he ordered the construction of an elaborate tomb for his

---

140. Ibid., 192.

141. Ibid., 192–93.

142. Young, *King James and the History of Homosexuality*, 693.

mother in Westminster Abbey, where her body was reinterred in 1612.[143] This rehabilitation of his mother coincided almost exactly with the 1604 commissioning, the production, and the 1611 initial printing of the King James Bible. In one sense, there is every reason to assume that the timing of these two sets of events was purely coincidental. In fact, it would have been impossible for James to take steps to rehabilitate his mother while Queen Elizabeth remained on the throne. On the other hand, James was under no political pressure to rehabilitate his mother's reputation, and, as we have seen, modern interpreters of James's efforts to rehabilitate his mother's reputation consider this to have been a very personal matter—a form of expiation, a means to still a guilty conscience. We suggest that his decision to commission the translation of the Bible, however politically expedient it may have been, was integral to this expiation process.

A clue in this regard, one that also has direct relevance to the effeminacy charge, is provided by Erik H. Erikson's discussion of passivity in *Young Man Luther*. Speaking of Luther's discovery that faith is not something that we do but something that is done for—and in—us, Erikson points out that many a young man

> becomes a great man in his own sphere only by learning that deep passivity which permits him to let the data of his competency speak to him. As Freud said in a letter to [Wilhelm] Fliess, "I must wait until it moves in me so that I can perceive it: *bis es sich in mir ruehrt und ich davon erfahre.*" This may sound feminine, and, indeed, Luther bluntly spoke of an attitude of womanly conception—*sicut mulier in conceptu.* Yet it is clear that men call such attitudes and modes feminine only because the strain of paternalism has alienated us from them; for these modes are any organism's birthright, and all our partial as well as our total functioning is based on a metabolism of passivity and activity.[144]

Erikson observes that before a man develops the active modes associated with his father, "a mother taught him to touch the world with his searching mouth and his probing senses. What to a man's man, in the course of his development, seems like a passivity hard to acquire, is only a regained ability to be active with his oldest and most neglected modes."[145] He concludes: "Intrinsic to the kind of passivity we speak of is not only the memory of having been given, but also the identification with the

143. Bergeron, *Royal Family, Royal Lovers*, 73–74.

144. Erikson, *Young Man Luther*, 207–8.

145. Ibid., 208.

maternal giver . . . I think that in the Bible Luther at last found a mother whom he could acknowledge: he could attribute to the Bible a generosity to which he could open himself, and which he could pass on to others, at last a mother's son."[146]

The translators' preface to the King James Bible captures this very sense of the Bible as a generous mother. To be sure, it does not use the maternal metaphor itself, but immediately following the military metaphor noted earlier, it offers a plethora of metaphors that focus on the Bible's life-bestowing qualities: "It is not an herb, but a tree, or rather a whole paradise of trees of life, which bring forth fruit every month, and the fruit thereof is for meat, and the leaves for medicine. It is not a pot of Manna, or a cruse of oil, which were for memory only, or for a meal's meat or two, but as it were a shower of heavenly bread sufficient for a whole host, be it never so great; and as it were a whole cellar full of oil vessels; whereby all our necessities may be provided for, and our debts discharged."[147] The idea that the Bible provides for all our necessities and discharges all of our debts seems particularly relevant to James, both because he lost his own mother in infancy, and also because he carried for years a profound sense of guilt for having failed her in her hour of need. The maternal image is made explicit in the observation, noted earlier, that the Bible's "penmen . . . were sanctified from the womb."[148] Thus, James's commissioning of the new translation of the Bible was an "identification with the maternal giver," the mother he had never known. It is not surprising, therefore, that the Bible verse with which he personally identified was Matt 5:9: "Blessed *are* the peacemakers: for they shall be called the children of God" (KJV).

Conclusion

In *The History of an Infantile Neurosis*, popularly known as the case of "the Wolf Man," Freud writes about a young Russian boy who, in the evening, would climb up on a chair in the bedroom and kiss the holy pictures that hung in the room.[149] In his concluding chapter of *Repressed Emotions*, Isador H. Coriat, an American psychiatrist who was an early advocate

---

146. Ibid.

147. McGrath, *In the Beginning*, 190.

148. Ibid.

149. Freud, *The History of an Infantile Neurosis*, 16. See Carlin and Capps, "Freud's Wolf Man," 153, 162–65.

of psychoanalysis, relates the dream of a woman who believed in "living religion." The woman dreamed that she began to explore a room she had discovered at the end of a long gallery, whose door was marked "Holy of Holies" just under the keyhole. In spite of a horrified protest from her mother, she opened the door and found that the room was all but empty, containing a cedar chest that held ceremonial robes. Coriat suggests that the room "symbolizes a forbidden erotic and unconscious wish carried over from childhood."[150] In this chapter, we have related the story of a king who commissioned the translation of the Holy Bible. Holy pictures, holy places, holy words—these three forms of the holy are examples of the role that symbolization plays in the process of sublimation.[151]

We are aware, of course, that symbols of the holy are used for purposes that are self-serving, disingenuous, and deceitful. While we are in no position to question the motives of those who use the holy word to claim that there is only one sexual identity that is acceptable to God, we are aware of the fact that books and articles have been written with the intention of refuting the idea that King James had homosexual tendencies, and that a motivation for doing so is to protect the special status of the King James Version of the Bible.[152]

In conclusion, we would hope that our readers would not assume that in our emphasis on the homosexual tendencies of King James we are in any sense attempting to demean the King James Version in any way. Of course, at times we have used other translations in our personal and professional lives, but we have not felt that this is a sign or expression of disloyalty to the King James Version. Moreover, for both of us, our introduction to the Bible was to the King James Version. Carlin remembers that his maternal grandmother read to him from the King James Bible, and although he was too young to understand its language, he did understand his grandmother's love for the Bible, for God, and for him. Capps knew no other version of the Bible until he was confirmed at the age of fourteen and received a Revised Standard Version (RSV) on that occasion from the church he attended. While he appreciated the gift, he continued to appreciate the fact that the King James Version did not use paragraphs, which made it easier to identify and memorize specific verses. Thus, we both have reasons, reaching back into our childhoods,

---

150. Coriat, *Repressed Emotions*, 204–5. See Capps and Carlin, "Sublimation and Symbolization," 779.

151. The classic work on the holy is Rudolf Otto, *Idea of the Holy*.

152. See, for example, Coston, *King James the VI of Scotland & the I of England*.

for according the King James Version a special status among the various translations that we have become acquainted with over the years. The homosexual tendencies of the man who commissioned this translation and the fact that the translation process was one that reflected his own identification with these words of Jesus—"Blessed *are* the peacemakers; for they shall be called the children of God"—are other reasons for viewing it as an incomparable expression of the idea of the holy.

3

Methuselah and the Sublimation of Envy

Introduction

IN THIS CHAPTER, WE focus on the disparity between women and men in
regard to longevity. Women live longer than men. This does not, of course,
mean that all women live longer than men, but, on average, they do. As we
will indicate in the following discussion, there are various environmental
reasons why this is so. But, as we also will show, women have a constitutional superiority over men as far as longevity is concerned. This being
the case, we assume that men, generally speaking, are envious of women's
superiority in this regard and we further assume that envy is not a good
thing either for the one who envies *or* for the one who is the object of this
envy. Thus, we suggest that the concept of sublimation can be very useful
in addressing the problem of men's envy of women, as it suggests that the
envy men experience of women may be transformed in a way that is ben-
eficial to men as well as women. We propose that one form or expression
of such sublimation is the transformation of envy into emulation.

Why Women Live Longer Than Men

Beginning in 2006, one of us (Capps) began monitoring the "100 Plus"
feature of the church denominational magazine that he receives monthly.

This feature identifies the members of the denomination who are one hundred or more years old and who celebrated birthdays in the previous month. Each person is identified by age. Over the next eighteen months, of the 354 persons cited, 307 were women and 47 were men (an 87-to-13-percent ratio). Since more church members are women than men, we would expect the women to outnumber the men, but does this factor alone account for the wide margin?

These statistics run counter to what the Bible tells us about the longevity of men and women. According to the book of Genesis, men lived much longer than women did. Methuselah (Adam's great-great-great grandson and Noah's grandfather) was 969 when he died; Jared lived to 962; and Noah lived to 950, despite a tendency to abuse alcohol (Gen 9:20–24). The first ten patriarchs (from Adam to Noah) lived an average of 838 years, while the next ten lived an average of 317 years, a rather dramatic reduction in life expectancy that has led to the proposal that the flood had something to do with it. We will return to the biblical statistics later.

The more immediate question was, why do women today live longer than men? The fact that the other of us (Carlin) is a colleague of a well-known expert in the field of aging proved to be extremely helpful. The expert is Thomas Cole, author of an important study of aging in America and coeditor of a widely used compendium on aging.[1] When Carlin asked why it is that women appear to live longer than men, Cole responded that "Women live on the average seven years longer than men. There's lots of speculation about why. I favor the view that women are biologically hardier because they have to carry and give birth to children."[2] Cole also noted that maximum life expectancy now is 115–120. Although various biogerontologists are working to extend it to 140 and beyond, the fact that more people are living into their eighties and nineties has not yet altered the maximum life span. Also, the person who has lived the longest—to the undisputed age of 122—is a woman, Jeanne Calment.

The following studies support Cole's view that, on average, women live seven years longer than men, and that the primary reason for this is that women are biologically hardier than men because they give birth to children. As we will see, this biological hardiness has become a constitutional given and means that there is no necessary correlation between the number of children that an individual woman bears and her life

1. Cole, *Journey of Life*; and Cole and Winkler, *Oxford Book of Aging*.
2. Personal communication, spring 2006.

expectancy. In fact, a woman who does not bear a child is not, for this reason, considered to have a shorter life expectancy; the hardiness is biological and thus a characteristic that goes with being a woman. As we will also see, however, there are other environmental factors that counteract this biological superiority over men as far as their longevity is concerned.

Women's Life Expectancy is 6–7 Years Greater Than Men's

In their article, "In Search of Methuselah: Estimating the Upper Limits to Human Longevity," S. Jay Olshansky, Bruce A. Carnes, and Christine Cassel note that since the mid-nineteenth century "the human population has experienced one of the most important and dramatic changes in the history of the species—a near doubling of the expectation of life at birth from 40 to nearly 80 years."[3] They also note that most of the mortality rates in younger and middle age groups are so low in the United States that the complete elimination of mortality before the age of fifty would increase life expectancy at birth by only 3.5 years. This means that the potential for additional increases in longevity depends upon progress in dealing with the diseases of older adulthood. A great deal of progress in this regard has, in fact, occurred over the past several decades. The question, then, is whether further advances are likely, and, if so, how will this affect the average life expectancy at birth?

To get a handle on this question, the authors point out that the life expectancy at birth in the United States increased from forty-seven years in 1900 to about seventy-five years in 1988. In 1900, just under twelve out of every one hundred female babies born in that year died before their first birthday; there was a pronounced increase in mortality among women during their reproductive years; and the survivors of high infant, child, and maternal mortality often died between the ages of fifty and eighty. For female babies born in 1985, most will die between the ages of seventy and ninety. The upshot is that deaths from infectious and parasitic diseases have been replaced by, to a great extent, deaths from chronic degenerative diseases. Thus, the answer to the question of whether life expectancy will increase in the future depends on progress in the cure of chronic degenerative diseases.[4]

3. Olshansky et al., "In Search of Methuselah," 634.
4. Ibid., 635.

On the basis of some rather complex computations of the available demographic data, the authors conclude that eliminating cancer and heart disease would increase life expectancy by only six to seven years, and that eliminating all circulatory diseases, cancer, and diabetes would increase life expectancy by about fifteen years. This means, in their view, that it is rather unlikely that life expectancy will exceed the age of eighty-five. Since life expectancy in 1988 was seventy-five years (in comparison to forty-seven years in 1900), this also means that "the period of rapid increases in life expectancy in developed nations has come to an end."[5]

Yet, the authors also point out, the size of the oldest old population will continue to increase. In fact, we can expect that the size of the population aged sixty-five and older in the United States will more than double by 2030. This, however, is the result of the aging of the large baby boom cohorts born in the United States between 1946 and 1964. A feature of this study that is especially relevant to our concern with the differences between the life expectancies of women and men is that the eighty-five years figure applies to women. The gap between women's and men's life expectancy (six to seven years) does not change as life expectancy increases. Thus, the figures for the upper limits to human longevity always apply to women, not to men.

Women Have Higher Mortality Rates Than Men

If women have higher life expectancy rates than men, we would think that there would be more women on this earth than men. This, however, is not true. In "More Than 100 Million Women Are Missing," Amartya Sen, an economist, agreed with the claim that females are biologically hardier than males but challenged the inference that this means there are more women than men in the world.[6] Sen writes:

> At birth, boys outnumber girls everywhere in the world, by much the same proportion—there are around 105 or 106 male children for every 100 female children. Just why the biology of reproduction leads to this result remains a subject of debate. But after conception, biology seems on the whole to favor women. Considerable research has shown that if men and women receive similar nutritional and medical attention and general

5. Ibid., 637.

6. Sen, "More Than 100 Million Women Are Missing."

health care, women tend to live noticeably longer than men. Women seem to me, on the whole, more resistant to disease and in general hardier than men, an advantage they enjoy not only after they are forty years old but also at the beginning of life, especially during the months immediately following birth, and even in the womb. When given the same care as males, females tend to have better survival rates than males.[7]

But *do* females receive the same care as males? Sen argues that in some places in the world they do, but in many they do not, and that this has a direct effect on the ratio of women to men: "Women outnumber men substantially in Europe, the U.S., and Japan, where, despite the persistence of various types of bias against women (men having distinct advantages in higher education, job specialization, and promotion to senior executive positions, for example), women suffer little discrimination in basic nutrition and health care."[8] In other parts of the world (especially in South and West Asia and North Africa), however, the mortality rates of females are much higher than those of males, owing largely to the relative neglect of females, especially in health care and medical attention. So much higher are mortality rates for females that there are over one million fewer women than there would be with equality in health care.[9]

In a follow-up study, Stephen Klasen and Claudia Wink concluded that the absolute number of missing women has actually increased since Sen's groundbreaking studies, but has fallen in terms of the ratio of women to men, due largely to improvements for women's survival in most of South Asia and the Middle East.[10] In other words, where females receive equal medical attention and health care to what males receive, their inherently superior biological hardiness leads to a lower rather than a higher mortality rate.

Sen suggests that women's biological advantage does not arise "after they are forty years old," but is present at the very beginning of life, "especially during the months immediately following birth, and even in the womb."[11] He does not offer reasons why this seems to be the case. We will not even try to speculate as to why this should be, though it is tempting to think that the explanation has something to do with the fact that they

7. Ibid.
8. Ibid.
9. Ibid.
10. Klasen and Wink, "'Missing Women.'"
11. Sen, "More Than 100 Million Women Are Missing," 1.

and their mothers are the same sex. We are more interested, however, in the relationships between life in the womb, biological hardiness, and the greater longevity of women. And this brings us to Cole's explanation for why women have a better life expectancy than men.

Childbirth: Key to Women's Greater Longevity

Various explanations for why women live longer than men have been proposed, such as the fact that men have traditionally worked in unhealthy environments, that women are more at home in their social and natural environments, that women take better care of their bodies, that men do not adjust well to retirement, that women maintain better social connections, and that women are more spiritually oriented than men. In comparison with these seemingly reasonable explanations, the idea that women live longer because they develop a biological hardiness from carrying and giving birth to children seems rather counterintuitive. For isn't it a fact that childbirth has historically been one of the major causes of death among women? And isn't it true that many women feel physically depleted after giving birth? Also, there is the issue of postpartum depression. Wouldn't these factors suggest that, if anything, carrying and giving birth to children would have the effect of shortening, not prolonging, a woman's life?

In their article "Fertility and Lifespan: Late Children Enhance Female Longevity," Hans-George Muller et al. investigated the relation between fertility and postmenopausal longevity by studying a sample of 1635 women from a historical French Canadian cohort who lived past age fifty.[12] They made use of an earlier article by E. Le Bourg et al. that presented well-documented statistics on the dates of birth and death of an even larger number of women and the birthdates of their children based on church records.[13] From this larger group of women, Muller et al. focused exclusively on women above age fifty (i.e., the "post-reproductive period").

Muller et al. found that of the 1635 women in this group, 78 percent had at least four, 55 percent had at least eight, and 22 percent had at least twelve children. One finding was that the mortality rate of women in the postmenopausal period declined with each additional birth. The

12. Müller et al., "Fertility and Life Span."

13. Le Bourg et al., "Reproductive Life of French-Canadians in the 17th–18th Centuries."

mortality rate for women with ten or more births is 13 percent lower than that of women with one birth. Put another way, the probability that a woman would die in a given year between ages fifty and eighty was greater for women who had between one and seven children, as compared with women who had eight or more children. Thus, the more children a woman had, the longer her life expectancy.

Why this increased life expectancy for the more fertile group? Muller et al. hypothesized that the "extended remaining life expectancy for mothers with many children confers an evolutionary advantage. Highly fertile women will tend to have small [i.e., young] children at age 50, and their increased longevity is likely to improve the chances of survival for their offspring."[14] A consequence of this hypothesis is the prediction that, for women aged fifty, remaining life expectancy increases with the decreasing age of the youngest child. This prediction was supported. They found, for example, that a mother with a child of one year at age fifty will live nearly three years longer than a fifty-year-old mother with a child of five years.

This study confirms that biological hardiness due to the carrying and bearing of children enhances life expectancy, but it also indicates that a mother's desire to ensure the survival of a young child also contributes to longer life expectancy. In other words, the whole maternal process is involved in a woman's life expectancy. Or, as the authors put it, "A high level of fertility increases the chance that young offspring need to be cared for after menopause, and that the probability of their survival is likely to be linked to the presence of the mother as a care-giver . . . Thus, it is plausible that extended longevity confers a selective evolutionary advantage to women with late children."[15] This means that the "age of the last child is a more significant predictor of remaining lifetime than the number of births, a fact which may slightly favor the care-giver hypothesis of postmenopausal life extension."[16]

In their discussion of these findings, Muller et al. note the obvious fact "that there is a large death toll directly associated with child bearing in this historical cohort."[17] The greatest likelihood of death occurs, however, with a woman's first pregnancy or delivery. The death-rate decreases

14. Müller et al., "Fertility and Life Span," B204.

15. Ibid., B205.

16. Ibid., B206.

17. Ibid., B204–5.

with later pregnancies, and this, too, is indirect evidence that the carrying and bearing of children produces greater biological hardiness. They also note that for this cohort group vulnerability to death occurred at around eighty years. As this vulnerable age occurred in the "more natural" reproductive setting provided by a historical group of women, it would be less likely to be observable "in a modern cohort under the conditions of birth control and largely improved medical care."[18] This suggests that under "natural conditions," the life expectancy of women who bear children is approximately eighty years, or thirty years beyond the reproductive period. If male life expectancy is some six to seven years less than that of women, this would mean that under "natural conditions," their life expectancy would be about seventy-two to seventy-three years.

The Central Issue

This leads us to the central issue of this chapter: If women's greater longevity than men is primarily due to the fact that they carry, bear, and care for children, this would mean that women, on average, have *always* lived longer than men, and there would appear to be relatively little that men might do to change this fundamental fact of life. We would expect that men would envy women's greater longevity, especially because conventional models of masculinity tend to encourage men not to think that they are inferior to women in matters of physical strength and endurance. We would also expect that this envy would be greatest among persons who think that longevity is a good thing. If longevity were not viewed as an inherently good thing, or if longevity were viewed as a curse, men would not be expected to be envious of women in this regard. But, as Cole points out in his cultural history of aging in America, the idea that longevity is an inherent good became a widespread belief between 1830 and 1870, and we have the religious evangelicals and health reformists, a seemingly unlikely coalition, to thank for this.[19] Thus, to set the context for our discussion of male envy of women's tendency to outlive them, we need to consider in greater detail the emergence of the belief in the inherent goodness of longevity.

18. Ibid., B205.
19. Cole, *Journey of Life*, 92–109.

Longevity and the Laws of God

As Cole points out, religious evangelicals in the middle decades of the nineteenth century emphasized the spiritual perfectibility of the individual, and this emphasis led them to suggest that physical perfectibility should accompany spiritual perfectibility. Health reformers joined the evangelicals, preaching "a physical perfectionism that dovetailed nicely with evangelical perfectionism."[20] In effect, "the Kingdom of God required perfect bodies as well as perfect souls. From this perspective, disease and suffering owed their existence not to God's inscrutable will but to human transgression. Sin alone—understood as ignorance or disobedience of God's natural laws—caused physical pain, disease, and infirmity. Since all individuals possessed the capacity for sinless perfection, all might achieve a state of perfect health."[21]

Sylvester Graham, author of *Lectures on the Science of Human Life*, published in 1839, claimed that matters of "life, health, disease, and diet" were ultimately governed by fixed laws and observable by the methods of science: "Our disquietudes, and diseases, and ultimately death must therefore spring not from the fulfillment, but from the infraction of the laws of God."[22] Thus, greater longevity is a sign of one's adherence to the laws of God. As Graham wrote, "The true principles of health and longevity, and the true principles of virtue and religion, are inseparable."[23] Also, as William Alcott, a physician, noted in his book *Forty Years in the Wilderness of Pills and Powders*, published in 1859: "Old age, whenever it is wretched, is made so by sin. Suffering has no necessary connection with old age, any more than with youth or manhood . . . If Methuselah suffered from what we call the infirmities of age, it was his own fault. God, his Creator, never intended it."[24]

Cole notes that hygienic perfectionists and evangelical perfectionists were unable "to maintain a realistic view of aging—neither could abide the uncontrollable contingencies of the body's temporal destiny."[25] On the other hand, their concern for the prolongation of human life made a great deal of practical sense, for, in midcentury Massachusetts, for ex-

20. Ibid., 94.
21. Ibid.
22. Ibid., 95.
23. Ibid., 92.
24. Ibid.
25. Ibid., 93–94.

ample, as many as three infants in ten died before their first birthday, and life expectancy at birth was roughly forty years for men and forty-three years for women.[26] (Note that women had a longer life expectancy even then.) But, as Cole points out, "Historical progress always carries a price. In this case, the popular legitimating and pursuit of longevity harbored evasive and hostile attitudes about the realities of aging. Rather than simply liberating them from orthodox dogma, the quest for perfect health eventually saddled many middle-class Americans with feelings of failure and shame in the face of physical decline."[27]

It seems plausible to suggest that men may well have felt such failure and shame even more than women, as the life expectancy of women, even with their vulnerability to death in childbirth, was several years longer than that of men. Men may also have concluded that because women's life expectancy was greater, women must therefore be closer to spiritual perfection than they were. Conceivably, the widespread belief among men themselves that women are more religious than men may itself be due, at least in part, to the fact that women live longer than men do.

How Long Are We Meant to Live?

As Cole observes, there were also discussions of how long "the perfectly healthy individual" might live:

> Answers to this question ranged from eighty years to a thousand, without unduly straining contemporary credulity. Before the days of life insurance records and vital statistics registration, even informed opinion enjoyed a degree of freedom unimaginable in today's world of demographic exactitude. Not statistical probability but examples of alleged individual longevity seemed to provide the most reliable source of knowledge. If Methuselah lived 969 years, or if Thomas Parr lived 152 years (William Harvey performed the autopsy in 1635 without doubting Parr's actual age), or Luigi Cornaro lived 98 years, then perhaps others could reach similar ages by obtaining the secrets of these prodigies.[28]

Cole cites Russell Trall's observation in *The Hydropathic Encyclopedia*, published in 1852, that "if it can be proved that one man may live two or three

26. Ibid., 95.
27. Ibid.
28. Ibid., 100–101.

hundred years under the most favorable hygienic circumstances, we want no further evidence of the existence of a physiological law that *all* may, under precisely similar circumstances."[29] Trall was supported in this belief by the eminent physician Benjamin Rush, who contended that extremely old people tend to regenerate certain functions and even organs. In his view, such "renovations" among older persons in his own time accounted for "the ancient achievement of 'antediluvian age,'" that is, the ages attributed to biblical persons who lived prior to Noah's flood.[30] Cole adds:

> As long as biblical literalism survived, and no one critically scrutinized the birth or baptismal certificates of pro-longevity's prodigies, belief in the incredible ages of various antediluvian patriarchs or hygienic heroes remained widespread. "Facts and testimony," wrote Sylvester Graham, "constitute our only authority on this point . . . The Sacred Books written by Moses are unquestionably the most ancient and perhaps the only authentic testimony."[31]

Cole also notes that on the basis of such scriptural testimony Graham confidently asserted that "good habits" would prolong life expectancy to several hundred years and would result in "a much greater degree of youthfulness" throughout the life span as well.[32]

Flawed Attempts to Explain
Biblical Patriarchs' Longevity

As Cole's discussion of pro-longevity authors active between the 1830s and 1870s indicates, the biblical claim that Methuselah lived 969 years was accepted as the gospel truth, and one author, William Alcott, even went so far as to suggest that, if Methuselah suffered "the infirmities of old age," this was his own fault. In point of fact, the book of Genesis doesn't indicate whether Methuselah suffered—or didn't suffer—the infirmities of old age.

Not being biblical literalists ourselves, at first we more or less assumed that just about everyone today believes that the ages attributed to the patriarchs are greatly exaggerated. In the case of Methuselah himself,

29. Ibid., 101.
30. Ibid.
31. Ibid.
32. Ibid.

we guessed that his age was exaggerated by about nine hundred years, and that he probably died at the respectable age of sixty-nine. This would square nicely with the statement in Ps 90:10: "The years of our life are seventy or perhaps eighty if we are strong." Interestingly enough, this particular psalm is attributed to Moses. And yet, as we have seen, the pro-longevity authors of 1830 to 1870 assumed that Moses wrote the books that tell of the advanced ages of Methuselah and the other antediluvian patriarchs.

Our assumption that virtually everyone today believes that the in-credible ages attributed to the patriarchs are greatly exaggerated, how-ever, proved to be wrong. One online encyclopedia[33] that we consulted noted that some creationists have speculated that human beings lived longer before the flood because much less ultraviolet light from the sun reached the earth, which enabled longer life spans. A variation on this theory is that a vapor canopy existed around the earth before the flood, which would have protected human beings from the sun's aging effects.

Another creationist, Carl Wieland, in an article titled "Living for 900 Years," offers a different explanation. In a section of his article, under the heading "Noah's New Environment," Wieland notes that it is natural to think that the reduction in life spans reported in Genesis was due to environmental changes. He acknowledges that there were some environ-mental changes and that fossil records suggest that carbon-dioxide levels (also possibly oxygen levels) were higher in the preflood world. Wieland also notes the suggestion that an atmospheric canopy of water vapor shel-tered the preflood world from cosmic radiation, but "whether this is so or not, there is little evidence that aging is *substantially* influenced by any of these factors."[34]

But, for Wieland, this environmental explanation "stumbles at one important point."[35] As he explains:

> Noah was already over 600 years old when he stepped out of the Ark. But this allegedly much more hostile environment did not cause him to rapidly wither and die in a few decades. Instead, he lived for another 350 years, outstripping the age of even his ancestor Adam. We don't know whether environmental factors perhaps only cause problems in the developmental phase of hu-man life. However, one simple explanation for why Noah still

33. We can no longer find this online reference, but we are working from our notes.

34. Wieland, "Living for 900 Years," 12.

35. Ibid.

lived for so long is that Noah's genetic make-up was what gave him the potential to live so long. And that perhaps most, if not all, people before the [f]lood were programmed for much longer lifespans than we are programmed for today.[36]

So what happened? Wieland suggests that we "remember that the whole population shrank to just a handful," and notes that there "are well known ways in which forms of genes (known as alleles), which could include any coding for longer life-spans, can be eliminated from a population that has gone through such a 'bottleneck'—down to eight people."[37] Wieland's assumption that the human population was reduced to eight people brings to mind the famous question that irreverent boys (such as Carlin and Capps!) love to ask their Sunday school teachers: If Adam and Eve were the only people on the earth, where did Cain get his wife? It was not until such boys went to seminary, however, that they learned that the story of Noah's flood was adapted from a Babylonian epic written around 2000 BCE about the ancient king Gilgamesh, which contains a similar flood account.

Other biblical literalists do not invoke scientific explanations but instead simply affirm that God set a specific life span for human beings immediately before the flood. They cite passages such as Gen 6:3: "Then the LORD said, 'My spirit shall not abide in mortals forever, for they are flesh; their days shall be one hundred twenty years.'" In this view, God simply decided on the upward limit, so there is no need to speculate about the deleterious effects of the flood itself on human longevity. Interestingly enough, the 120 year figure is virtually identical to the view expressed by Cole that maximum life expectancy is now between 115 and 120 years.

The divine-fiat explanation, however, is confronted with the somewhat troubling "fact" that the flood did not immediately result in the reduction of longevity to the 120-year mark. Several of the postdiluvian patriarchs are said to have lived much longer than that: The book of Genesis indicates that Noah's son Shem died at age 600 (Gen 11:10–11); Shem's son Arpachshad died at 438 (Gen 11:12–13); Arpachshad's son Shelah died at age 433 (Gen 11:14–15); and Shelah's son Eber died at age 464 (Gen 11:16–17). These ages were roughly half the age of their antediluvian predecessors, so a decline in the ages of the patriarchs does occur after the flood, but it is nowhere near the 120-year limit that God announced just before the flood.

36. Ibid.
37. Ibid.

Interestingly enough, however, there is another significant decline after Eber: his son Peleg died at age 239 (Gen 11:18); Peleg's son Reu died at age 239 (Gen 11:20–21); and Reu's son Serug died at age 230 (Gen 11:22–23). After this threesome—who clustered around the 230 mark—the next three patriarchs (Nahor, Terah, and Abraham) died, respectively, at 148, 205, and 175 years. Pretty impressive from our own contemporary point of view, but a far cry from the 900+ years of seven of the first ten patriarchs, and almost double the 120-year maximum that God set prior to the flood. Apparently, even God, who was said to have used environmental disasters (floods, fires, and so forth) to teach humans a lesson, had to wait patiently as the genetic bottleneck took full effect.

The same online encyclopedia noted above also alludes to the speculation that the unusually high longevity of the patriarchs is the result of an error in translation. In this view, lunar cycles were mistaken for the solar ones, so the actual ages were 12.37 times less. This would mean that Methuselah lived seventy-eight years. Yet, this source also noted, two antediluvian patriarchs (Mahalalel and Enoch) fathered their male descendents at the age of sixty-five. If the lunar cycle were accepted, this would translate to an age of about five years and two months. If the antediluvian patriarchs' ages at death seem incredible, the notion that a five-year-old boy might father a son seems even more so.

The First Act of Fatherhood and Personal Longevity

Others may be impressed by one or another of these explanations for why the book of Genesis claims that the biblical patriarchs lived hundreds of years, but our own skepticism caused us to cast about for another explanation, and our own tendency to prefer psychosocial explanations led to some speculations of our own.

If, as Muller et al. show, late children enhance female longevity, is it possible that the writers of Genesis have a somewhat similar belief with regard to male longevity? Specifically, did they believe that fathering a descendent son later than earlier would mean that these men would live longer? Table 3.1 provides the data relevant to this question. Unfortunately, it does not support this or, for that matter, any other theory that would suggest a relationship between fathering a descendent son and personal longevity. Mahalalel fathered his son Jared at age sixty-five and lived to age 895, while Lamech fathered his son Noah at age 182 (117 years older) and lived to age 777 (118 years younger). Of course, a more comparable test of findings from Muller et al. would be the biblical patriarch's age when he fathered his *last* child. Unfortunately, the book of Genesis does not provide this "data." It typically asserts that other children, both male and female, were born to a patriarch after the birth of his descendent son, but the birthdates of later children relative to the age of the patriarch are not provided. Abraham's fatherhood of Ishmael and Isaac is the sole exception to this in Genesis.

Table 3.1

Patriarchs' Age at Birth of Descendent Son and Age at Death

Name	Age at Birth of Son	Age at Death	Intervening Years
Antediluvian Patriarchs			
Adam*	130	930	800
Seth	105	912	807
Enosh	90	905	815
Kenan	70	910	840
Mahalalel	65	895	830
Jared	162	962	800
Enoch	65	365	300
Methuselah	187	969	782
Lamech	182	777	595
Noah	500+	950	450
Postdiluvian Patriarchs			
Shem	100	600	500
Arpachshad	35	438	403
Shelah	30	433	403
Eber	34	464	430

Name	Age at Birth of Son	Age at Death	Intervening Years
Peleg	30	239	209
Reu	32	239	207
Serug	30	230	200
Nahor	29	148	119
Terah	70	205	135
Abraham**	86/100	175	89/75

* Adam fathered his sons Cain and Abel before he fathered Seth, but only the date for Seth is provided. Cain (the bad son) killed Abel (the good son) before Abel fathered a son of his own. A new descendent was needed in place of Abel, and Seth was his replacement (Gen 4:25–26).

** Two dates are provided here. Abraham was 86 when Ishmael was born (Gen 16:16) and 100 when Isaac was born (Gen 21:5).

Table 3.1 suggests that some realistic figures for the age at which a patriarch fathered a descendent son began to occur after the flood. Beginning with Arpachshad and continuing for the next six generations (Nahor), the ages at which patriarchs fathered descendent sons are in the upper twenties and early thirties. However, these more realistic figures seem to have no obvious relationship to the age of death, as the ages at death remain incredibly high. Yet they may explain why Abraham scoffed at the notion that he would father a son at age 100, though it is also worth noting that Abraham's own father Terah was 70 when Abraham was born and Abraham had fathered Ishmael just thirteen years earlier.

Methuselah: Hero of Pro-Longevity Enthusiasts

The fact that our speculation about a possible connection between age of first fatherhood and longevity led nowhere prompted us to focus our attention on the longevity issue itself and, more specifically, on the fact that the authors of Genesis seemed to share the same pro-longevity bias as the religious evangelicals and health reformists of the mid-1800s. This brought us to Methuselah, the biblical patriarch who was 969 years old when he died. To get a sense of how impressive this was, we imagined that we attended his funeral in 2015 and the eulogy focused on the fact that, having been born in 1046, he would have been 463 years old when John Calvin was born, and 657 years old when John Wesley was born. We imagined him reminiscing on his deathbed about all the changes he had seen in the course of his lifetime, and perhaps of the difficulties he had experienced in trying to adapt to all of them. We also thought of asking him what was the one thing he missed the most of all the things that had become obsolete in the course of his lifetime: Roasting a rabbit over a spit? Witnessing a criminal hanging from a noose? Writing with a feather? Wearing a monocle?

As we noted, Methuselah is the antediluvian patriarch who lived longer than anyone else: 969 years. He is therefore the hero of those who celebrate longevity—though honorable mention should be given to Jared, who lived to age 962 (just seven years less than Methuselah), and also to Noah, who, as we mentioned earlier, made it to 950 (Gen 9:20–24). But who *is* Methuselah? And what does the Bible say about him? As we have seen, Genesis 5 traces his ancestry back to Seth, the third son of Adam and Eve. According to Gen 5:3, "When Adam had lived a hundred and thirty years, he became the father of a son in his own likeness, after his image, and named him Seth." As Table 3.1 notes, Adam lived another 800 years, and died at age 930, just 39 years short of Methuselah's 969. Seth fathered Enosh, who fathered Kenan, who fathered Mahalalel, who fathered Jared, who fathered Enoch, who fathered Methuselah. When Methuselah was 187 years old, he fathered Lamech, and he lived another 782 years, and had other sons and daughters: "Thus all the days of Methuselah were nine hundred and sixty-nine years; and he died" (Gen 5:27). When Lemech was 182 years old, he fathered Noah, and Noah had his three sons—Shem, Ham, and Japheth—after he reached 500 years. So, as we noted earlier, Methuselah was Adam's great-great-great-great grandson and Noah's grandfather. His father, Enoch, lived only 365 years, which was abnormally short for antediluvian patriarchs, but this was because Enoch "walked with God; and he was not, for God took him" (Gen 5:24). God seems to have let Methuselah be.

First Chronicles summarizes this antediluvian patriarchal history in four short verses. Methuselah is mentioned one more time in the Bible, in the genealogy of Jesus in Luke 3:23–38. According to Luke, there are six-ty-nine generations between Methuselah and Jesus. Matthew's genealogy

(Matt 1:1–17) notes nothing about Methuselah because it begins with Abraham.

It seems noteworthy that the hero of the book of Hebrews—and the progenitor, as it were, of Jesus—is not the man, Methuselah, who lived longer than any other man, but Melchizedek (mentioned in Gen 14:18–20 and Ps 110:4), who is said by the author of Hebrews to be "without father, without mother, without genealogy," and who "has neither beginning of days nor end of life, but resembling the Son of God, he continues a priest forever" (Heb 7:3). Thus, if Jesus is symbolic of endless longevity, Methuselah is overshadowed by Melchizedek.

Still, humanly speaking, Methuselah is the hero of pro-longevity enthusiasts, and one does not have to be a biblical literalist to invoke his relevance today. We found more than a dozen books published in the last decade whose titles include the name Methuselah. Almost all of them tend to idealize him: *The Methuselah Potential for Health and Longevity*; *New Methuselahs: Can We Cheat Death Long Enough to Live Forever?*; *Hello Methuselah! Living to 100 and Beyond*; *The Methuselah Manual: The 3% Formula for Staying Young, Healthy and Sexy*; and *Waltzing Methuselah: Practical Steps to Paying for a Longer Life*. It seems noteworthy that the last of these titles substitutes the name of a man, Methuselah, for the name of a woman, Matilda. ("Waltzing Matilda" is the unofficial anthem of Australia.) This substitution serves as a clear indication that men want what women have. Judging from these books, the pro-longevity ideology that came to prominence in 1830–1870 is still very much with us, and a 969-year-old man is at the head of the pack.

What about Sarah?

In the foregoing, we have focused on the fact that the ages of biblical men are greatly exaggerated. But aren't the ages of biblical women also exaggerated? And, if so, couldn't we assume that, had women's ages at death been recorded, these would have been greatly exaggerated as well—that, in other words, we are making too much of the fact that male longevity is emphasized in the Bible? It is true that in the single case in Genesis when a woman's age is emphasized—that of Sarah, Abraham's wife—an exaggerated age is ascribed to her. According to Gen 23:1, Sarah died at age 127. However, the story of Sarah seems to be primarily concerned with the ability to conceive a child at an advanced age, especially when the woman was unable to conceive during the period of normal fertility (Gen 16:1; 18:11). And even in this story, the male is ten years older than the female, suggesting that it is at least as remarkable that Abraham was able to father a child as it was that Sarah was able to bear a child. Furthermore, whereas Sarah died at age 127, Abraham lived to age 175, and after Sarah's death, Abraham remarried (Gen 25:1), and his second wife, Keturah, bore him six children, which suggests that his ability to father children actually *increased* after he reached the age of 137. This, then, is not a story about a woman's longevity but about how a man outlived his first wife, remarried, and fathered more children than ever before.

Male Envy of Women's Procreative Powers

As we noted earlier, our dissatisfaction with the environmental, genetic, and solar-year-versus-lunar-year explanations for the exaggerated ages ascribed to biblical patriarchs, and our tendency to prefer psychosocial explanations for unusual human behaviors, led us to seek such a psychosocial explanation for why the Bible exaggerates the life spans of men. In simple terms, we believe that women have always outlived men for the reasons already cited: (1) that women are made biologically hardier by carrying and giving birth to children, and this hardiness leads to increased longevity; and (2) that the maternal desire to ensure the survival of their late-born child or children also enhances their lifetime expectancy. Because men are not involved in carrying and giving birth to children, and because they tend to be less involved than women in ensuring the survival of children, the most important means of enhancing their own life expectancy is difficult to attain. Various reactions to women's advantage in this regard are possible—and likely—but we think that envy is the most central one.

A valuable—if indirect—clue to the existence of male envy of women's longevity is provided in Bruno Bettelheim's *Symbolic Wounds: Puberty Rites and the Envious Male.*[38] In the introductory paragraphs of his chapter "The Men-Women," Bettelheim notes that men have developed two ways of emphasizing their own contribution to childbearing: "Using the positive approach, [a man] can claim directly or symbolically to give birth to men."[39] The "negative way is to de-emphasize the impor-

38. Bettelheim, *Symbolic Wounds.*
39. Ibid., 109.

tance of the woman's contribution (illustrated by the biblical promise of God to make of Abraham a great nation, with no mention of Sarah)."[40] Traditional initiation rites are examples of the former, while the custom of the couvades is illustrative of the latter.

In initiation rites, there is often "a frank acting out of childbirth."[41] In an Indonesian initiation ritual, for example, a group of boys is taken to an oblong wooden shed in the dark forest, and each boy is taken individually into the shed. Once all the boys are gathered in the shed, a fearful cry rings out at the close of the rite, and a sword or spear dripping with blood is thrust through the roof of the shed. The sight of the sword or shed becomes a token that each boy's head has been cut off and that the devil has carried each away to the other world. At the sight of the bloody sword, the boys' mothers, who have followed the procession into the forest, weep and wail: they return to the village crying that the devil has murdered their children. Then, still back in the forest, the chief, who has been acting the part of the devil, warns the boys never to reveal the fact that no harm has been done to them. Two days later the men who had initially taken the boys into the woods return to the village in a totally exhausted state and declare the glad tidings that the devil, through the intercession of the priests, has restored the novices to life.[42]

Bettelheim notes that the exhausted state of the men suggests the exhaustion of childbirth, and that the dark forest and oblong hut probably represent the womb, to which the boys had returned to be reborn. But the most impressive evidence that the men are reenacting childbirth is their behavior. They "afterwards pretend to be as disoriented as newborn infants. When they return to their homes, they act as if they had forgotten how to walk, tottering and entering the house backward. If food is given to them, they hold the plate upside down. Their sponsors have to teach them all the common acts of life, as if they were newborn children, including how to talk."[43] Thus, in the initiation rites, the men reenact the experience of childbirth, thus answering, in their own paternalistic way, the rhetorical question that Nicodemus put to Jesus when Jesus said that a person needed to be born anew: "How can a man be born when he is old? Can he enter a second time into his mother's womb and be born?" (John 3:4).

40. Ibid.
41. Ibid., 113.
42. Ibid., 114.
43. Ibid.

The custom of the couvades surrounds childbirth itself with an elaborate ritual, but it is a ritual that focuses on the father, not the mother. In it the woman works until a few hours before birth and then goes to the forest with a few other women as the birth takes place. In a few hours, she returns to work. But as soon as the child is born, "the father takes to his hammock, and abstains from work, from meat and all food but weak gruel of cassava meal, from smoking, from washing himself, and above all, from touching weapons of any sort, and is nursed and cared for by all the women of the place . . . This goes on for days, sometimes weeks."[44] Bettelheim suggests that the man either "wishes to find out how it feels to give birth, or he wishes to tell himself that he can."[45] In either case, "he tries to detract from the woman's importance; but he copies only the insignificant externals and not the essentials, which indeed he cannot duplicate. Such an aping of superficials only emphasizes the more how much the real, essential powers are envied. Women, emotionally satisfied by having given birth and secure in their ability to produce life, can agree to the couvades; men need it to fill the emotional vacuum created by their inability to bear children."[46] Thus, in Bettelheim's view, what the initiation rites and the couvades have in common is that they are expressions of men's envy of women's ability to bear children.

The biblical illustration to which Bettelheim alludes—a case in which Abraham's fatherhood of Isaac greatly eclipses Sarah's role in the birth of Isaac—suggests a similar envy. But it is envy with a twist. As David Bakan points out in *The Duality of Human Existence*,

> One of the pervasive themes that runs through the Bible is that there is *a biological role for the male in conception*. We may presume that there was a time in history prior to Biblical times in which this was not known. It is certainly not "obvious." Sexual intercourse can take place without conception. The interval between conception and either the signs of pregnancy or the birth of a child is considerable. And whether a particular woman has had intercourse or not often remains her "secret."[47]

---

44. Ibid., 109–10.

45. Ibid., 110.

46. Ibid., 111.

47. Bakan, *Duality of Human Existence*, 202 (italics original).

Thus, we can presume "that there was an early 'scientist' who made the discovery of the relationship between sexuality and pregnancy."[48]

This discovery would have two important implications. One is that the man could take credit for the fact that there even *was* a baby. After all, without his "seed," there would be no baby, meaning that the mother could therefore be viewed as little more than the soil in which the seed germinates. As Bettelheim notes, the Pilaga of South America believe that the man's ejaculation projects "a complete homunculus" into the woman, which grows in her until it is large enough to come out.[49] Similarly, the story of how Onan deprived his deceased brother Er of offspring by spilling his semen on the ground "when he went into his brother's wife" (Gen 38:9) illustrates the importance of the male seed.

The other implication of the discovery of the relationship between sexuality and pregnancy is that a man may not be certain about the identity of the child's biological father. This implication is the focus of Bakan's discussion of Abraham's relationship to Isaac under the heading, "Doubt Concerning Paternity and Infanticide." Bakan centers on the visit of the three men to Abraham's camp in Genesis 18 and the fact that biblical scholars believe that verses 10–15 are a substitution by a later author for the original verses.[50]

Sublimation through Emulation

Bettelheim and Bakan provide some rather powerful evidence that men have a tendency to envy women and that when they do, they go to rather extraordinary lengths to counteract the grounds for their envy. We suggest that this is also the case with male envy of women's greater longevity. There does not appear to have been a "scientist" back in the days of the patriarchs who made an association between childbirth and female longevity, so we will not attempt to make a direct connection between men's obvious envy of women's procreative powers and their envy of women's greater longevity. But because women have always been the ones who have carried and given birth to children, there is reason to assume that women have always had a greater life expectancy than men, and that men

48. Ibid., 202.

49. Bettelheim, *Symbolic Wounds*, 131.

50. Bakan, *Duality of Human Existence*, 212–18. See also Bakan, *Disease, Pain & Sacrifice*, 104–10.

have been aware of this fact. Indeed, there were probably many matriarchs around to confirm that this was, in fact, the case. We think that the greatly inflated ages of the patriarchs (both antediluvian and postdiluvian) are therefore a reflection of male envy, and that these inflated ages are the functional equivalent for longevity of the same tendency of men to exaggerate their role in the creation of new human life.

Of course, it *might* be argued that the exaggerated ages of the biblical patriarchs are simply an expression of the honor or of the esteem in which these patriarchs were held. Making them several centuries older than ordinary men would have been a way of honoring them in much the same way that Christians honor their saints. But like Bettelheim, who thinks that the anthropologists tended to overlook the deeper psychological conflicts that prompted men to create initiation rituals and the couvades, we believe that the exaggerated ages of the biblical patriarchs have a deeper, psychological motivation than that of honoring the ancestors. This, we are suggesting, is the motivation of envy.

We also believe that these deeper psychological conflicts are with us today. It seems significant that contemporary books that invoke Methuselah are overwhelmingly written by men. And, of course, this chapter is written by two men. This seems to suggest that whereas women *have* a longer life expectancy than men, men *think* more about longevity than women do, and one of the things they are likely to think about is *why* their life expectancy is several years less than that of women. On the one hand, such thinking may lead them to formulate plans to ensure that their wives will be cared for after they die. On the other hand, such thinking may also lead them to feel a certain amount of envy that their days on earth are several years shorter. To be sure, their wives (in cases of heterosexual marriages or relationships) can—and do—respond that life without their life partner is hardly a life worth living, and men (especially those who believe that they are fun to be with) see no reason to challenge this response. But if a person has gotten used to living, the idea that he belongs to a cohort that is predestined to die six or seven years prior to another cohort is likely to make him feel envious of members of that other cohort.

So the question is, what can men do about their envy? The basic argument of this book is that sexual desires and impulses that are considered illicit or personally demeaning may be sublimated to take a more elevated or socially constructive form. To explore this possibility in the case of men's envy, which, as Bettelheim's illustrations suggest, is sexual (i.e., libidinal), we suggest that Capps's discussion of envy in *Deadly Sins and Saving Virtues* offers a way to conceive of such a sublimation in the case of male envy of female procreative powers.[51] Capps notes that from the fourth century to the present, Christianity has considered envy to be one of the deadly sins.[52] In its most basic meaning, envy "is a feeling of discontent and ill will because of another person's advantages or possessions."[53] In the case that concerns us here, the "advantage" is greater life expectancy (which is likely to have positive effects in the here and now) and the "possession" is significantly more years of life. (If it were only a month or two, there would be little cause for envy.) The feelings that envy manifests are discontent and ill will. In this case, this suggests that men, to the extent that they envy women's longevity, do not celebrate women's advantage in this regard. In fact, if they do give women recognition for this advantage, they tend to make light of it or suggest that it is not really a benefit because, after all, old age brings with it all sorts of sufferings, pains, and inconveniences.

The parson in Geoffrey Chaucer's "The Parson's Tale" in *The Canterbury Tales* refers to envy as "sorrow at the prosperity of others and joy in their hurt," and also suggests that envy "is the worst of sins as it sets itself against all other virtues and goodness, and is flatly against the Holy Ghost, source of Bounty."[54] Also, in his study of the deadly sins in the present era, Henry Fairlie suggests that envy "must always try to level what it cannot emulate."[55] Thus, the initiation rites and the couvades described by Bettelheim can be seen as attempts by men to emulate women's childbearing abilities, and their inability to truly emulate women has a leveling effect on women's own achievement.

On the basis of these and other writings on envy, Capps concludes that envy "is more than seeing that someone else has something that we want for ourselves. Envy forms when we believe that the other person's advantage or possession diminishes or brings disgrace on us. Once we believe that, we try to divest those we envy of their advantage, usually by trying to 'pull the other person down' (e.g., by intimating to other interested parties

---

51. Capps, *Deadly Sins and Saving Virtues*, 39–44.

52. Ibid., 11–12.

53. Ibid., 40.

54. Chaucer, *Canterbury Tales*, 487–88.

55. Fairlie, *Seven Deadly Sins Today*, 65.

that the envied person's advantage is spurious or ill-gotten)."[56] Capps also notes that envy may "produce a psychological reaction of dejection or resentment that eventually results in apathy, one of the other deadly sins [commonly mistranslated as "sloth"]. Here the envious person sadly and grudgingly 'accepts' the self-diminishment caused by the advantage of the envied person and is unable to do anything to change it."[57]

Capps observes that envy is not always a bad thing, that there are times when it has positive effects. For instance, envy can become a resource for protesting the injustices of life. Since society is so organized as to make it possible for some to benefit and others, equally deserving, to be deprived, envy may spark the awareness that one's group is unfairly disadvantaged. This awareness may become the basis for social and political action. The danger here, however, is that the protest against the injustice may degenerate into revenge, or, if such revenge is impossible, envy may become a smoldering resentment that is never appeased.[58]

Another positive effect of envy occurs when our awareness of another person's goods or qualities arouses in us the desire to acquire goods and qualities by meritorious effort: "This is a benign form of envy because it does not direct any hostile attention toward the better-off. And because this form of envy is emulative rather than aggressive, it channels our resentments into legitimate activities. Rather than taking revenge against persons we envy, we emulate them. And, by emulating them, *we hope to acquire in time the qualities they possess or the advantages they enjoy*."[59] Thus, while Fairlie indicates that envy "must always try to level what it cannot emulate," Capps suggests here that the inability to emulate is not necessarily a foregone conclusion. In effect, in cases where the other person has a quality or capacity that seems beyond our reach, the effort to emulate the other person, despite the feeling that one will never fully acquire what the other person has, may initiate a process of sublimation that enables one to transform one's envy into something that is personally freeing and socially constructive.

The emulation of childbirth itself is not, however, the kind of emulation we have in mind. As we have seen, this leads to the spurious, deceitful, and self-degrading rituals that Bettelheim discusses. Instead, men

---

56. Capps, *Deadly Sins and Saving Virtues*, 40–41.

57. Ibid., 41.

58. Ibid. See also Lyman, *Seven Deadly Sins*, 186.

59. Capps, *Deadly Sins and Saving Virtues*, 41 (italics added).

can emulate women's behavior *following* childbirth for, as we have seen, this behavior also contributes to the greater longevity of women. In a word, men can become the paternal counterpart to what D. W. Winnicott terms "good-enough mothers."[60]

Women's maternal care for the child following birth is only part of the reason they live longer than men, and, as the literature we have reviewed on women's longevity suggests, it is not the major reason for biological hardiness: the process of carrying and giving birth to the child is far more important. Thus, in emulating women's maternal capacities, men should not do so under the illusion that they will thereby increase their chances of living longer, much less close the gap between their longevity and that of women. Instead, they will discover that emulation of women's maternal qualities and capacities is inherently rewarding, both for the "good-enough father" and for the child who is the recipient of his attentions.

We are aware that the father will not be able to emulate the mother in all respects. Yet it is noteworthy that for Winnicott the "good-enough mother" is "not necessarily the infant's own mother."[61] On the contrary, "she" may be anyone "who makes active adaptation to the infant's needs, an active adaptation that gradually lessens, according to the infant's growing ability to account for failure of adaptation and to tolerate the results of frustration."[62] To be sure, Winnicott notes that "the infant's own mother is more likely to be good enough than some other person, since this active adaptation demands an easy and unresented preoccupation with the one infant; in fact, success in infant care depends on the fact of devotion, not on cleverness or intellectual enlightenment."[63] It might seem that the next most logical candidate for "good-enough mothering" would be the child's father, as he would have a similar investment in this child's survival and general well-being.

However, Winnicott quite unintentionally identifies here two major reasons why fathers may not make good candidates for the "good-enough mother" role. One reason is that they may resent the infant. Bakan discusses this very problem in his consideration of the ambivalence reflected in biblical accounts of men's relationships to their firstborn child. He suggests that males, prior to the birth of their first child, have tenuously

---

60. Winnicott, *Home Is Where We Start From*, 119–20; see also Winnicott, *Playing and Reality*, 10–11.

61. Winnicott, *Playing and Reality*, 10.

62. Ibid.

63. Ibid.

moved toward a greater integration of their "agency" (or achievement orientation) and "communion" (or relational orientation) in their relations with their wives, and that the firstborn is the critical test of this integration; but the communion of the mother that has been directed toward him tends to turn in the direction of the child, and, when this happens, he regresses toward his earlier emphasis on agency.[64] Bakan suggests that this regression can take the rather extreme form of rejection of the child—"You are not my son."[65] We suggest that it may also take the form of resentment. The father, in effect, says to the infant, "Your mother loves *you* more than she loves *me*. After all, *you* are *her* child, and *I* am the child of another woman, probably one that she doesn't especially like."

The other reason why fathers may not make good candidates for the "good-enough mother" role is that a father is more likely to think that "cleverness" and "intellectual enlightenment" are more effective methods of infant care than simple "devotion." Thus, their interactions with the infant may be quite different from those of the mother, and this difference may be of such significance that it nullifies the potential life-prolonging effects of child care.

There are reasons, therefore, to be skeptical that fathers will become such "good-enough mothers," and thus to believe that the envy they feel toward women with regard to longevity will not undergo the sublimation that we envision here. But if the desire to emulate is there, the development of a large cohort among men of "good-enough mothers" is not out of the question. In any case, this is surely a better approach to the problem of male envy of women's greater longevity than, say, pretending to possess the procreative powers of women through rituals, or seeking to reduce the gap through a *decrease* in women's life expectancy (e.g., enacting social policies of unequal access to medical assistance), or adopting an antilongevity view based on godless hedonism (e.g., "Eat, drink, and be merry, for tomorrow we may die").

Let us, instead, join company with our predecessors who recognized that longevity has inherent value. But let us also accept the fact that the Bible has two visions of longevity—the vision of 120 years expressed in Genesis and the vision of eighty years expressed in Psalms. As far as we know, no human male has lived 120 years, but many have lived 80 years.

64. Bakan, *Duality of Human Existence*, 211–12.

65. Ibid., 212.

And perhaps we can learn a lesson from taking into account the fact that the vision of 80 years is presented in a discussion of God's anger and wrath:

> For all our days pass away under your wrath;
>   our years come to an end like a sigh.
> The days of our life are seventy years,
>   or perhaps eighty, if we are strong;
> even then their span is only toil and trouble;
>   they are soon gone, and we fly away. (Ps 90:9–10)

Yet the psalm does not conclude on this unhappy note. Instead, it asks God to "Teach us to number our days that we may get a heart of wisdom," and also asks God to "satisfy us in the morning with thy steadfast love that we may rejoice and be glad all our days" (Ps 90:13). And, finally, it asks God to establish "the work of our hands" (Ps 90:17). We would simply add to this final request that those who make it may consider child care an especially significant and life-giving work. And, as we have suggested here, there is no shame in the fact that this work may have its origins in men's envy of the procreative capacities of women.

PART 2

Moral, Sexual, and Religious Issues

---------- 4 ----------

Masturbation, Homosexuality,
and Moral Disapproval

Introduction

OVER THE PAST SEVERAL decades, those who engage in homosexual acts have been singled out, especially in American religious culture, as moral reprobates, whereas in the nineteenth century and in the early decades of the twentieth century they shared this dubious honor with those who engaged in self-masturbatory practices. Masturbation no longer receives the attention that it formerly received, having virtually fallen off the moral opprobrium radar screen. As a result, those who engage in homosexual acts bear a greater burden as the object of moral disapproval than before, and homosexual behavior receives much greater scrutiny. Moreover, it is the subject of much more moral and theological debate and is also the target of considerably greater moral condemnation than before.

In *Whatever Became of Sin?* Karl Menninger, perhaps the most influential American psychiatrist of the mid-twentieth century, notes that masturbation, long considered the "great sin of youth," is barely mentioned, much less discussed, today. Prior to the late twentieth century, however, "almost no other activity was so regularly condemned and punished as erotic self-stimulation, autoeroticism. For centuries, school children, prisoners, sailors, and slaves were savagely punished when detected in or even suspected of 'the solitary vice' of 'self-abuse.'"[1] Menninger cites a study by E. H. Hare on masturbation published in the *Journal of Mental Science* in 1962 that shows both the degree and intensity of moral condemnation directed toward masturbation and those who practiced it.[2] For example, Hare quotes T. Pouillet, writing in 1876: "Of all the vices and of all the misdeeds which may properly be called crimes against nature which devour humanity, menace its physical vitality and tend to destroy its intellectual and moral faculties, one of the greatest and most widespread—no one will deny it—is masturbation."[3] Menninger also notes that while the moral taboo against masturbation is thousands of years old and attempts at deterrence by punishment have gone on for centuries, a strong "intimidation curb" from the medical profession began about 250 years ago. A famous book by an unknown author (Menninger suggests that he was a quack doctor), bearing the title *Onania, or The Heinous Sin of Self-Pollution*, published in 1716, went through eighty editions. Forty years later Samuel Tissot, a renowned Swiss physician, claimed a direct causal relationship between masturbation and various physical diseases and mental disorders.[4] It had a profound effect on medical thought, resulting in numerous medical articles on masturbation. According to Hare, "By the end of the eighteenth century the masturbatory hypothesis for much disease was widely accepted throughout Europe and America."[5]

Immanuel Kant

Medical doctors, however, were not the only official opponents of masturbation. Hare notes that major philosophical writers, like Voltaire and Rousseau, who were otherwise known for their liberality, also wrote condemnations of masturbation. And Immanuel Kant (1724–1804), a highly influential German philosopher, identified masturbation, homosexual acts, and sodomy (sexual acts with other species) as the three major sexual "crimes" against our "animal nature."[6] If masturbation is no longer subject to moral disapproval, and if sodomy (i.e., bestiality) is a

1. Menninger, *Whatever Became of Sin?*, 31.
2. Hare, "Masturbatory Insanity."
3. Menninger, *Whatever Became of Sin?*, 31.
4. Tissot, *Treatise on the Diseases Produced by Onanism.*
5. Menninger, *Whatever Became of Sin?*, 31.
6. Kant, *Lectures on Ethics*, 169.

relatively rare occurrence, this leaves homosexual acts as the unrivaled focus of sexual moral condemnation, at least as far as these three "crimes" are concerned.

In a section on "Duties towards the Body in Respect of Sexual Impulse" in his *Lectures on Ethics*, Kant discusses what he calls *crimina carnis* (or crimes against the body) and defines them as acts that are "contrary to self-regarding duty because they are against the ends of humanity" and "consist in abuse of one's sexuality."[7] He distinguishes two forms of *crimina carnis*. One is *crimina carnis secundum naturam*, or acts that are contrary to sound reason. The second is *crimina carnis contra naturam*, or acts contrary to our animal nature. The former include concubinage, incest, and suicide. The latter include onanism (or masturbation), homosexuality, and sodomy (sexual acts committed with other species).

Kant describes onanism as "the abuse of the sexual faculty without any object, the exercise of the faculty in the complete absence of any object of sexuality," and writes that this "practice is contrary to the ends of humanity and even opposed to animal nature. By it man sets aside his person and degrades himself below the level of animals."[8] Homosexuality is "intercourse between *sexus homogenii*, in which the object of sexual impulse is a human being but there is homogeneity instead of heterogeneity of sex, as when a woman satisfies her desire on a woman, or a man on a man." Kant asserts that this "practice too is contrary to the ends of humanity; for the end of humanity in respect of sexuality is to preserve the species without debasing the person; but in this instance the species is not preserved (as it can be a *crimen carnis secundum naturam*) but the person is set aside, the self degraded below the level of the animals, and humanity is dishonored."[9] The third, sodomy, "occurs when the object of desire is in fact of the opposite sex but is not human . . . This, too, is contrary to the ends of humanity and against our natural instinct. It degrades mankind below the level of animals, for no animal turns in this way from its own species."[10]

Kant concludes that acts contrary to our animal nature are worse than acts against our sound reason because these acts "degrade human nature to a level below that of animal nature and make man unworthy of

7. Ibid.
8. Ibid., 170.
9. Ibid.
10. Ibid.

his humanity. He no longer deserves to be a person."[11] Kant acknowledges that suicide is "most dreadful," though it is not as "dishonorable and base" as *crimina carnis contra naturam*. The latter, in fact, are "so abominable" that "they are unmentionable, for the very mention of them is nauseating, as is not the case with suicide."[12]

This presents teachers with a dilemma. Should they mention these acts, so as "to warn their charges against them"? Or should they refrain from mentioning them "in order that people should not learn of them and so not have the opportunity of transgressing? Frequent mention would familiarize people with them and the vices might as a result cease to disgust us and come to appear more tolerable."[13] Kant advises teachers to "mention them only circumspectly and with disinclination" so that "our aversion from them is still apparent."[14] An especially important reason for exercising restraint in mentioning them is that "each sex is ashamed of the vices of which its members are capable. Human beings feel, therefore, ashamed to mention those things of which it is shameful for humanity to be capable. These vices make us ashamed that we are human beings, and, therefore, capable of them."[15]

Two things are especially noteworthy about Kant's discussion. One is his view that masturbation, homosexual acts, and sodomy are inherently worse than concubinage, adultery, incest, and suicide, as they are acts that "degrade" those who engage in them "below the level of animals."[16] Why are these acts more degrading? Why are masturbation and homosexual acts worse than incest? Kant's reasoning here is that the purpose of sexuality "is to preserve the species," and, therefore, although the crimes against sound reason are "contrary to our self-regarding duty," they are not contrary to "the ends of humanity," which, as far as sexuality is concerned, are to preserve the human species. Our disgust with acts against our animal nature is an effective deterrent, but the basic reason why these acts are "degrading" is that there is no intention to preserve the species by them. Thus, Kant places an extremely heavy burden on

11. Ibid.

12. Ibid.

13. Ibid., 171.

14. Ibid.

15. Ibid.

16. Ibid., 170.

species preservation as the basis for making moral judgments about the behaviors with which he is concerned.[17]

Another noteworthy feature of Kant's discussion is that he identifies three crimes against "man's animal nature": masturbation, homosexual acts, and sodomy (i.e., sexual acts with other species). His identification of these crimes against "man's animal nature" (and only these) raises the question of what happens when one of these three crimes (masturbation) comes to be viewed in the latter half of the twentieth century not as a serious moral crime but as, at most, a moral misdemeanor. The answer, we suggest, is that it makes practitioners of the other two crimes more vulnerable to moral opprobrium, social stigmatization, and personal abuse. Since sodomy with animals would appear to be a relatively rare behavior whereas homosexual acts are far more prevalent, we should expect that the moral disapproval previously expended on masturbation would be redirected toward those engaged in homosexual acts. Homosexuality would then be viewed as a singular example of what Kant considers the worst form of crimes against the body (worse than concubinage, adultery, incest, and suicide). The contentiousness that has prevailed in recent decades in American religious culture over homosexual behavior—a contentiousness far more prevalent and sustained than in the case of, say, adultery and incest—indicates that many religiously identified persons share Kant's view that homosexuality is the worst crime against the body.

Nineteenth-Century Views on Masturbation

If masturbation is no longer held to be the heinous crime against the body it was once held to be, the obvious question is, why not? Why did moral disapproval of masturbation decline? There are various reasons for this decline, and an attempt to identify all or even most of them would require a much more extensive investigation into the history of masturbation than is possible here.[18] However, one important reason for this decline is that, in the first decades of the twentieth century, psychiatrists and other doctors began to challenge the view that masturbation causes

17. We could, of course, point out that not all sexual acts between a man and a woman are for the purpose of preserving the species. If Kant were to make preservation of the species an absolute condition for engaging in sexual acts, then sexual acts involving women who are beyond the childbearing years would also be morally degrading.

18. See Engelhardt, "Disease of Masturbation."

physical disease, mental disorders, and moral degeneracy. A minority view at first, this challenge gained support through the 1930s and 1940s. By midcentury, the view that masturbation causes physical disease, mental disorders, and moral degeneracy was thoroughly discredited. Today the fact that virtually the whole nineteenth-century medical community assumed that masturbation has these effects is almost beyond belief.

Hare cites several nineteenth-century authors who made a direct association between masturbation on the one hand and personality defects and moral degeneracy on the other. R. H. Allnatt reported in 1843 that when one of his patients "entered the room with a timid and suspicious air and appeared to quail like an irresolute maniac when the eye was fixed steadily on him," there was no doubt of the cause of the patient's problems.[19] When Allnatt "directly charged" a patient with masturbatory behavior, he would usually admit it, thus seeming to confirm the association of masturbation with personality problems and moral degeneracy.

Another author, C. F. Lallemand, also cited by Hare, emphasized the cold and callous qualities of the masturbator: "He has no other interests; he loves no one; he is attracted to no one; he shares no emotion before the grandeur of nature or the beauties of art; still less is he capable of any generous impulse or act of loyalty; he is dead to the call of his family, his country, or of humanity."[20] In an essay on "onanism in females," T. Pouillet held that there is no single sign of masturbation in girls, but that a number of them, taken together, "create a strong, even an almost certain, presumption of this vice, in spite of denials."[21] These signs included "an unsteady and peevish disposition tending toward anger, an exaggerated timidity in the presence of parents and a surly attitude toward strangers, a profound idleness, and a tendency toward lying."[22]

The Case of William James

While these authors especially emphasized the role of masturbation in the creation of a morally weak (and even degenerate) character, others emphasized its role in mental disease. Beginning in the early decades of the nineteenth century, masturbation was deemed a major cause of

19. Menninger, *Whatever Became of Sin?*, 32.
20. Ibid.
21. Ibid., 33.
22. Ibid.

mania, melancholy, and dementia. In *The Varieties of Religious Experience*, originally published in 1902, William James (1842–1910), the American philosopher and psychologist mentioned in chapter 1, describes his experience in his late twenties of "the worst form of melancholy," that of "panic fear." It occurred at a period in his life when he was living at home and seemed to be devoid of career plans, despite having completed his medical degree at Harvard. He writes:

> Whilst in this state of philosophic pessimism and general depression of spirits about my prospects, I went one evening into a dressing-room in the twilight to procure some article that was there; when suddenly there fell upon me without any warning, just as if it came out of the darkness, a horrible fear of my own existence. Simultaneously, there arose in my mind the image of an epileptic patient whom I had seen in the asylum, a black-haired youth with greenish skin, entirely idiotic, who used to sit all day on one of the benches, or rather shelves against the wall, with his knees drawn up against his chin, and the coarse gray undershirt, which was his only garment, drawn over them inclosing his entire figure. He sat there like a sort of sculptured Egyptian cat or Peruvian mummy, moving nothing but his black eyes and looking absolutely non-human.[23]

At that moment, James felt his image of the youth and his own panic fear coalescing, and realized, to his utter horror, that the "shape" he had seen in his mind was potentially himself: "There was such a horror of him, and such a perception of my own merely momentary discrepancy from him, that it was as if something hitherto solid within my breast gave way entirely, and I became a mass of quivering fear."[24] The fear was "so invasive and powerful that if I had not clung to scripture-texts like 'The eternal God is my refuge,' etc., 'Come unto me all ye that labor and are heavy-laden,' etc., 'I am the resurrection and the life,' etc., I think I should have grown really insane."[25]

---

23. James, *Varieties of Religious Experience*, 159–60. James does not say that this is his own case. In fact, he represents it as having been written by a French correspondent of his. But he informed his son, Henry James III, that the case was his own and no James scholar has had any reason to question this. In fact, there is a footnote reference to a similar experience reported by his father Henry James Sr. in his book *Society the Redeemed Form of Man*, published in 1879.

24. Ibid., 160.

25. Ibid., 161.

In her biography of James, Linda Simon suggests that the "mental patient James recalled was notable because he suffered not from the common pathology of moral insanity (alcoholism and excessive masturbation, for example) but from epilepsy, which, although often misdiagnosed and misunderstood, could not be cured by strengthening a patient's will. An epileptic patient was at the mercy of his own biology."[26] This would seem to suggest that James did not associate his own crisis with his (perhaps unsuccessful) struggle to "hold in check certain bad habits, tendencies to 'moral degradation' (another allusion, probably, to auto-eroticism)," as R. W. B. Lewis puts it in his study of the James family.[27] However, in *Manhood at Harvard*, Kim Townsend contends that James himself believed masturbation to be the cause of the young mental patient's madness: "When a man fears or experiences the dissolution of his financial and professional and public life, it would not be surprising if his private or intimate or sexual life seemed to lack all purpose or definition as well. How specifically James was applying this diagnosis to himself we cannot say, but into his darkest imaginings there seem to have come the figure—perhaps the very figure a nineteenth-century medical student (like James himself) might have in mind—of a man driven to insanity by masturbation."[28]

Townsend cites a text—Jean Etienne Dominique Esquirol's monumental and standard treatise on mental illness, published in 1838—which may well have explicitly informed James's vision of madness. It contains "an illustration of an idiot, in a coarse undershirt, his hair black, his eyes wild, and 'his knees drawn against his chin.'"[29] This illustrative image "is of one Aba, a man who has no memory, who can do nothing other than feed himself, and whose only utterances are the sounds 'ba ba ba'—all the result of his being 'a masturbator,' Esquirol says."[30]

Townsend notes, however, that "James would not have needed Esquirol's text. If the image haunting him sprang out of his visits to the state insane asylums in Northampton or Worcester, it might well have

---

26. Simon, *Genuine Reality*, 125.

27. Lewis, *Jameses*, 201. Lewis cites James's diary entry of January 10, 1870, in which he wrote: "Today, I about touched bottom, and perceive plainly that I must face the choice with open eyes: shall I frankly throw the moral business overboard, as one unsuited to my innate aptitudes, or shall I follow it, and it alone, making everything else merely stuff for it?" (ibid., 201).

28. Townsend, *Manhood at Harvard*, 52.

29. Ibid., 53.

30. Ibid.

been an image of a masturbator, for according to an influential report on idiocy presented to the Massachusetts state legislature by the superintendent at Worcester, 32 percent of the population was there because of 'self-pollution.'"[31] Townsend guesses that the authors of the report were "so dismayed by seeing madmen masturbate" that "they assumed their self-indulgence had driven them mad."[32]

Townsend also cites a 1968 article by Cushing Strout, who speculates that as a medical student James would probably have been familiar with William Acton's *The Functions and Disorders of the Reproductive Organs* and "would have been struck by Acton's warnings that the habit of introspection could lead not just to 'the suicidal view of life' but to masturbation and madness as well."[33] In his diary from this period, James mentions that he has been reading Henry Maudsley, the British psychiatrist, who, as Townsend notes, was also an "authority" on "the relationship between masturbation and the morbid brooding of those who are unable to chart a straight course through life."[34] Townsend acknowledges that it may seem far-fetched to attribute James's experience of "quivering fear" to his unsuccessful struggles to curb his masturbatory habits, but he notes that when James "was a boy he was told about the dire consequences of 'that horrible pollution' by his own father—and when the appropriate time came, he duly passed on his father's warnings to one of his sons. 'If any boys try to make you *do* anything dirty,' he told him when he went off to boarding school, 'either to your own person, or to other persons . . . you must both preach them and smite them. For that leads to an awful habit, and a terrible disease when one is older.'"[35]

Noting that James determined to do something about his habit of "self-abuse" by setting out on a course of "moral hygiene," Wendy Graham points out in her study of his younger brother Henry James that he was therefore very much in tune with the moral leaders of his time. She suggests that "William's reflections on moral hygiene should be read in light of nineteenth-century descriptions of sexual neurasthenia and masturbatory insanity."[36] She indicates that Samuel Tissot's 1758 text

31. Ibid.

32. Ibid.

33. Ibid. Strout's article is titled "William James and the Twice-Born Sick Soul."

34. Townsend, *Manhood at Harvard*, 53.

35. Ibid., 53–54. Townsend is citing here Perry, *Thought and Character of William James*, 145.

36. Graham, *Henry James's Thwarted Love*, 41.

on masturbation "inaugurated a booming market for publications of this kind" and that William Acton's *The Functions and Disorders of the Reproductive Organs* "was widely available after its publication in 1857, and his ideas were rapidly disseminated by boarding school administrators, priests, and doctors."[37] She adds: "In William's case the drive for self-control and clean living appears to have been internally generated, but it also stemmed from terrifying medical and popular reports on the consequences of self-abuse. William's malaise, inanition, indigestion, and lack of concentration are all symptoms of what was then termed sexual neurasthenia. As an invalid given to solitary contemplation and bed rest, he was a prime candidate for this 'vice.'"[38]

Graham also cites an article by Charles Rosenberg on sexuality, class, and role in nineteenth-century America that shows that from the 1830s on "self-control, the need to repress childhood and adolescent sexuality, became issues of paramount importance in America."[39] Another article, by Peter Cominos, "argues that Victorian men were socialized to conform to a program of 'strict and extreme continence' and 'exaggerated asceticism'"; and specifically, "masturbation was decried as the cause of impotence, sexual neurasthenia, immorality, madness, and failure in professional and business pursuits."[40] She also cites G. J. Barker-Benfield's chapter on "The Spermatic Economy and Proto-Sublimation," which summarizes the content of Victorian advice-books such as *The Student's Manual* that "warned against the enervating effects of masturbation owing to the loss of vital fluids" and "recommended tonics, stimulants, exercise, and cold showers as methods for controlling the base impulse to self abuse."[41]

Graham's discussion of masturbation occurs within a larger consideration of William James's brother Henry's struggles with his homosexual desires. She notes that William, owing to his medical training as well as his position as an instructor in physiology and psychology at Harvard, served throughout his life as Henry's informal consulting physician. She

---

37. Ibid. She cites Cohen's comment in *Talk on the Wilde Side*: "As the topic of frequent sermons, lectures, advice sessions, and disciplinary actions, masturbation became a primary focus for the enactment of pedagogical authority over middle-class adolescent boys" (Cohen, *Talk on the Wilde Side*, 44).

38. Graham, *Henry James's Thwarted Love*, 41–42.

39. Ibid., 43. See Rosenberg, "Sexuality, Class and Role in 19th-Century America."

40. Graham, *Henry James's Thwarted Love*, 43–44. See Cominos, "Late-Victorian Sexual Respectability and the Social System."

41. Ibid., 44. See Barker-Benfield, *Horrors of the Half-Known Life*.

thinks that it is likely that he advised his brother to control his homosexual desires for essentially the same reasons that he sought to control his own masturbatory urges. In any case, "Henry's fears of psychological, physical, and moral disintegration carried greater weight" in "his renunciation of physical passion" than did "codes of respectable behavior."[42]

Medical Treatment of Masturbation

The medical journals of the late nineteenth century were replete with articles describing procedures designed to eradicate masturbation. Writing in *The Boston Medical and Surgical Journal* in 1883, Dr. Timothy Haynes described a surgical procedure that he had developed for curing "hopeless cases of masturbation and nocturnal emissions."[43] Haynes indicated that he was frequently called upon to care for victims of self-abuse; his normal procedure was to help the "perverted" state of mind of the victim by advising marriage and even, at times, adultery. But some cases were so utterly desperate that he began to wonder whether some help could be provided even at the expense of the procreative powers. Judging the scar of castration to be an intolerable stigma, he developed a less extreme surgical procedure that involved removing parts of the spermatic duct in which he would make an incision midway between the external inguinal ring and the testicles. This incision provided access to the duct, from which a half inch was cut off, and the "slight wound" was then closed with a suture.[44]

Haynes cites three cases in which positive results were achieved. An eighteen-year-old "confirmed masturbator" who had spent nearly a year in the New Hampshire Asylum for the Insane did not experience full recovery from his demented state but was so much relieved by the treatment that he became a very useful farm hand. A thirty-six-year-old man, addicted to masturbation and also suffering from nocturnal emissions for several years, was of such disordered mind that he was totally unfit for any business. Symptomatic of his deranged mind was the fact that when he embarked on a journey, he was more than likely to turn up miles from the place he intended to reach. After the surgery, he began to improve in physical strength and appearance, and at the time of Haynes's writing

---

42. Ibid.

43. Haynes, "Surgical Treatment for Hopeless Cases of Masturbation and Nocturnal Emissions."

44. Ibid., 130.

was "a correct, healthy business man." His testicles are normal in size and appearance, but his sexual desire is "entirely destroyed." The third man, aged thirty, had practiced "self-abuse" for years and also suffered from nocturnal emissions. He was very emaciated and had been confined to his room for months. While not insane, his mind was impaired, and at times it was difficult to get him to eat sufficiently. After the surgical procedure, he gained weight and improved markedly in physical strength. Haynes commends this procedure as having the same desired results as castration without the genital deformity. The price of these men's improvement in mental and physical donation was the permanent eradication of any sexual appetite.[45]

In *The Therapeutic State*, published in 1984, Thomas Szasz discusses an article published in the *New Orleans Medical and Surgical Journal* in 1879 in which the author, Dr. B. A. Pope, describes the case of a fourteen-year-old boy whose "syndrome" was allegedly caused by masturbation.[46] The patient's presenting problem was the loss of sight, together with anemia and mental weakness. Judging that his blindness had a "cerebral" or mental cause, as the retina and optic papillae appeared healthy, Pope proceeded to ask the boy about his masturbatory habits. He extracted a "confession," though with "great difficulty," and the patient promised to discontinue the habit. Then he injected morphine into his arm and a month later the boy was dismissed from treatment, the very "picture of health," his sight restored and "every type of anemia and mental imbecility" eradicated.

Szasz contends that the case history presented by Dr. Pope is nothing but a "caricature" of medical diagnosis: "The patient is a pubertal boy brought to the doctor by his father. Presumably, the father has been warned throughout his life that self-abuse causes weakness, blindness, and madness, and he has duly transmitted this warning to his son. The boy reaches puberty—and, presto, he presents a textbook case of masturbatory insanity."[47] In Szasz's view, Dr. Pope's "diagnosis" of the fourteen-year-old boy is not science—he establishes no causal connection between the boy's masturbatory habits and his symptoms—but is, rather, pure rhetoric. The pathogenic powers of masturbation rests upon the absence of a clear distinction between distress and disease.

45. Ibid.

46. Szasz, *Therapeutic State*, 348–49. See Pope, "Opium as a Tonic and Alternative."

47. Ibid., 349.

Masturbation: Convenient Scapegoat

Szasz's main concern in *The Therapeutic State* was to challenge contemporary arguments that masturbation is therapeutic. For him, the medical profession has no more grounds for claiming its therapeutic value now than it previously had in claiming its pathogenic powers. Given this concern, he did not develop his critique of the earlier pathogenic view in detail. However, in a more recent article, "Remembering Masturbatory Insanity," published in 2000, he returned to the subject, noting that from the very beginning of scientific medicine, masturbation (or "self-abuse") was a handy scapegoat when medical practitioners could not identify the cause of a particular disease. He notes that by the end of the 1700s physicians assumed that masturbation caused blindness, epilepsy, gonorrhea, tabes dorsalis (a chronic disease of the nervous system), priapism (persistent erection of the penis without sexual excitement), constipation, conjunctivitis (inflammation of the mucous membrane lining the inner surface of the eyelids), acne, painful menstruation, nymphomania, impotence, consumption, anemia, insanity, melancholia, and suicide.[48] Szasz also notes that among the widely accepted treatments for masturbation, the most popular were restraining devices and mechanical appliances, circumcision, cauterizing of the genitals, clitoridectomy, and castration. He adds that as recently as 1936 a widely used pediatric textbook recommended some of these methods. The primary "beneficiaries" of these treatments were children and persons with mental illness because they were unable to resist "being fitted with grotesque appliances, encased in plaster of Paris, having their genitalia cauterized or denerved, or being castrated—for their own good."[49]

In a concluding section of the article, titled "Error or Arrogance?" Szasz suggests that this scapegoating of masturbation provides a valuable warning against similar abuses of power today. Noting that young men have always experienced nocturnal emissions, he asks, what was it that turned these emissions into dreaded "symptoms" of dangerous spermatorrhea? He suggests that it is the same thing that in our own day has turned young male exuberance into the dreaded symptoms of dangerous attention deficit disorder: "parental annoyance and anxiety combined with medical imperialism and furor therapeuticus."[50] In Szasz's view,

48. Szasz, "Remembering Masturbatory Insanity," 2.

49. Ibid.

50. Ibid., 3. *Furor* means "fury, rage, or frenzy, and may suggest a craze or state of

these are not innocent medical errors. Instead, the belief in masturbatory insanity and its treatment "enhanced the identity and self-concept of the believers. Ostensibly, such beliefs assert facts; actually, they credential believers." Thus, "none of psychiatry's classic mistakes—from masturbatory insanity and its cures, to the disease of homosexuality and its compulsory treatment with 'aversion therapy,' and to the attention of the cause of schizophrenia to reverberating circuits in the frontal lobes and its cure with lobotomy—are innocent errors."[51] Rather, these are instances of arrogance, the abuse of power, and "the false belief and the medical interventions it appears to justify serves the needs of the believers, especially the relatives of 'patients[,]' who seek control over the misbehavior of their 'loved ones,' and the physicians who gain prestige and power by 'diagnosing' and 'treating' misbehavior as if it were disease."[52]

Twentieth-Century Views on Masturbation

As we indicated, Szasz points out that as recently as 1936 a widely used pediatric textbook advocated some of the medical treatments described above for masturbation. He also notes that as recently as 1938 Menninger, "the undisputed dean of American psychiatry in mid-century," declared: "In the unconscious mind, it [masturbation] always represents an aggression against someone."[53] In effect, a psychodynamic understanding had replaced the nineteenth-century view that masturbation is the cause of mental insanity, but it was still being viewed as a form of psychopathology, one that invited psychotherapeutic treatment in cases where the habit persisted. As Menninger notes, Freud considered masturbation "the primary addiction" and suggested that other addictions (alcohol, tobacco, morphine, and so forth) are a substitute for and means of withdrawal from masturbation. His physician-biographer, Max Shur, noted that Freud viewed his compulsive addiction to smoking, which he could not relinquish in spite of near-cancerous lesions in his mouth for

---

excitement of confusion" (see Agnes, *Webster's New World College Dictionary*, 575). In other words, Szasz is suggesting that the medical profession needs to exhibit a calmer and more measured disposition as far as children's and adolescents' behaviors are concerned.

51. Szasz, "Remembering Masturbatory Insanity," 4.

52. Ibid., 3.

53. Ibid. See Menninger, *Man against Himself*.

which he submitted to many painful operations the last fourteen years of his life, as a substitute for the primary addiction of masturbation.[54]

Masturbation as Immoral and Sinful Behavior

Most important for our purposes here, however, is the fact that, as the view of masturbation as the cause of various physical diseases and mental disorders was being abandoned in the first several decades of the twentieth century, the view that it is immoral—a vice or sin—showed little signs of abating. Freud is instructive in this regard. As Szasz shows, Freud did not view masturbation as a cause of mental insanity but he did contend that neurasthenia (a condition whose symptoms include lack of motivation, feelings of inadequacy, and psychosomatic symptoms) may be traced back to a condition of the nervous system caused by excessive masturbation or frequent emissions.[55] Freud also considered masturbation "perverse" because "it has given up the aim of reproduction and pursues the attainment of pleasure as an aim independent of it."[56] Thus, masturbation is problematic on moral grounds because it departs from conventional, genital, heterosexual intercourse aimed at procreation. Menninger notes that when one of Freud's own sons came to him with worries about masturbation, he issued a strong parental warning against engaging in the practice, and this, according to another of Freud's sons, led to an estranged relationship between them.[57]

Menninger's account of his own father's advice to young boys is also instructive. He notes that "in the high schools of this country until well after the turn of the century it was widely customary to have 'sex talks,' made by local doctors once a year, given to boys and girls separately. The themes were usually the dangers of pregnancy, venereal disease, and masturbation."[58] Menninger writes that he has "always been rather proud of the fact that my own father, when doing his turn at this civic chore about 1906, told the boys that while not to be recommended (this would have been scandalous!) masturbation was not as harmful as some books and speakers described and was nothing to worry about. For this

---

54. Menninger, *Whatever Became of Sin?*, 34.
55. Szasz, *Therapeutic State*, 349.
56. Ibid.
57. Menninger, *Whatever Became of Sin?*, 33.
58. Ibid., 34.

audacious affront to the popular and professional code he was much censured."[59] The very fact that Menninger's father was greatly censured even though he told the boys that masturbation was "not to be recommended" and "was not as harmful" as commonly asserted—hardly a radical position—suggests that even the most "enlightened" doctors were unwilling to declare that there is nothing wrong with masturbation or that it is a morally neutral behavior.

Menninger also notes that Havelock Ellis, the British author of a multivolume text on the psychology of sex and cited by Freud in his lectures at Clark University in 1909 as having coined the term "autoeroticism,"[60] complained in 1901 that Tissot's book on the disorders produced by masturbation had "raised masturbation to the position of a colossal bogey, and accused Tissot of combining his reputation as a physician with religious fanaticism."[61] To Ellis, it was clear that a major force behind the pathologizing of masturbation was the religious culture of the time. Thus, while the association of masturbation with various physical diseases and mental disorders declined in the first several decades of the twentieth century, its association with immorality and sinfulness did not.

Citing his own experience of growing up in America at the turn of the twentieth century, Menninger notes that "in America the masturbation taboo has always been, until recently, very explicit." It was never a crime, but it was considered a moral offense of such seriousness that many authorities joined hands in ensuring its prohibition: "To help stem the temptation of evil-doing, threats or inflictions of dire punishment were commonly made to children by all and sundry."[62] Parents and school teachers both looked for signs of this sin: "To an extent difficult for the present-day reader to grasp," masturbation was "the *major sin* for middle- and upper-class adolescents a century and less ago."[63] Because it was secretly indulged in by the vast majority of adolescents, it was "an ever-present, easily reached source of guilt feelings, often exploited by religious leaders. Consider the emotional conflict in a boy (or girl), instructed in the faith, that Jesus, the good man, the Son of God, died 'for

59. Ibid., 34–35.

60. Rosenzweig, *Historic Expedition to America*, 428.

61. Menninger, *Whatever Became of Sin?*, 33.

62. Ibid., 34.

63. Ibid., 35.

your sins,' whose chief preoccupation was his propensity for repeating this dreadful act."[64]

What made it especially dreadful was the fear that one would be found out (either because one was directly observed engaging in masturbation or because one's body began to manifest one or more of its telltale signs). And, of course, religious leaders emphasized that God knows our "secret sins," that nothing can be hidden from the all-knowing Father. Menninger notes that he once witnessed "a large room full of university men bowed on their knees in prayer for forgiveness and for strength to resist the temptation of (this) sin."[65]

Masturbation as Sin: Disappearance or Displacement?

Menninger claims that an "amazing circumstance" occurred sometime after the turn of the twentieth century—namely, this ancient taboo, "for the violation of which millions had been punished, threatened, condemned, intimidated, and made hypocritical and cynical—a taboo thousands of years old—vanished almost overnight! Masturbation, the solitary sin, the SIN of youth, suddenly seemed not to be so sinful, perhaps not sinful at all; not so dangerous—in fact, not dangerous at all; less a vice than a form of pleasurable experience, and a normal and healthy one!"[66] He views this "sudden metamorphosis in an almost universal social attitude" toward masturbation as "more significant of the changed temper, philosophy, and morality of the twentieth century than any other phenomenon that comes to mind."[67] When the view that masturbation is a sin "disappeared," it seems that all sin other than crime disappeared along with it: "This, in a way, now seems regrettable. For masturbation lost its quality of sinfulness through a new understanding, but there was no new understanding of ruthlessness or wastefulness or cruelty." To be sure, "a small amount of the disapproval of masturbation may have been displaced by previously undervalued 'sins' such as those mentioned, but,

64. Ibid.

65. Ibid. Kant's suggestion that teachers should mention masturbation "only circumspectly and with disinclination" was typically addressed by religious leaders' suggestion that one's body is the temple of the Holy Spirit and that one should not do anything to defile this temple. Adolescents understood that this was an implied reference to masturbation.

66. Ibid., 36.

67. Ibid.

in general, it seems as if the great phenomenon of a deadly sin suddenly disappearing—and disappearing 'without anyone noticing it'—affected our attitude toward other disapproved behavior."[68]

Two points need to be made regarding the contention that the view of masturbation as sinful suddenly disappeared soon after the turn of the twentieth century. First, Menninger's story of his father's experience of being censured for downplaying the alleged physical and moral effects of masturbation would seem to indicate that the change was far more gradual. In fact, Szasz's account of changing attitudes toward masturbation in the twentieth century presents a very different, and more accurate, picture. In his reconstruction, there was a fundamental change in social attitudes toward masturbation, but it occurred during and after the sexual revolution of the 1960s. He views William Masters and Virginia Johnson's *Human Sexual Response*, published in 1966, and their subsequent book, *Human Sexual Inadequacy*, published four years later, as especially influential in this regard.[69] If Tissot's book on onanism played a major role in shaping nineteenth-century attitudes toward masturbation, these books by Masters and Johnson had a similar influence in the latter decades of the twentieth century. While Freud had contended that the aim of sexual activity is reproduction and that a sexual activity is perverse if it "pursues the attainment of pleasure as an aim independent of it," Masters and Johnson "maintain the opposite view—namely, that the aim of human sexuality should be the procuring of pleasure."[70] Thus, for Masters and Johnson, masturbation is not only acceptable, it is also highly recommended (for example, for release of tension), and the problem that may require treatment is not engagement in masturbation but the failure to experience pleasure through masturbation.

Of course, there were members of the therapeutic community— Szasz included—who did not endorse this new understanding of masturbation. Szasz's opposition was based on his contention that, even as psychiatrists had no business endorsing the view that masturbation is immoral, neither do they have any warrant—scientific or otherwise—for endorsing the idea that it is a healthy activity. Many religious leaders also

68. Ibid.

69. Masters and Johnson, *Human Sexual Response*; Masters and Johnson, *Human Sexual Inadequacy*.

70. Szasz, *Therapeutic State*, 338. It is interesting to note that the brief chapter of *The Therapeutic State* in which this quotation occurs is titled "The Case against Sex Education" and was originally published in *Penthouse* in 1981.

opposed it. However, Szasz quotes the following declaration by the evangelist Ruth Carter Stapleton, sister of former president Jimmy Carter, in the *Atlanta Journal* in the early 1980s: "The Lord wants us to experience whole, complete lives, and He offers this gift (masturbation) to each of us as we surrender to Him."[71] A clearer indication of how the moral and theological landscape relating to masturbation was changing is difficult to imagine. It did not, however, happen overnight—as Menninger claims—and it did not occur shortly after the turn of the twentieth century. If there were indications of changing attitudes at that time, the "almost universal" change to which Menninger refers took another sixty years.

Second, Menninger indicates that, for the most part, the idea that masturbation is an immoral or sinful behavior simply disappeared, and there was little displacement of the moral disapproval of masturbation onto other behaviors that are, in his view, clearly sinful, such as ruthlessness, wastefulness, or cruelty. Rather, the disappearance of masturbation as a sin reflects the "changed temper, philosophy, and morality of the twentieth century."[72] We would agree that moral disapproval of masturbation was not displaced onto ruthlessness, wastefulness, or cruelty, but in our view such a displacement *did* occur in the last several decades of the twentieth century: a displacement of moral disapproval of masturbation onto homosexual behavior. As moral disapproval of masturbation has declined, moral disapproval of homosexual behavior has increased. Moral disapproval does not simply "disappear." Rather, it gets displaced. It is as though there is a constant amount of moral disapproval in American society, and if it ceases to be directed toward one behavior and its practitioners, it shifts to another behavior and *its* practitioners.

The Displacement of Moral Disapproval

The argument that the moral energy directed against masturbation was displaced onto a new object of moral disapproval—homosexual behaviors—makes sense at a purely theoretical level, as the psychoanalytic theory of displacement refers to the redirection of an emotion or impulse from its original object (for example, a person or an idea) to another. It also assumes that this is an unconscious process, that the person (or, in this case, the religious culture) that engages in this displacement is largely

71. Ibid., 346. See Stapleton, "God Gave Man a Variety of 'Gifts.'"
72. Menninger, *Whatever Became of Sin?*, 36.

unaware of the fact that it has done so.[73] It knows, of course, what and who are its current targets of moral disapproval. But the original target of its moral disapproval is a distant memory. On the other hand, the two objects need to have something in common—while being sufficiently distinctive—for the displacement to do its work. Since, as we have seen, masturbation and homosexual behavior *do* have something in common that is deemed very important by those who engage in moral disapproval of both (i.e., the fact that both are sexual activities that do not serve the purpose of reproduction), homosexual behavior becomes a useful target for those who, for one reason or another, have relinquished their moral disapproval of masturbation. The very fact that one of these behaviors is a solitary act (mutual masturbation between heterosexuals was rarely mentioned in the moral case against masturbation) while the other involves sexual behavior between two individuals enables the displacement to work, as this serves the purpose of ensuring that the connection between them will remain unconscious. The purpose of this chapter is to bring it to consciousness.

The Mishandled Sex Life

Empirical support for this theoretical argument is provided by a book by Leslie D. Weatherhead, published in 1932, titled *The Mastery of Sex through Psychology and Religion*.[74] While Weatherhead was an English clergyman, his book was published in New York as well as London, and went through at least eleven printings between 1932 and 1947. The book cover of the 1947 edition quotes from a review in *Methodist Recorder* that exclaims, "Without any exaggeration it can be said that tens of thousands of young people will be deeply grateful for [Mr. Weatherhead's] latest. Nor will gratitude be confined merely to young people. It is a book for which parents and the unmarried will also be thankful. Many in middle life will wish that twenty years ago such a book had come into their hands." The back cover goes on to claim that the book "should be of immense value to clergymen and parents, as well as to men and women of college age."

73. Freud introduced the concept of displacement in his first major book, *The Interpretation of Dreams*. He discusses displacement in his chapter called "The Dream-Work." Here he suggests that "Dream-displacement and dream-condensation are the two governing factors to whose activity we may in essence ascribe the form assumed by dreams" (ibid., 343).

74. Weatherhead, *Mastery of Sex through Psychology and Religion*.

The reference to "men and women of college age" suggests that the book targets the middle- and upper-class young people for whom, according to Menninger, masturbation was "the major sin."

The Mastery of Sex through Psychology and Religion has chapters on the mistake of silence and ignorance about sexual matters, on comradeship and flirting, on the true approach to marriage, on the unhappy marriage, on the question of birth control (which Weatherhead strongly endorses), on those who do not marry, on the mishandled sex life, on sex and society, and on healthy-mindedness. The chapter that most concerns us here is chapter 8, "The Mishandled Sex Life," which covers the subjects of masturbation, homosexuality, fetishism, sadism and masochism, scoptophilia and exhibitionism, and venereal disease. Composed of 44 pages, this is the longest chapter in the book, and over half of the chapter (26 pages) is devoted to masturbation. The section on homosexuality ranks second, but at seven pages it is about 27 percent the length of the masturbation section.

This suggests that when Weatherhead's book first appeared, masturbation was by far the most important topic requiring treatment in a chapter on the mishandling of one's sex life. (Given the prominence of masturbation in the chapter, we may wonder whether the double entendre in the word "mishandled" was intentional.) Not only was homosexuality a very distant second, but the fact that Weatherhead devoted nearly half as many pages each to fetishism and to venereal disease, and more than half as many to sadism and masochism, suggests that homosexuality was not a subject that he felt was of concern to his typical reader. This attitude is reflected in his citation of authors whose statistics on the prevalence of the practice of masturbation ranged from 95 to 99 percent, though he states that "my own experience would go to show the percentage much lower, both in men and women, but much higher than most people imagine."[75] In contrast, while he asserts that homosexual behavior is "an exceedingly common one especially among unmarried women," it is probably the case that "true homosexuals are not more than three percent of the population."[76]

In his discussion of masturbation, Weatherhead distances himself from the view promoted "in olden days—not so very olden either" that this practice is "the blackest of all possible sins" and that anyone "who

75. Ibid., 122.
76. Ibid., 152.

practiced it was pretty sure of hell."[77] He notes that "our grandfathers, including our medical grandfathers," taught that it was "not only a dreadful sin, but that it also had physical and mental consequences which were terrible; these consequences being regarded as the just punishment of God for human wickedness. It was said that the victim of this habit invariably brought disease upon himself and that if he did not speedily check it he would go mad. Asylums were said to be full of people brought there by this cause alone."[78] Evidence that such views were still held in Weatherhead's own day was a youth's query of Weatherhead whether it is true that the substance of the brain runs down the spinal column and escapes with the seminal fluid; another believed that masturbation compromised the morality of marriage because masturbation rendered its victim impotent.

Weatherhead assures his readers that, fortunately, "most of what was held to be true in regard to masturbation, physically, psychologically, and theologically, we now know to be vulgar nonsense."[79] Physically, its effects are negligible: "A person may masturbate daily for twenty years and suffer no more physical disability than a slight and temporary devitalization." On the other hand, we cannot so easily dismiss the psychological consequences of masturbation, for "masturbation in the adult is nearly always due to a maladjustment to sex and its continuance maintains such maladjustment."[80] Weatherhead largely faults "the Victorian taboo on the discussion of sex problems" as the primary cause of such maladjustment, as the reason for it is due less to the act itself and more to "the false emotions with which it has been surrounded"—emotions "the intensity of which are out of all proportion to the seriousness of the habit."[81] These emotions are guilt, shame, inferiority, self-loathing, horror, and fear.

Masturbation as Potentially Sinful

But however much he regrets the sexual maladjustment that arises from the false emotions generated by "the Victorian taboo," Weatherhead believes that there is another consideration that needs to be addressed—namely,

77. Ibid., 123.
78. Ibid.
79. Ibid., 124.
80. Ibid.
81. Ibid.

the theological question whether masturbation is a sin. While condemning the older theological view that masturbation has dire consequences (for example, that anyone who practices it may go to hell for this), he considers it potentially sinful to the degree that it conjures up "mental pictures." It is not the mental pictures per se, but what one does with them that determines whether masturbation is a sinful act. Because these pictures "come from the depths of the unconscious mind," we have no moral responsibility for the mere fact that they appear. We do, however, have responsibility for what our conscious mind does with them. It isn't necessary that we act on these pictures in the world around us. Rather, "masturbation becomes sin when such thoughts are *deliberately entertained.*"[82] Thus, what makes masturbation sinful "is not the act itself, but the conscious reliving of imaginative pictures conjured up by the mind which accompany the act and produce the first stirrings of sex excitement."[83] Weatherhead cites the case of a young man who masturbated five or six times a day and on every occasion "the act was accompanied by the working out of an imaginative scene in which he took a lustful part."[84] He notes in this connection Jesus's condemnation of the imaginative "looking" on a woman with intent to seduce her as "a way of committing adultery."[85]

Weatherhead sees two dangers in the conscious entertaining of such imaginative scenarios. One is that a person may dwell on these mind pictures so long that one has no self-control when circumstances similar to the fantasy present themselves. The other is that one may come to believe that the mental picture has actually occurred, and this can lead to false allegations of seduction or rape. Not surprisingly, Weatherhead implies that men are more susceptible to the former danger while women are more prone to the latter.

While Weatherhead views masturbation with conscious fantasy as sinful, he cautions that it is "no worse in the sight of God than, say, to lose one's temper."[86] He also notes that everyone who has come to him for help has nearly always suffered from "an exaggerated sense of guilt," often referring to masturbation as "the unpardonable sin." He cannot believe that a sin which only harms the person who engages in it "can be so bad

---

82. Ibid., 126 (italics original).
83. Ibid.
84. Ibid., 126–27.
85. Ibid., 127.
86. Ibid., 130.

in the sight of Heaven as a sin such as spiritual pride," which often results in "social cruelty."[87]

Cures for Masturbation

Weatherhead believes that masturbation is curable. He sets forth a series of suggestions in this regard under the three headings of the psychological, the religious, and the physical. We will not discuss these suggestions in detail, but we do want to draw attention to his observation that, under the heading of the psychological, masturbation is an expression of narcissism and for this reason is a form of "misdirected" sexual energy. Defining *narcissism* "as a psychological term which means self-love that has become morbid," he encourages the adult masturbator to view the habit as a means of satisfying "an undeveloped, infantile self-love."[88] Thus, he advises looking for and identifying one's hidden, thwarted, and egoistic desires, and redirecting them toward more adult expressions of sexual desire. As the prevailing psychoanalytic view of homosexuality was that it is narcissistic,[89] Weatherhead was aware, no doubt, that he was making an indirect association of masturbation and homosexuality, both of which are thus contrasted with mature heterosexuality.

Under the heading of the religious, Weatherhead suggests that because sex and religion are closely associated, religion provides excellent means for the sublimation of the desire to masturbate. He recommends training one's mind to focus on the face of Christ when it wants to picture sex fantasies, and notes that picturing Jesus blessing the little children, or as smiling and radiant, is better than picturing him as sad, anguished, and covered with thorns.[90]

87. Ibid.

88. Ibid., 134.

89. Freud wrote in his *Introductory Lectures on Psycho-Analysis*: "Homosexual object-choice originally lies closer to narcissism than does the heterosexual kind. When it is a question, therefore, of repelling an undesirably strong homosexual impulse, the path back to narcissism is made particularly easy" (ibid., 530).

90. Weatherhead, *Mastery of Sex through Psychology and Religion*, 139–40. In his article on snake handling, titled "When the Spirit Maims and Kills," Ralph W. Hood points out that the practice of religious snake handling emerged within the first decade of the twentieth century and quickly spread throughout the Appalachian and Southern Bible Belt states. Since serpent handlers typically hold and stroke the snake at the level of their own genitals while hopping and dancing about, it may be argued that this practice was also a religious form of sublimation.

In his discussion of physical cures, Weatherhead recommends adult circumcision on the grounds that, in men, quite often "the foreskin is long, or tight, and rubbing on the clothing sets up an irritation to relieve [in] which the organ is tickled, scratched or rubbed and the habit [of masturbation] begins . . . It is obvious enough that if the cause of such irritation can be removed it is the first thing to be done."[91] It is well worth speculating whether the dramatic increase in circumcision of Gentile newborns from the late nineteenth century and into the twentieth in the United States was not only to serve hygienic purposes (to prevent infections and the like) but also to reduce the incidence of masturbation from childhood through adulthood.

Innate and Acquired Homosexuality

Weatherhead views homosexuality as another example of the "misdirection" of the sexual instinct, for the "sex energies, instead of going out to the member of the opposite sex, are directed towards a member of the same sex."[92] He identifies two forms of homosexuality—innate and acquired—and acknowledges that in its present state psychological treatment can do little to help those who are afflicted with the innate form. Alleviation through the use of hypnosis has been somewhat successful, but treatment "is generally directed to the deflecting of the sexual energies, the avoidance of all sex stimulation and the removal of the guilt feelings which make the homosexual of this class feel a kind of outcaste or leper."[93] In other words, the sexual energies are redirected (i.e., sublimated) and "feelings of self-loathing and revulsion" are challenged on the grounds that this is a "congenital abnormality," probably "due to remote prenatal causes," and therefore is neither vice nor sin.[94]

Acquired homosexuality is more akin to masturbation in that it is not an innate "psychological disharmony" but a "practice" in which one "indulges" with members of the same sex. Weatherhead focuses on the question of whether such practices are wrong among consenting adults. Citing his "unhappy case" of a forty-year-old woman who considered herself "married" to a young girl of eighteen, he advances three points

91. Weatherhead, *Mastery of Sex through Psychology and Religion*, 141.
92. Ibid., 148.
93. Ibid., 149.
94. Ibid.

in favor of the argument that it is, in fact, wrong. First, any "perversion—here differing from a sublimation—always makes exceedingly difficult and frequently impossible the redirection of the sex energies to the biological [i.e. reproductive] channel if ever the way is opened up."[95] While the forty-year-old woman could respond to this objection that this does not concern her, it *does* concern the eighteen-year-old girl, "who has a reasonable expectation of normal marriage"; it is "not right to do fellow beings an injury even if they welcome the injury."[96] Weatherhead does not indicate whether he would therefore be approving of a sexual relationship between two postmenopausal women.

Second, the fact that the older woman raised the question with him indicated her "uneasiness of mind," and subsequent inquiry showed that her uneasiness derived not from outmoded taboos but from the fact that her "religious feelings were hurt," as her behavior was inconsistent with her "ideals and aspirations."[97] That these hurt feelings, ideals, and aspirations were shaped to a significant degree by the outmoded taboos is an issue that Weatherhead does not address.

Third, and most potent for Weatherhead, is the psychological argument that in "inverted practices" the "sex instinct is roused and yet is not satisfied." He compares it to bringing a hungry man to a hotel grill room so that he can smell the food, then not allowing him to eat it. While not wanting to seem "alarmist," Weatherhead observes that very few people have any idea of what an awakened and unsatisfied sex desire can do: "The passion becomes sometimes uncontrollable and may lead in extreme cases to that unpleasant kind of nervous disorder called nymphomania in women and satyriasis in men."[98] Weatherhead "has seen cases of nymphomania—uncontrollable passion in women—and I can only say I do not want to see another. Women of good birth and breeding have been driven by it to give themselves to anybody and even to have relations with animals to satisfy the pangs aroused with them."[99] Here, Weatherhead makes a causal connection between homosexuality and sodomy—the third of Kant's crimes against our animal nature.

95. Ibid., 150.
96. Ibid.
97. Ibid., 151.
98. Ibid., 152.
99. Ibid.

Weatherhead believes that unless the "inversion" is innate, the very same methods recommended for the cure of masturbation may effect a cure for acquired homosexuality. He recognizes that it may be resistant to treatment, and that in many cases the most that can be done "is the removal of morbid emotions and self-loathing, the reduction of sexual hyperaesthenia [i.e., unusual or pathological sensitivity of the skin], the fear that inversion is a sign of mental deficiency, and the strengthening of the patient's spiritual life so that he may not cause others to acquire the perversion or endanger their well-being."[100] Significantly, Weatherhead's argument that masturbation may be sinful when it is accompanied by a conscious entertaining of mental scenarios is avoided in the case of both forms of homosexuality. In fact, he contends that the "modern attitude must not be to label inversion as a loathsome vice . . . but as a psychological disharmony the causes of which we must investigate and the sufferers from which, with pity and skill, we must try to help."[101] Of course, Weatherhead does not normalize homosexuality, nor does he even consider the argument that homosexual behavior may be an expression of adult sexual desire and of "harmonious satisfaction" in its own right. But the fact that masturbation is so singularly and unqualifiedly narcissistic; that it typically involves the conscious entertaining of lustful mental pictures that may either be acted out in the real world or affect one's ability to discriminate between what is real and what is imagined; and that it is so universal makes it an especially pernicious practice, even to a person like himself who wants to set aside the "old taboos" and view it from the perspective of "a modern attitude."

The Redirection of Moral Disapproval

If, for Weatherhead, the primary forms of "the mishandled sex life" are masturbation and homosexuality, and if, for Menninger, masturbation has "disappeared" as a major sexually related sin, it should not surprise us if the moral disapproval directed against masturbation should be directed instead toward homosexual behavior. As Weatherhead himself emphasizes, the other forms of misdirected sexuality (fetishism, sadism and masochism, voyeurism, and exhibitionism) are primarily matters that require more technical discussion than is appropriate for a text whose

100. Ibid., 154.
101. Ibid.

intended readership includes young persons, their parents, and the clergy. That is, the other forms of mishandled sexuality clearly fall within the domain of psychiatry. Weatherhead does not make similar caveats with respect to masturbation and homosexuality, thus implying that these two forms of misdirected sexuality are the concern of nonspecialists.

This, in fact, is precisely the situation we find today. While nonexperts may continue to defer to the specialists on fetishism, scoptophilia, and so forth, they do not hesitate to express their opinions and views on homosexuality. Indeed, they sometimes invoke "studies" by "specialists" to buttress these opinions, as we will see in chapter 5. Lack of expertise is no deterrent to making one's views known on this particular form of so-called "misdirected" sexuality. Homosexuality is therefore the only issue, aside from masturbation, that remains from Weatherhead's forms of "the mishandled sex life" for the nonspecialists who wish to engage in moral disapproval. It alone satisfies the need to engage in the "social cruelty" fueled by spiritual pride. Weatherhead's view that persons who are "dreadfully shocked" by sex scandals are perhaps engaging in "a form of sex-gratification" may also apply to many who are currently engaged in morally inspired attacks on persons who engage in homosexual practice. In any event, the one virtue of the view of masturbation as a sinful act is that it aroused the vast majority of members of American religious culture to be morally introspective (even if this introspection was itself misdirected), whereas the current focus on homosexual behavior as sinful enables the vast majority of contemporary members of American religious culture to externalize their sense of sinfulness and engage, instead, in moral disapproval of others. The displacement of moral disapproval is largely other-directed.

The Reproductive Criterion

The very year (1879) that Dr. Pope reported on his use of morphine to cure a fourteen-year-old boy of masturbation, and exactly 100 years before evangelist Ruth Carter Stapleton issued her rather stunning theological endorsement of masturbation in the *Atlanta Journal* (1979), Mark Twain delivered a brief satirical talk on masturbation before a small group of American expatriates in Paris. Szasz notes that the talk was considered so scandalous that it did not see print until eighty-five years later. Here is an excerpt from this talk:

Cetewayo, the Zulu hero, remarked, "A jerk in the hand is worth two in the bush." The immortal [Benjamin] Franklin has said, "Masturbation is the mother of invention." He also said, "Masturbation is the best policy." Michelangelo said to Pope Julius II, "Self-negation is noble, self-culture is beneficent, self-possession is manly, but to the truly grand and inspiring soul they are poor and tame compared to self-abuse.[102]

Menninger views Ellis as "brave" and "far-visioned" for having complained in 1901 that Tissot's supposedly scientific views on masturbation were heavily influenced by "religious fanaticism."[103] But Twain had made essentially the same point several decades earlier. What could have been a liberating word was instead silenced.

This history should be instructive for those who have moral objections or religious objections, or both, to homosexual behavior. As we have seen, these objections have essentially the same moral basis as previous objections to masturbation—that is, that the primary purpose of sexual activity is reproduction and that neither masturbation nor homosexuality meets this criterion. However, if the vast majority of sexual acts between heterosexual adults do not eventuate in reproduction of the species, and if excessive or indiscriminate reproduction is itself subject to moral censure, why should the reproductive purpose of sexual behavior have such prestige among the various other purposes that sexual behavior may serve, such as affording pleasure or as expression of intimacy and love?

One plausible explanation is that the preeminence of reproduction as an aim of sexual behavior was an effect of the discovery that the male has a role in conception. In chapter 3, we noted David Bakan's observation in *The Duality of Human Existence* that

one of the pervasive themes that runs through the Bible is that there is a *biological role for the male in conception*. We may presume that there was a time in history prior to Biblical times in which this was not known. It is certainly not "obvious." Sexual intercourse can take place without conception. The interval between conception and either the signs of pregnancy or the birth of a child is considerable. And whether a particular woman has had intercourse or not often remains her "secret." If we consider a two-way table with pregnancy-no pregnancy on one axis and

102. Quoted in Szasz, *Therapeutic State*, 351.
103. Menninger, *Whatever Became of Sin?*, 33.

intercourse-no intercourse on the other, observation would show that there are instances of pregnancy and no pregnancy with intercourse; and definitive data in the no intercourse cells are hard to come by. We can presume that there was an early "scientist" who made the discovery of the relationship between sexuality and pregnancy.[104]

Bakan further imagines that this "discovery" would have at first been resisted, as "the natural development of the male ego does not usually encompass the ejaculated semen."[105] He suggests that the Bible expresses the effort of males to come to terms with this "discovery" by extending the boundary of their ego to include their semen or "seed," thereby developing the idea that the male is even more important in procreation than the female, "as seed is the determining factor of the nature of the plant, with the soil, water, and sun playing only enabling roles."[106] Onan's act of spilling his semen on the ground to avoid consumating intercourse with his brother's widow, thus refusing to provide his brother an heir, is described as a refusal to "give seed to his brother" (Gen 38:9). (*Onanism* is thus a term for both coitus interruptus and masturbation.) Onan's refusal was so "displeasing" to the Lord that he slew him. By emphasizing the value of their "seed," and thus their (literally) seminal role in reproduction, males could assert their biological priority in the reproductive process and hence their superiority in procreation. The primacy of patrilineal descent was itself the heir of this "scientific" discovery.

If Bakan's argument is correct, this would help to explain why religious culture has such a stake in defending heterosexual sexual behavior against homosexual behavior. At the same time, it exposes the rationale behind the reproductive argument. The survival of the species is not the crucial issue. (After all, nuclear or biochemical catastrophe poses a much greater threat to its survival than the fact that a percentage of men and women do not engage in the reproductive process.) This is a smokescreen erected to disguise the deeper motivation behind it: the assertion of male superiority and privilege.

May we expect that the religious culture will soon abandon its moral disapproval of homosexual behavior? Freud's suggestion that the leadership structures of the army and the church are remarkably similar bears

104. Bakan, *Duality of Human Existence*, 202 (italics original).

105. Ibid.

106. Ibid., 203.

on this question, as it appears that these two inherently traditionalist and conservative institutions tend to view this issue in remarkably similar ways and to use similar procedures in handling cases of "deviance" from the prescribed—that is, heterosexual—norms.[107] Whether this similarity is grounds for hope or despair may depend on social forces beyond the control of either institution. But, in any event, these two institutions have rarely in the past been numbered among the vanguard as far as the abandonment of long cherished traditions of privilege and prejudice is concerned. As the suppression of Twain's 1879 satire on masturbation would seem to suggest, the religious institutions, in taking themselves— and their deliberations—so seriously tend, in the end, to make *themselves* a laughingstock, fair game for ridicule and the all too familiar charge of moral hypocrisy.[108]

Conclusion

In this chapter, we have endorsed Szasz's view that the sexual revolution of the 1960s dealt a crippling blow to the moral disapproval of masturbation and have suggested that the effect of this crippling blow to moral disapproval of masturbation was the displacement of this moral disapproval onto homosexuality. It is noteworthy in this connection that an article by Thomas J. Bigham, titled "Pastoral and Ethical Notes on Problems of Masturbation," was published in *Pastoral Psychology* in 1960.[109] In the article, Bigham argues against theologian Emil Brunner's engagement in "ethical simplifications" with regard to masturbation and against pastoral theologian Seward Hiltner's reduction of masturbation's psychological complexity to a matter of the will. Bigham also contends against the "tradition of punitive disapproval" that emphasizes the "evil consequences of masturbation" and that fails to recognize its more positive indications. If it is a "retreat from life," it is a retreat that is "only possible because there has been some advance, and therefore [it] is a positive sign." This

---

107. Freud, *Group Psychology and the Analysis of the Ego*, 32–39.

108. See Saroglou and Jaspard, "Does Religion Affect Humor Creation?" They found that exposure to a religious video inhibited humor whereas exposure to a humorous video promoted it.

109. Bigham, "Pastoral and Ethical Notes on Problems of Masturbation."

advance, Bigham suggests, is the achievement of puberty, and masturbation is a sign of a desire for something better—namely, full growth.[110]

Bigham's effort to provide a more sensitive, enlightened approach to masturbation is significant in itself, as it supports our argument that moral disapproval of masturbation was becoming a relic of the past in the 1960s. But even more striking is that the journal has an advertisement for a new book on how to counsel "the homosexual" on the top right corner of the last page of Bigham's article.[111] The advertisement proclaims: "Without mincing words, the Rev. Robert W. Wood here becomes the first to offer a way for homosexuals to enter the Christian community and join the Church, yet remain homosexuals without fear or guilt or apology." As represented by the advertisement, the author's position was clearly liberal for its time. Yet the message conveyed is that "the homosexual," not the Christian community itself, requires pastoral counsel (and the word "mincing" may also betray some unconscious feelings toward homosexual persons). However one views the content of the advertisement, its placement on the last page of an article on masturbation is striking evidence in support of our argument in this chapter: An era was ending, a page was turning.[112]

110. Ibid., 23.

111. Wood, *Christ and the Homosexual.*

112. If, in the future, many or most churches come to embrace homosexuality, one wonders if masturbation would again become the target of moral disapproval. The thesis of this chapter suggests that this is not inconceivable.

---------- 5 ----------

Eleven Gay Men
A Case of Unexceptional Sublimation

Introduction

THIS CHAPTER CONSIDERS THE efforts of leaders and lay members of Christian churches to change men from a homosexual orientation to a heterosexual orientation by means of religious interventions. It does so by focusing on a study by E. Mansell Pattison and Myrna Loy Pattison, titled "'Ex-Gays': Religiously Mediated Change in Homosexuals," published in the *American Journal of Psychiatry* in 1980.[1] The article presents the authors' "evaluation" of eleven white males who "claimed to have changed [their] sexual orientation from exclusive homosexuality to exclusive heterosexuality through participation in a Pentecostal church fellowship."[2] This article has been routinely cited in literature in which the "conversion" of males from a homosexual to a heterosexual orientation is advocated.[3] In light of its continuing influence, we felt it would be useful to provide an assessment of the study itself by focusing on the research design, the findings, and the authors' conclusions. And because Pattison and Pattison claim that what happened to these eleven men was

1. Pattison and Pattison, "'Ex-Gays.'"
2. Ibid., 1553.
3. See, e.g., Loder, *Logic of the Spirit*; and Glesne, *Understanding Homosexuality.*

a form of "folk therapy"—one in which they moved from psychologically immature to psychologically mature men—we also felt that it would
be useful to evaluate the "religiously mediated change" that the authors
report having happened in the case of these eleven men.

References to the Pattison and Pattison Study

In *The Logic of the Spirit*, published in 1998, James Loder makes the following statements: "From the standpoint developed here, one may be able
to see that there is no such thing as a homosexual. There are only persons
who have this resolution to the sexual aspect of their identity."[4] He adds,
"The principle point of my observation is not an attack on persons who
practice homosexuality, but it is in opposition to what this practice does
to persons."[5] Moreover, "a careful examination of sexuality reveals that
no one's identity is ultimately determined by sexuality; rather, it comes
from their walk in the Spirit of God."[6] Following these and similar statements, he cites the article by Pattison and Pattison, noting that "one study
in the *American Journal of Psychiatry* corroborates my work in counseling
and will make this point more concretely."[7] As our primary focus here
is the Pattison and Pattison study itself, we will not take time to critique
Loder's claims, though it seems obvious to us that his discussion is replete
with misleading, if not spurious distinctions (persons/practices, sexual-
ity/spirit) and ambiguous ("no such thing," "ultimately determined") and
pejorative ("does to") phrases. It is, however, noteworthy that he cites the
Pattison and Pattison study in support of his "work in counseling," which
largely centered on seminary students.

In the first chapter of *Understanding Homosexuality: Perspectives
for the Local Church*, published in 2004, David Glesne presents "four
common myths" about homosexuality: (1) the myth that ten percent
of the adult population is homosexual; (2) the myth that homosexuals[8]

4. Loder, *Logic of the Spirit*, 222.

5. Ibid.

6. Ibid., 223.

7. Ibid.

8. The fact that Glesne and others (such as Pattison and Pattison) refer to persons as "homosexuals" is problematic in part because it reduces personhood to one
aspect of identity—sexual identity. The following phrasing seems more appropriate:
homosexual persons or *persons with a homosexual orientation*. This chapter retains the
word *homosexuals* in some places because it reflects the writing of the sources being

are "born that way," (3) the myth that homosexuals lead happy lives, and (4) the myth that homosexuals cannot change. In his discussion of the "myth" that homosexual persons cannot change, Glesne cites several studies from 1962 to 2001 that report a success rate of 30–79 percent in the "improvement" or "cure" rate of "homosexuals" by means of psychotherapy.[9] While he stresses that change is difficult, he suggests that "the three values" necessary for success in the attempt "at sexual reorientation, or at least sexual control" are "a strong, unswerving commitment to Jesus Christ," "the establishment of a long-term relationship with a professional therapist," and "an accepting environment in which progress and healing toward sexual wholeness can be made."[10] In his view, the third value is where churches come in. He asks: "Can our churches be the kind of communities that offer a supportive, understanding environment in which people can struggle for wholeness in this sexual area?" He answers: "It is my strong conviction that life change is more likely to take place through interaction within a caring, supportive community, than in the isolated setting of the psychiatrist's couch."[11]

This conviction is taken up in the last section of the book, which considers "the church's attitude toward the homosexual."[12] The Pattison and Pattison study is cited in the chapter called "Communities of Grace," in the section headed "Helping Someone Change."[13] Before citing this study, Glesne suggests that the church "ought to be a community within which change can take place," and adds, "it is to be an environment within which repentant believers prone to certain sins are striving against their inner and outward expression. Hopefully, this is what the person with a homosexual orientation within the church is doing. Hopefully, that is what we

---

cited. However, the term *homosexual practice*, while it does not reduce personhood to one aspect of identity, seems heterosexist because (1) it does not seem to give proper weight to the relationship between one's sexuality and one's identity; and (2) scholars who write against so-called homosexual practice tend not to use the term *heterosexual practice*. All this is to say that terms relating to sexuality are often contested and debated, and terms that are considered appropriate—politically and intellectually—change over time.

9. Glesne, *Understanding Homosexuality*, 30–31. His citations are not, however, to the original studies but to secondary sources such as, for example, to Green et al., *Church and Homosexuality*.

10. Glesne, *Understanding Homosexuality*, 32.

11. Ibid., 32–33.

12. Ibid., 145.

13. Ibid., 164–68.

all are doing—struggling against sins, repenting daily, asking the Holy Spirit to make us more like Christ."[14] This, however, raises the troubling question: "But what about the one who cannot change very much? What about the one who is battling against his homosexual orientation but still finds it a strong and difficult tendency? What is such a one's calling?"[15] He answers: "In light of the biblical teaching, I think we can only say that maybe this one has to view this as a call to celibacy. If one has called upon God's strength to help him change but there is little change, he may be called to trust God's grace to be sufficient to live the celibate life."[16] Celibacy, then, is for those for whom change is not attainable.

But change, according to Glesne, *is* possible, and the study by Pattison and Pattison provides evidence of "the possibility of change." Glesne writes:

> By way of underscoring the possibility of change for the homosexual, there was a very interesting paper published some years ago in the *American Journal of Psychiatry* by two Christian psychiatrists, E. Mansell Pattison and Myrna Lloyd Pattison. In the article the authors describe the change that occurred in 11 white, exclusively homosexual males. For all these men, before coming into contact with the church, the average rating on the Kinsey scale was six. This is the highest number on the Kinsey scale. The average age of the men was 23, with ages running between 17 and 35. They all had strong homosexual orientations since they were about age 11.[17]

Then, these men joined a Pentecostal church. Glesne continues:

> The members of this church accepted them, loved them, and as a result they all became Christians. They were given loving acceptance in the context of small fellowship groups of prayer and Bible study. They were taught the Scriptures and were helped to repent and to forgive others and themselves, to deal with their pasts and to go on dealing from day to day with their homosexual orientation. Most of them came to find out that they were psychologically immature in relationships, which is something they hadn't realized before. But within the context of

14. Ibid., 166.

15. Ibid., 166–67.

16. Ibid., 167.

17. Ibid. We will explain the Kinsey scale in our discussion of the Pattison and Pattison study.

the non-erotic relationships with men and women in the group, they were able to change.[18]

Glesne concludes that at the time the article was written, "Seven of the eleven were happily married and had already been so for four years. The other four wanted to be married. On the Kinsey scale rating, five of them were now at zero. The other six varied on the scale between one and three. Not only did their overt behavior change, but their fantasy and dream life changed remarkably also."[19] Readers of *Understanding Homosexuality* are presented here some very impressive findings.

Or are they? A closer look at the study itself provides a rather different picture.[20]

The Pattison and Pattison Study

In the following consideration of the Pattison and Pattison study, we will focus on the research methods employed, noting several problems with the way that the study was conducted and reported, as well as the comparisons drawn between this study and another study of homosexual males. We also will take up the question of the nature of the change that the men experienced in light of Freud's concept of sublimation.

An early version of the Pattison and Pattison article was presented at the annual meeting of the American Psychiatric Association in May

18. Glesne, *Understanding Homosexuality*, 167.

19. Ibid., 167–68.

20. As we will see, Glesne's account of the study is replete with factual errors. He states that the average age of the men was 23, when in fact it was 27. He also indicates that the men all had strong homosexual orientations since they were about eleven, when in fact the age at which they began to identify themselves as homosexually inclined ranged from 8 to 15 years. He notes that seven of the eleven men were married following the religious intervention and had been married for four years, when in fact six of the men were married, and the years of marriage ranged from two to seven years. Glesne indicates that their average Kinsey score ratings was originally 6, when in fact it was 5.7; and that for those whose Kinsey score was not currently zero, their scores ranged from 1 to 3, when in fact they ranged from 1 to 2. Finally, he claims that "the members of this church accepted them, loved them, and as a result they all became Christian," while it is more accurate to say that, according to Pattison and Pattison, there was a two-stage process. While it is true that the church initially welcomed them, the experience of acceptance and love followed their own acceptance of "the invitation to commit their life to Christ and his church," and this acceptance and love primarily occurred in their participation in small fellowship groups (see Pattison and Pattison, "'Ex-Gays,'" 1558).

1979. It was submitted to the *American Journal of Psychiatry* in June. A revised version was resubmitted the following April, and it was accepted for publication in May 1980 and published in the December 1980 issue. Thus, the original research was conducted in the late 1970s. The thirty-three references to other books and articles range in dates from 1956 to 1979. Citations to earlier articles authored or coauthored by E. Mansell Pattison include studies of possession, faith healing, and exorcisms; a study of mental health functions of community groups; and an article on "confusing concepts about the concept of homosexuality," published in the *American Journal of Psychiatry* in 1974.[21]

The article begins with the observation that the "possibility that homosexual orientation can be changed, or may change over time, is in vigorous debate," adding,

> The gay-liberation movement asserts that any fundamental change is rarely possible. Most behavioral therapists and psychotherapists conclude that changes in sexual behavior may be attained or [that] anxiety and conflict about homosexuality can be reduced, but they, too, doubt that basic change in sexual orientation is generally feasible. Some psychotherapists suggest that in highly motivated persons a basic change can be accomplished but only through long-term intensive psychotherapy. The general tenor of professional opinion is given by [D. J.] West, who stated, "Permanent eradication of all homosexual inclinations appears to be rather rare."[22]

They note, however, that "occasional autobiographical reports have described a spontaneous change in sexual orientation through salutary life experience, which usually includes religious conversion," and "there are individual case reports of spontaneous change without psychotherapy. However, such reports seem to be the exception."[23]

A Natural Experiment: The Problem of Controls

Continuing, the authors state that they recently came into contact with a religious hotline crisis program sponsored by a Pentecostal church that offers lay crisis services to homosexuals:

21. Pattison, "Confusing Concepts about the Concept of Homosexuality."
22. The authors are quoting from West, *Homosexuality Re-examined*.
23. Pattison and Pattison, "'Ex-gays,'" 1553.

This program claimed to involve a number of persons who were "ex-gay," that is, these people had experienced a basic change in sexual orientation from exclusive homosexuality to exclusive heterosexuality. The term "ex-gay" had been deliberately selected by them to denote an ideological position in opposition to "gay liberation." This change was said to have occurred within the context of the church fellowship without any psychotherapy or other professional intervention. The program seemed to offer an "experiment of nature" by which we could investigate this apparently spontaneous change from homosexuality.[24]

In *The Conduct of Inquiry*, Abraham Kaplan discusses experiments "where the changes are produced, not by the scientist's intervention, but by that of the policy maker or practitioner."[25] He indicates that Daniel Katz refers to these as "natural experiments."[26] Kaplan expresses some discomfort with the term "natural experiments" because it might be confused with what are called "nature's experiments," which are naturally occurring anomalous events or deviants (such as geniuses, psychotic experiences, and so forth), and he suggests that the term "social experiments" might be better, "though this might wrongly suggest that the change was made for the sake of experimentation, which is true very seldom, if ever."[27] In any event, Kaplan notes,

> Whatever they are called, and whatever their motivation, such interventions as the evacuation of London's children during the blitz, the relocation of California's Japanese, or the desegregation of schools in the southern United States, can serve as experiments in behavioral science, and have in fact been subjected to intensive study as such. The great advantage of such experiments, as Katz points out, is that the manipulation of the variables is much more powerful than would otherwise be possible or even desirable, and the changes produced much more clear and drastic.[28]

Yet the same criticism that applies to "nature's experiments" applies to "natural experiments" where the changes are made by a policy maker or practitioner, namely, that "the problem of controls is likely to be a much

24. Ibid.
25. Kaplan, *The Conduct of Inquiry*, 164.
26. Festinger and Katz, *Research Methods in the Behavioral Sciences*, 78–79.
27. Kaplan, *The Conduct of Inquiry*, 164.
28. Ibid.

more serious one, for 'we generally lack a control group whose comparability to the experimental group is assured.'"[29]

Obviously, serious ethical questions would have been raised (one hopes) if the federal government would have authorized the desegregation of some schools and not others in order to compare the test scores of African American children in the segregated schools and African American children in the desegregated schools. Similarly, ethical questions were raised in the 1980s concerning the policy of the Food and Drug Administration to use a control group in experiments on the effectiveness of medicines designed to combat HIV/AIDS, on the grounds that persons with HIV/AIDS had nothing to lose and everything to gain by being administered the drugs in question. Withholding the drugs from some (the control group) in order to conduct an experiment was considered inhumane, so, after receiving considerable pressure from gay activist groups, the Food and Drug Administration changed its normal experimental procedures in this instance.

Pattison and Pattison, however, do not comment on the fact that this "experiment in nature" afforded by the program sponsored by the Pentecostal church did not meet the usual experimental criterion of a control group. Nor did they make an effort to address this problem by creating a control group of their own. This would be a comparable number of gay men who were similar in all respects to the men in the study, but who were not recipients of the Pentecostal church's lay crisis services.

Method: The Problem of Sampling Bias and Instability

The article continues with an account of the method that Pattison and Pattison employed. First, the authors "obtained written permission from the church program to review all their crisis program records and to conduct personal interviews with their clients."[30] The crisis program records for a five-year period included three hundred individuals ("clientele") who had sought its services. Of these three hundred, there were "30 cases [who] claimed to have changed from homosexuality to heterosexuality."[31] Thus, 10 percent of the total clientele made this claim. The authors note that these thirty cases "were reviewed in detail with the program staff,

---

29. Ibid. Kaplan is quoting Daniel Katz.

30. Pattison and Pattison, "'Ex-gays,'" 1553–54.

31. Ibid., 1554.

who knew all the subjects," and that this review "produced a set of corollary data that confirmed the subjects' claims that they had changed in sexual orientation."[32] How this "review" was conducted, however, is not described, nor was the possibility of program-staff bias addressed. We would assume that the staff would have much to gain from "confirming" the subjects' claims, as this would support their own claims that the program itself was effective. We would therefore expect that the investigators (i.e., Pattison and Pattison) would have provided an account of their own procedures for "reviewing" the case materials provided by the program staff. A standard procedure would have been to secure the assistance of independent judges to review the materials so that the issue of the authors' own possible bias might also be laid to rest.

The authors then contacted the thirty men who claimed to have "changed in sexual orientation," and they note that "of these 30 cases we were able to obtain the cooperation of 11 men and to collect personal interview data on them."[33] Thus, the authors' own study was based on 37 percent of the men who claimed to have changed in sexual orientation, or about 4 percent of the original clientele.

The fact that the Pattison and Pattison study centers on only 10 percent of the total clientele group, and that only 37 percent of those selected agreed to cooperate with their own study, raises the obvious question of whether there was a sampling bias. As Kaplan notes:

> We cannot say whether a sample is a fair one or not without referring at least tacitly to the process by which it was obtained ... What is required is that the sampling plan should not be one which preferentially selects specimens differing from the rest of the population in some respect significant for the inquiry, or at any rate, that the higher probability of their being chosen be sufficiently determinate—and determinable!—so that it can be corrected for. We say otherwise that the sample is a *biased* one— the expected values in the sample differ from the true values of the parameters in the population being studied.[34]

The authors could have addressed the issue of sampling bias by randomly selecting another thirty men from the rest of the clientele of 300 (n=270) who did *not* claim to have changed in sexual orientation as a result of

32. Ibid.
33. Ibid.
34. Kaplan, *Conduct of Inquiry*, 241.

the lay crisis ministry, and to conduct a study in which the two groups of thirty men each were compared on several measures relevant to their having solicited the help of the crisis ministry. For all we know, these men may well have believed that they were significantly helped by the crisis ministry *despite* the fact that they did not perceive themselves to have changed their sexual orientation.[35] Whether such claims to have been helped would have been welcomed by the program staff is, of course, open to question, but we can imagine that some lay crisis ministry practitioners might have viewed such claims as evidence of their program's effectiveness.

According to Kaplan, avoidance of sampling bias is only one of two requirements of a sampling plan. Another is the assurance of sampling stability. By stability, he means that we need "to know how likely it is that other samples produced by the same plan will yield essentially the same results."[36]

> Instability is most easily seen with regard to very small samples: they may be selected without any bias at all, but because of their size it may very well happen that repeated samples will show large differences among themselves. The use of unstable samples is a failing especially common in behavioral science, with its reliance on case studies, clinical observations, and the like. Even if the samples have been chosen without bias (rather than, say, because they are the most striking or the more easily accessible), they often do not provide a basis for reliable generalizations about the entire population of cases which they are supposed to represent.[37]

As Kaplan points out, random sampling is the widely accepted method for ensuring against sampling bias and instability. He contrasts random sampling with grab sampling, which is "like taking a handful of beans from a sack, or the next ten patients to enter the clinic," and notes that "such samples are likely to be too homogeneous, and therefore also

35. This is no idle speculation. One of the authors (Capps) recalls reading a newspaper article about a psychotherapist in New York City who offers one-session counseling. His rationale for this minimalist approach is based on his own study of persons who sought psychotherapy but did not return for the scheduled second session. When contacted and asked why they did not return, one-third of the dropouts said that they had gained considerable clarity concerning their problem in the initial session and felt that they could deal with it without further need for therapy (Coleman, "Therapists Say").

36. Kaplan, *Conduct of Inquiry*, 242.

37. Ibid.

insufficiently stable."[38] He provides the following illustration: "Suppose, for example, we wish to study what is said by patients during psychoanalysis. If we select one month's records, much may depend on whether it is a month near the beginning or near the end of the therapy. The records of an equal number of hours distributed throughout the whole course of the treatment would be much more representative."[39]

Random sampling may follow different patterns, but the important thing is that the sample is representative of the larger group of which it is a smaller (usually, considerably smaller) subgroup. Are the eleven men that Pattison and Pattison studied representative of the total clientele of of three hundred men? There is no reason to believe that this is the case. We know only that they are representative of the thirty men who claimed to have experienced a change in sexual orientation, and that they themselves differ from the other nineteen in regard to the fact that the authors of the study were able to "obtain the cooperation" of these men and not the others. Why the other men did not cooperate is not explained. Were the authors unable to contact them? If they were able to contact them, would they have refused to participate in the study? We simply do not know, but if any *did* refuse to cooperate, such refusal would seem to be significant: Did it mean that their claim to have changed in sexual orientation was no longer valid? Or did it mean that the change was still valid but that they were reluctant to be interviewed for one reason or another? Given the very claim that the article makes—that change in sexual orientation is possible—we would have liked to have known more about the 19 men who did not cooperate with the study.

Method: The Question of Interview Bias

The Pattison and Pattison study was based on interviews with the eleven men who agreed to cooperate. In addition, for the six men who were married, "corollary data" was obtained from their wives. The interviews were "structured and detailed," and included the following items: current mental status; developmental history; past and present sexual history; sexual fantasies, dreams, and impulses; social relations; homosexual and heterosexual experience; heterosexual marital experience; and details of alleged change in sexual orientation. According to the authors, "we

38. Ibid., 243.
39. Ibid., 242.

found no substantial discrepancies in the data we collected from the staff, from interviews, or from spouses."[40] As "substantial discrepancies" is not defined or explained, we take it to mean that all parties involved confirmed that the men's sexual orientation had changed from homosexual to heterosexual. The authors also claim that the data they collected was reliable: "Although the subjects knew we were investigating their changes in sexual orientation, we do not believe that this substantially biased the data; they were forthright about the details of their past and present life and did not attempt to distort their life experience."[41]

While we might simply accept the authors' assurances that the fact that the subjects knew the investigation concerned their changes in sexual orientation did not substantially bias the data, it seems appropriate to want to know how the authors came to this belief. And would it not have been better had they not revealed this fact to the interviewees, and instead had allowed it to emerge in the course of the interview itself? A more neutral approach—one that asked how they were or were not helped by the lay crisis ministry they had received—would seem to have been a better strategy, as this would have laid to rest the suspicion that the interviewees, in their desire to say what they believed the investigators wanted to hear, were in fact "distort[ing] their life experience."[42]

Basic Findings

The study did include one objective measure relative to the question of change in sexual orientation (the Kinsey scale), and this objective measure may be viewed as a basis for confirming the authors' belief that the interviewees were not in fact distorting their life experience, and this brings us to the section of the article on results.[43] There is a certain irony in the fact that the Kinsey scale is the objective measure employed in support of the argument that homosexual men may, through religious mediation, experience a change in sexual orientation for, when Kinsey's original study of the sexual behavior of the human male first appeared (in 1948), church leaders generally ridiculed its contention that few men

---

40. Pattison and Pattison, "'Ex-gays,'" 1554.

41. Ibid.

42. Ibid.

43. Kinsey et al., *Sexual Behavior in the Human Male*.

are exclusively heterosexual.[44] The Kinsey rating scale is described by Pattison and Pattison as follows:

> A rating of 0 is defined as the subject having no physical contact with the same sex producing erotic arousal, no psychic erotic arousal to the same sex, and sociosexual contact exclusively with the opposite sex. A rating of 1 involves only incidental physical or psychic response to the same sex. A rating of 2 includes definite same-sex response but strong and predominant reaction to the opposite sex. A rating of 3 is midway. A rating of 4 is a predominant response to the same sex, with definable heterosexual response and relationships. A rating of 5 is predominantly homosexual, with occasional psychic response to the opposite sex. A rating of 6 is an exclusively homosexual physical and psychic response.[45]

In order to place their data in a meaningful context, the authors juxtapose their data with comparable data from two large sample studies of homosexual persons.[46] In effect, this juxtaposition makes their much smaller sample appear representative of the larger population of homosexual men despite the fact that, as we have seen, the eleven men in the study were not representative of the total clientele of the lay crisis ministry of the Pentecostal church itself.

The Saghir and Robins study was based on eighty-nine white homosexual men (drawn from volunteer recruits from the Chicago and San Francisco homosexual communities) whom they described as "healthy

---

44. Kinsey's work was the center of a controversy a decade ago among American historians regarding the sexual orientation of Abraham Lincoln. In *The Intimate World of Abraham Lincoln*, C. A. Tripp, a former associate of Kinsey, argued that Lincoln would have scored 5 on the same scale employed in the Pattison and Pattison study; in other words, "predominantly homosexual, but incidentally heterosexual" (Tripp, *Intimate World*, 20). In his review of Tripp's book in the *New Republic* titled "Log Cabin Republican: How Gay Was Lincoln?" Andrew Sullivan agrees with Tripp that Lincoln was more homosexual than not, but assigns him a 4 ("predominant response to the same sex, with definable heterosexual response and relationships"). Tripp's posthumously published book contains reactions and comments from two historians (Michael Burlingame and Michael B. Cheeson) who take opposite positions on the question of Lincoln's homosexuality; and from psychologist Alice Fennessey, who observes that "according to the Kinsey criteria which Dr. Tripp uses, Lincoln was definitely bisexual" (Tripp, *Intimate World*, 247).

45. Pattison and Pattison, "'Ex-gays,'" 1554–55.

46. Saghir and Robins, *Male and Female Homosexuality*; and Bell and Weinberg, *Homosexualities*.

homosexuals," and whom Pattison and Pattison describe as "essentially hard core confirmed homosexuals who have made some adjustment to their homosexuality and the world at large."[47] They ranged in age from nineteen to seventy, and their mean age was thirty-five. The Bell and Weinberg study was based on a sample of 575 white homosexual men (drawn from volunteer recruits from the San Francisco homosexual community) whose ages ranged from under twenty to over seventy, with a mean age of thirty-seven. The eleven men in the Pattison and Pattison study ranged in age from twenty-one to thirty-five, with a mean age of twenty-seven, and all were white.

The major difference between the Pattison and Pattison study and the two previous studies is that about 50 percent of the subjects in the earlier studies were over thirty-five years of age. Pattison and Pattison comment on this age difference in the "Discussion" section of their article, suggesting that the other samples "may well represent homosexual populations beyond the optimal age for change in sexual orientation."[48] They cite a study by R. R. Troiden which states "that between the ages of 21 and 24 there is a major period of critical evaluation about assuming a homosexual identity."[49]

In the Pattison and Pattison study, all eleven men in the study experienced "defined homosexual proclivities" before age fifteen. (Comparable figures are 90 percent in the Saghir and Robins study and 82 percent in the Bell and Weinberg study.) Among the eleven men, the age range was from eight to fifteen years old. The age at which they changed to heterosexuality ranged from nineteen to twenty-eight years old, and the years as a heterosexual ranged from one to seven. Among the six married men, four were heterosexual before they married, and two became heterosexual after marriage. The years of marriage ranged from two to seven. Regarding "intra-psychic evidence of current homosexuality" (dreams, fantasies, and impulses), three of the eleven men indicated that they experienced none, seven indicated experiencing one, and one indicated experiencing two of the three. Of the eight who experienced at least one form of homosexual interest, one had dreams, three had fantasies, and five had impulses.

---

47. Pattison and Pattison, "'Ex-gays,'" 1554. The difference in wording—Saghir and Robins's "healthy homosexuals" and Pattison and Pattison's "essentially hard-core confirmed homosexuals"—is noteworthy.

48. Ibid., 1559.

49. Ibid.; Troiden, "Becoming Homosexual," 19.

Against the argument that "any evidence of intra-psychic homo-sexual proclivity in these men suggests that their homosexuality had not been resolved," the authors claim that

> this argument overlooks the fact that heterosexuality or homo-sexuality is not an either/or, mutually exclusive phenomenon. Indeed, Kinsey convincingly showed that even among lifelong heterosexuals there were occasional homosexual dreams, fantasies, and impulses. Similarly, Saghir and Robins reported that among exclusively heterosexual men, 94% had experienced pla-tonic feelings toward other men, and 11% had wanted physical, congenital contact. Thus, our data do not suggest some magical change or massive denial or repression, but rather they suggest the gradual development of a rejection of the homosexual object choice and an increased cathexis of the heterosexual object is developed.[50]

While the fact that five of the eleven men are not married does not necessarily challenge the claim that "an increased cathexis of the heterosexual object" has occurred in all of the cases—after all, the unmarried men may have succeeded in the cathexis of the heterosexual object without having this cathexis result in marriage—it is interesting to note that among the three men who have been heterosexual the longest (for six to seven years), two are unmarried. We may also wonder how gradual the process of rejection of the homosexual object and the cathexis of the heterosexual object is expected to be, and whether the two men who have been heterosexual for only a year (and are unmarried) have had sufficient time to complete this gradual process. The ages of the eleven men in the study are also relevant, for six of the men are between age twenty-one and twenty-six. Might we not wonder, therefore, whether the "cathexis of the heterosexual object" is, in fact, firmly established and not subject to future reversal? Of course, only a follow-up study of the eleven men would lay this question to rest.

Our greatest concern, however, is that the objective test employed in the study is the Kinsey scale. Pattison and Pattison note that this is the most widely used scale for assessing degrees of heterosexuality and ho-mosexuality, and they assert its reliability: "Although this is a gross mea-sure dependent on rater judgment, the scale represents the continuum of degree of psychic inclination and behavior toward either direction."[51]

50. Pattison and Pattison, "Ex-gays," 1555.
51. Ibid., 1554.

As we noted earlier, the scale consists of six ratings, ranging from 0 for an exclusively heterosexual physical and psychic response (i.e., no physical contact with the same sex producing erotic arousal, no psychic erotic arousal to the same sex, and sociosexual contact exclusively with the opposite sex) to 6 (i.e., no physical contact with the opposite sex producing erotic arousal, no psychic erotic arousal to the opposite sex, and sociosexual contact exclusively with the same sex). Although the authors discount the fact that the Kinsey scale is based on rater judgment, this is a potential problem, especially when there is no evidence provided in the article itself that more than one person performed the rating. A more serious problem is the fact that the ratings of the men were made before the change itself occurred (with nine receiving a rating of 6, and one each receiving a rating of 5 and 4), and that such ratings would have had to be based on retrospective reporting by the men themselves. In light of Kinsey's research findings that few men are either totally homosexual or totally heterosexual (an argument that Pattison and Pattison themselves agree with in principle), how do we know that nine of the men were totally homosexual before the religious intervention took place? Was the change as dramatic as the prechange rating of 6 suggests?

There are also apparent discrepancies in the ratings given the men following the change. In three of the five cases where the individual received a rating of 0, there was intrapsychic evidence of current homosexuality, whereas among those who received a rating 1, one of the three did *not* evidence intrapsychic dreams, fantasies, or impulses. Among the three who received ratings of 2 (definite same-sex response but strong and predominant reaction of the opposite sex), all three had sexual impulses (probably the strongest evidence of current homosexuality), but so did one of the men who received a rating of 0 and one of the men who received a rating of 1. These discrepancies raise questions concerning the accuracy of the ratings. The article's abstract claims that "8 men became emotionally detached from homosexual identity in both behavior and intra-psychic process" while "3 men were functionally heterosexual with some evidence of neurotic conflict."[52] This statement would lead readers to assume that only three of the men continued to experience current homosexual impulses (the strongest of the three indications of current homosexuality). But, in fact, five (or nearly half of the total sample) were experiencing current homosexual impulses. On the basis of the evidence

52. Ibid., 1553.

provided, we would have placed several of the men at the 3 (or mid-way) rank, which would raise questions as to whether a decisive change in sexual orientation had occurred; or, alternatively, assuming that an identifiable change did occur, what kind of change was it? We will return to this question later.

Psychological Status

In a section of the article headed "Psychological Status and Social Relations," Pattison and Pattison compare their sample with the 575 men with a homosexual orientation studied by Bell and Weinberg on several indicators of "mental status," including feelings of exuberance, self-acceptance, loneliness, worry, depression, tension, paranoia, and happiness. As we noted earlier, the Bell and Weinberg sample was drawn from volunteer recruits from the San Francisco homosexual community. Pattison and Pattison conclude that, in comparison with the Bell and Weinberg subjects, their subjects "demonstrated a remarkable state of psychic well-being, with an absence of negative affects and the presence of strong feelings of self-acceptance and happiness."[53] They note that the exceptions were the three subjects who rated 2 on the Kinsey scale and, as we noted previously, "manifested neurotic symptoms." In contrast, "the homosexual men from the Bell and Weinberg sample demonstrated overall much more psychological distress."[54] For example, the corresponding scores for self-acceptance (low, medium, and high) are 73 percent high, 27 percent medium, and 0 percent low for the Pattison and Pattison study; and 21 percent high, 40 percent medium, and 39 percent low for the Bell and Weinberg study. Similar differences are reported for exuberance and happiness, and similar differences (in the reverse) are reported for loneliness, worry, depression, tension, and paranoia.

These are very impressive findings, but they are weakened by two significant problems in the research and in the reporting of the research. First, there is the problem of the comparability of the two sample groups. The Bell and Weinberg sample (n=575) is much larger than the Pattison and Pattison sample (n=11), and the Pattison and Pattison sample is less than 4 percent of the original group of persons who had solicited the assistance of the lay crisis ministry, and only 37 percent of the 10 percent of

53. Ibid., 1556.
54. Ibid.

this larger group who had claimed a change in sexual orientation. If Bell and Weinberg had selected 4 percent of their 575 subjects (twenty-three men) who were deemed by them (through interviews) to have accepted their homosexual orientation with minimal misgivings, we would have a truer basis for comparison of the two groups. Also, the table in the Pattison and Pattison article that presents the differences between the two studies (Table 2) is titled: "Psychological State of 11 Male Homosexual Subjects Who Changed to Heterosexuality after Religious Participation Compared with 575 Male Homosexuals Studied by Bell and Weinberg." For a true comparison to be made, a subset of the Bell and Weinberg sample would need to be identified, one that focused only on the men who, *through religious participation*, had *accepted* their homosexual orientation.

Later, in the section of their article headed "Religious and Social Attitudes," the authors note that only 6% of the Bell and Weinberg sample were "very" religious, 51% were "not at all" religious, and 78% were "not too" religious. The more appropriate comparison on psychological states, therefore, would be one that compared the eleven men in the Pattison and Pattison study with this 6 percent (n=35) of "very" religious men in the Bell and Weinberg study. It is also quite conceivable that there were men among the 270 who sought the services of the lay crisis ministry but instead of changing their sexual orientation moved to greater acceptance of it. It is also conceivable that the religious services that they were provided may have helped them, despite the intentions of the lay ministers, to accept their homosexual orientation.

Another problem with the data on the psychological state of the eleven men is that the authors do not tell us how they arrived at these percentages. Were they based on the subjects' own self-scoring, or on the judgment of the interviewer? If the latter, this presents the same difficulty that occurs in the case of the Kinsey scale ratings, namely, that there is no evidence of the use of multiple judges to insure reliability.

Similar problems arise with respect to the authors' claim that there were marked differences between the two sample groups in terms of the effort of subjects to "hide" their homosexuality. The authors make the following rather blanket assertion: "Another significant difference in our data from the Bell and Weinberg data is that our subjects did not attempt to hide their homosexuality; instead they sought to inform and include their spouse in the further elaboration of their heterosexuality. Consequently, rather than the demands of heterosexuality producing conflict, as is often reported in marriages involving one homosexual, our subjects reported that their heterosexual marriages further solidified and developed their heterosexual identity and sexual preference."[55]

As this point relates specifically to the six men who were in heterosexual marriages, the appropriate comparison group in the Bell and Weinberg study would be those who were similarly in heterosexual marriages. Their very inclusion in the study, however, would seem to conflict with Pattison and Pattison's description of the Bell and Weinberg sample as having been drawn "from volunteer recruits from the San Francisco homosexual community"—unless, of course, Pattison and Pattison are referring here to individuals in the Bell and Weinberg study who were living dual lives (both homosexual and heterosexual). If Pattison and Pattison are referring to men living with a sexual double identity, this is not directly stated. Therefore, the question of how many of the men in the Bell and Weinberg study were attempting to "hide their homosexuality" (and from whom) is not addressed. We would have thought that living in a known homosexual community would itself have been a visible disclosure of their homosexual orientation, and that the men in that study would not have felt that additional disclosure was necessary.

Social Relations

In the section headed "Psychological Status and Social Relations," Pattison and Pattison initiate a discussion of the role played by the Pentecostal church in the eleven subjects' change in sexual orientation. This discussion is continued in the following sections of the article, on "Heterosexual Marital Experience," "Homosexual Background," and "Other 'Therapies.'" Here, the authors argue that the "religious ideology" of the subjects' church was a major factor in their change from a homosexual to a heterosexual orientation. We believe that this claim is quite accurate.

First, the eleven men in Pattison and Pattison's study were presented with the beliefs that premarital and extramarital sexual experience are immoral, that heterosexual promiscuity is as immoral as homosexual promiscuity, and that one should not engage in sexual intercourse to "prove" masculinity or to "overcome" homosexuality.[56] Second, they were presented with the idea that the condition of homosexuality is an emotional problem due to psychological maldevelopment. Pattison and

55. Ibid.
56. Ibid.

Pattison note the following: "All of our subjects remarked that they soon became aware that they were psychologically immature and had poor interpersonal relationships. In essence, then, these subjects were exposed to an ideological expectational set demanding growth in personal and interpersonal maturity."[57] Pattison and Pattison add that their eleven subjects attributed this psychological mal-development to unsatisfactory relations with their parents. They also note that eight subjects stated that their fathers were "distant, aloof, and uninvolved with them," and that as a result they identified more with their mothers, developed effeminate manners, and felt like "sissies" because they were insecure about their own identity as males. The authors report that these eight men "saw homosexual behavior as a search for a masculine identity through identification with the male sex partner," while the other three subjects "reported the same psychodynamics and identity conflicts but focused their dynamic conflict on their mothers, whom they experienced as harsh, controlling, and demasculinizing."[58]

These beliefs were not, of course, presented in a social vacuum. In fact, a second major factor in the subjects' change in sexual orientation was the fact that they were involved in a church. The authors note:

> When our subjects came in contact with the church's crisis service for homosexuals, they found a welcome reception as homosexuals. No attempt was made to make them change their homosexuality. Rather, they were presented with the invitation to commit their life to Christ and the church. All subjects had an explicit Christian conversion or rededication. They were then invited into small church fellowship groups where they studied the Bible and learned expected Biblical patterns of mature lifestyles. This included an expectation to engage in loving, non-erotic relationships with both men and women in the fellowship groups.[59]

Especially through these groups, all of the subjects "soon became aware that they were psychologically immature and had poor interpersonal relationships."[60] Thus, the "ideological expectational set demanding growth in personal and interpersonal maturity" was coupled with "a great deal of actual interpersonal experience, behavioral rehearsal, and behavioral practice," and all the subjects "said they were surprised to

57. Ibid., 1558.
58. Ibid.
59. Ibid.
60. Ibid.

experience acceptance, non-judgmental evaluation, and non-erotic love from both men and women. These were new experiences for them, and in turn they began to learn and practice these new styles of interpersonal relationships."[61] As a result, "they began to identify with those they considered 'mature Christian men,' and they began to experience and practice nonerotic relationships with Christian women in the church. Thus, they felt they were growing in mature object relations with both men and women."[62] In their section on "Conclusions," the authors state that "cognitive change occurs first, followed by behavioral change, and finally intra-psychic resolution."[63]

The Men's Beliefs Regarding the Causes of Their Homosexual Orientation

We see no reason to question the veracity of this account of how the men changed from a homosexual to a heterosexual orientation. Some combination of a credible belief system and a hospitable social environment is the normal way in which persons become affiliates of a group. If one of these features is missing, the enduring affiliation is likely to be a tenuous one at best. Moreover, it is very common for a religious group to present itself as an alternative to an individual's original primary group (the family) where one can assume a new identity that is different from one's attributed identity or the identity that is ascribed by one's social position, family of origin, and so forth.[64] We suggest, therefore, that a crucial feature of the change that these eleven men experienced was their belief that they were maldeveloped as children and that the cause of this mal-development was their parents.

This, however, raises a very interesting question that Pattison and Pattison do not address: Eight of the men believed that the primary cause of their "mal-development" was "a distant, aloof, and uninvolved father," which led them to identify with their mothers instead. Are we therefore to assume that only men who have had fathers who fit this description become

61. Ibid., 1559.

62. Ibid.

63. Ibid., 1562.

64. Andries van Aarde discusses the differences between attributed identity, subjective identity, and optative identity as they relate to Jesus himself in van Aarde, "Social Identity, Status Identity, and Jesus' Abba." See also Capps, *Jesus: A Psychological Biography*, 267–71.

homosexual? If so, this flies in the face of the claims of various authors that the majority of boys experience their fathers as distant, aloof, and uninvolved. For example, Frank Pittman discusses the common experience of "father hunger," Samuel Osherson writes about the common experience of "father absence," and William Pollack writes about both.[65] Or, alternatively, are we to assume that what makes homosexual men unique is that they react to the distance and aloofness of their fathers by identifying with their mothers and developing effeminate manners whereas heterosexual men handle their fathers' emotional distance in some other way?

On the other hand, three of the men offered a different explanation for their homosexuality: They believed that the primary cause was their dynamic conflict with their mothers, whom they experienced as "harsh," "controlling," and "demasculinizing." Again, are we to conclude from this that only boys who had harsh, controlling, demasculinizing mothers are likely to develop a homosexual orientation? This, too, would fly in the face of evidence that many heterosexual boys have had harsh, controlling, demasculinizing mothers.

In any event, the causal factors that the two groups of subjects put forward to explain their original homosexual orientation seem to contradict one another, leading us to conclude that there is a deeper issue involved here, and that this deeper issue has to do with the fact that a boy's relationships with his parents are necessarily eroticized. Thus, we think that the key factor in the change that the men experienced was the fact that the relationships they experienced in the fellowship groups were evidently "non-erotic" ones, and that "non-erotic" relationships were believed to be more "mature" than erotic ones.

Religiously Mediated Change as a Form of Sublimation

If so, this raises the question, what was the nature of the change that the eleven men experienced? We agree with Pattison and Pattison that the change they experienced was not "some magical change or massive denial or repression."[66] But we question whether their alternative explanation—that the men experienced a "gradual development of a

---

65. Pittman, *Man Enough*, 128–33; Osherson, *Finding Our Fathers*, 28–33; and Pollack, *Real Boys*, 124–25.

66. Pattison and Pattison, "'Ex-gays,'" 1555.

rejection of the homosexual object choice as an increased cathexis of the heterosexual object [was] developed"—is accurate.[67] As Freud used the word, "cathexis" implies a libidinal (or erotic) attachment,[68] and if the men were "actively prohibited" from engaging in sexual behavior of any kind short of marriage, "cathexis of the heterosexual object" applies, at best, to the six married men. No conclusions can be drawn from the cases of the five unmarried men because the active prohibition of sexual behavior toward women outside of marriage means that their "cathexis of the heterosexual object" remains in doubt. As for the six married men, it is noteworthy that in only one case was there no indication (dreams, fantasies, impulses) of intrapsychic evidence of current homosexuality, and in three of the cases there was evidence of homosexual impulses. Two of the six married men were given a rating of 2 on the Kinsey scale (while only one of the unmarried men scored 2 on the Kinsey scale). To be sure, Pattison and Pattison note Kinsey's "convincing" evidence "that even among lifelong heterosexuals there were occasional homosexual dreams, fantasies, and impulses,"[69] so the fact that five of the six married men experienced homosexual dreams, fantasies, or impulses is not necessarily evidence of their *not* having made a "cathexis of the heterosexual object." But the fact that the married men are not different from the unmarried men with regard to "intra-psychic evidence of current homosexuality" is certainly grounds for wondering whether the heterosexual "cathexis" is as fully "developed" as the authors suggest.

We believe, therefore, that Freud's concept of sublimation is the most accurate label for the "change" that has occurred in the eleven men. We have discussed the concept of sublimation in the previous chapters, but it may be useful here to review the succinct definition of sublimation, which was noted in chapter 1, provided by Nick Rennison in *Freud and Psychoanalysis*. He indicates that sublimation is distinguished from repression, and, as we have seen, Pattison and Pattison reject the notion that the change in the eleven men was due to repression. Repression is "the process by which unacceptable impulses, ideas, memories and emotions, products of the conflict between the pleasure principle and the reality principle, are forced into the unconscious. There they remain active, influencing action and experience, without themselves returning to

---

67. Ibid.

68. Freud, *New Introductory Lectures on Psycho-analysis*, 80, 96.

69. Pattison and Pattison, "Ex-gays," 1555.

consciousness." In contrast to repression, sublimation is the process "by which instinctual, socially unacceptable energy or libido is transferred to a non-instinctual, socially acceptable activity, e.g. Freud believed that the sublimation of unsatisfied libido was behind the creation of great art and literature."[70] Freud considers both repression and sublimation to be unconscious processes. Whereas the eleven men in the Pattison and Pattison study are actively engaged in what the authors call "the rejection of the homosexual object choice," sublimation comes closer than repression to describing what is going on, namely, the transfer of socially unacceptable energy or libido to a noninstinctual, socially acceptable activity (i.e., involvement in fellowship groups that seek to foster nonerotic relationships with the men and the women in these groups).

Still, what remains unclear is whether the libidinal energy previously directed toward "homosexual objects" has been fully transferred to "a non-instinctual socially acceptable activity," or whether some of it *has* in fact been "repressed," forced into the unconscious, where it continues to be active, influencing action and experience. The fellowship groups, after all, are composed of men as well as women, and it is not therefore out of the question that the men do, in fact, have homosexual fantasies and impulses toward other men in the group. Since only three of the eleven men experienced no "intra-psychic evidence of current homosexuality," we may appropriately wonder if the dreams, fantasies, or impulses of the others are now directed toward other men in the group itself. Had Pattison and Pattison asked the men to identify the "homosexual object" of their dreams, fantasies, and impulses, they may have discovered that the fellowship groups were not as "non-erotic" as they were represented to be. In fact, it is not unreasonable to wonder whether the men's awareness of the fact that there were other men with homosexual backgrounds in the church may have been an important factor in their commitment to the church itself, and, more specifically, to involvement in the fellowship groups. To be sure, Pattison and Pattison note that "8 of our subjects participated in helping their peers as ex-homosexuals," and that they "reported no homosexual arousal in these contacts, which they interpreted as evidence of their solid heterosexuality."[71] This, however, could also be interpreted as an indication of an endorsement of the church's

---

70. Rennison, *Freud & Psychoanalysis*, 89.

71. Pattison and Pattison, "'Ex-gays,'" 1562.

prohibition of sexual promiscuity and of the fact that these particular men evoked no sexual arousal.

Whatever case might be made for repression, we nonetheless believe that Freud's concept of sublimation provides an accurate explanation of these men's "religiously mediated change." This means that the change is not a spurious one, but neither is it especially unique. Such sublimations may occur, for example, among heterosexual men who have experienced the deaths of their spouses and choose to remain faithful to their memories. It also occurs among heterosexual men who make a conscious decision *not* to engage in extramarital affairs lest they jeopardize their marriages or the intactness of their families. Sublimation may occur in various other situations, as when their wives are seriously ill, temporarily absent, or simply indisposed to engage in sexual activities. Or it may occur because the men themselves are engaging in activities (such as work) that they believe to be more essential or interesting.

But perhaps the best analogous situation is that of heterosexual men who do not marry. In his book on the psychology of men who haven't married, Charles A. Waehler identifies three types of bachelors: flexible, entrenched, and conflicted. Flexible bachelors are those who "create their independent lifestyle out of a benign indifference to marriage rather than as an apprehensive reaction to and retreat from women. These men could have gotten married, but instead their priorities led them to make other choices."[72] Waehler cites the case of a flexible bachelor for whom "fulfilling his ambition has been more important than committing to a relationship."[73] He was once in a serious relationship for about seven months, and thought she would be his wife, but then he moved away to take a new job, "and the relationship took a quick turn downhill as I became consumed by the new challenges I was facing."[74] Entrenched bachelors "withdraw into their own private worlds . . . These are shy men who withdraw from deep relationships and are inhibited in their ability to express their feelings . . . Their ability to experience sexual desire is directly linked to their sense of personal autonomy. That is, if they feel their independence encroached on, their desire for sex will diminish or may stop altogether."[75] Conflicted bachelors "have mixed feelings about being

---

72. Waehler, *Bachelors*, 78. We realize that this discussion reflects a heteronormative bias, which we do not want to support.

73. Ibid., 109.

74. Ibid., 88.

75. Ibid., 95, 97.

single. These men are dissatisfied with their single status, but they are reluctant to give up the independence that they imagine they would have to compromise in marriage." Yet they are "quite uncomfortable. Their opposing internal forces cause stress. Conflicted bachelors are sincere about wanting to be married, but back away from taking the plunge. They say that they are seeking to make a serious commitment to an intimate relationship, but then find reasons (excuses?) why this is not happening. Their reluctance to fully engage in one position or the other leaves them despondent."[76] While some of these bachelors are sexually active, many of them are not. Given that the sexually inactive frequently choose not to be sexually active because they have other priorities, it seems appropriate to say that they are engaging in sublimation, and doing so on a relatively permanent basis.[77]

The Issue of Psychological Immaturity

As we have seen, one of the tenets of the Pentecostal church (and one that the men themselves endorsed) is that homosexuality is inherently an expression of psychological immaturity, and heterosexuality is inherently an expression of psychological maturity. Here, too, comparison with the heterosexual bachelors is instructive. These men, Waehler notes, make up only 3 million of America's male population. But does their minority status suggest or imply that they are therefore psychologically immature? Waehler suggests that there is some evidence of "interpersonal passivity,"[78] and certain "psychologically protective qualities,"[79] but the primary psychological themes in the lives of bachelors are the importance of independence, a tendency toward consistency and preference for the status quo, and a tendency to prefer pursuing one goal at a time, especially when they are in their mid- to late twenties. In our view, these characteristics do not warrant the judgment that they are psychologically immature; these same characteristics and qualities are also found among men who marry.

Males with a homosexual orientation are also a minority group, but does this make them psychologically immature? We have seen that the

76. Ibid., 109.
77. Ibid., 165.
78. Ibid., 44–46.
79. Ibid., 20–23.

men in this study tended to attribute their alleged psychological immaturity to their early relationships with parents, yet we have also noted
that these relationships were not significantly different from those of
heterosexual males. If the causes that are deduced for their homosexual
interests are not unusual but rather shared with heterosexual males, this
in itself raises serious questions as to whether they are, in fact, psychologically immature in comparison with heterosexual males. The Pattison
and Pattison study assumes psychological immaturity on the grounds
that some homosexual males are sexually "promiscuous," especially in
their late teens and early twenties, but is this evidence of psychological
immaturity, or is it rather evidence of the same search for a more permanent relationship in which heterosexual men of the same age are also
"promiscuous"? Religious groups may, for theological reasons, believe
that homosexuality is inherently immoral, but we see no reason why they
should support this judgment with the claim that homosexuality is also
an expression of psychological immaturity.

Is That All There Is?

As we have noted, the sublimation that the eleven men have achieved has
essentially taken the form of participating in a fellowship group and, as
Pattison and Pattison suggest, of encouraging other gay men to do as they
have done. But these men could have experienced fellowship with other
groups without undergoing this change in their sexual orientation; or,
alternatively, if we accept the authors' contention that the men received
acceptance without strings attached, it would appear that they could have
remained members of the fellowship group even if they retained their
homosexual orientation. This raises the obvious question as to whether
the change served other ends, and whether these ends may have been
acted upon without the change? Or are we to accept the notion that the
change is a worthy end in itself?

Churches, like any other social group, cannot do everything that
needs doing in the world, and they need to establish their priorities. If
the sublimation of sexual impulses is deemed a priority, it would seem
that those who deem it a priority would need to indicate what purposes
the sublimation is intended to serve. Freud, after all, believed that sublimation of sexual impulses may result in great art, as in the case of
Leonardo da Vinci, who was brought to court on the charge of sodomy

and subsequently avoided homosexual behaviors; in great literature, as in the case of Henry James, who may have had homosexual relationships but felt that such relationships were a distraction from his work as a novelist; and in important scientific discoveries, which, in Freud's view, were even more impressive in Leonardo da Vinci's case than his artistic achievements.[80]

The table on the "psychological state" of the eleven subjects in the Pattison and Pattison study claims that they were more exuberant, self-accepting, and happy, and less lonely, worried, depressed, tense, and paranoid than their homosexual counterparts. While we have raised questions about the comparison itself, we see no reason to challenge the authors' view that these qualities suggest that their subjects have realized "a remarkable state of psychic well-being."[81] But to what end? We would have expected that an article that refers to the "religiously mediated change" that these men experienced would have had more to say about the ends these men's sublimation of sexual impulses was intended to foster or to serve. We would also have expected that a case would have been made that these ends, whatever they might be, could not have been realized if the men had *not* changed. Absent such a discussion, we find the authors' account of these eleven men interesting but not, at least as presented by the authors, particularly inspiring.

At the risk of sounding a bit preachy, we would suggest that there is another group of men of roughly equal size—the men whom Jesus called his disciples—which is both interesting *and* inspiring.[82] They experienced fellowship among themselves, but they would not be remembered if they did not follow their leader's example and heal those who were truly sick and confront those who believed that they were more exemplary in the sight of God than others. We would suggest that these initiatives were expressions of religious sublimation.

Back to Kinsey

Earlier, we noted the irony of the fact that Pattison and Pattison used the Kinsey scale as a basis for their article on the "religiously mediated

---

80. Freud, *Leonardo da Vinci and a Memory of His Childhood.*

81. Pattison and Pattison, "'Ex-gays,'" 1556.

82. It might be worth pointing out that the size of the two groups is exactly equal if we take into consideration Judas's betrayal of Jesus.

change" of eleven gay men. The Kinsey scale assumes that human sexuality follows a continuum between same-sex and other-sex desires. If the Kinsey scale is a reliable indicator of who we are, would it not have made more sense to focus an article on "religiously mediated change" on those who proclaim themselves to be thoroughly heterosexual (thus scoring 0 on the Kinsey scale) and to attempt to help them become more aware of their same-sex desires and, by doing so, to become more tolerant of those who score higher on the Kinsey scale than they do? Would this not have been a more promising project for demonstrating the role of religion in mediating change?

We believe that it would, and we suggest that one way to address the inevitable resistance to *this* effort to achieve change would be to introduce those who resist our proposal to Harry Stack Sullivan's "chumship" concept: the idea that all preadolescent boys form a very strong emotional attachment to one other boy his own age.[83] Thus, if early adolescent boys in the chumship period were given the Kinsey test, they would all be 5s or 6s. And, as Sullivan describes this period, it is one of remarkable psychological maturity. He writes:

> The preadolescent frames of reference are, at least in our culture, about the clearest and workable ones that we have. They do not include lust as a complicating and distorting factor—generally, a confusing and misleading element. Love is new and uncomplicated. The parental complex is viewed from this new angle and, while there may still be aspects which do not make sense, the appraisal is often more valid than is the view which will be adopted some five or six years hence.[84]

Sullivan continues:

> The relatively uncomplicated experience of love is entirely ennobling. Sympathy flows from it. Tolerance as a respect for people—not as an intellectual detachment from prejudice—follows it like a bright shadow. Authoritarian figures in the home and elsewhere are recast as of good intention, however stupid and uninformed. A remedy has been found for many thwartings and humiliations, for sundry prohibitions. One looks about one at one's compeers, without sentimentality but with a feeling that they have come naturally by their assets and deficiencies.[85]

83. Sullivan, *Conceptions of Modern Psychiatry.*

84. Ibid., 55.

85. Ibid.

He goes on to note,

> A new form of participation develops, in part from sympathy
> and understanding, in part from awe at the newly expanded
> world. The preadolescent evolves the practice of *collaboration*,
> a valid functional activity as a person in a personal situation.
> This is a great step forward from cooperation—*I* play according
> to the rules of the game, to preserve *my* prestige and feeling of
> superiority and merit. When we collaborate, it is a matter of *we*.
> The achievement is no longer a personal success; it is a group
> performance—no more the leader's than the led.[86]

Sullivan concludes that in this brief phase of preadolescence, "the world
as known gains depth of meaning from the new appraisal of the people
who compose it," and although the "imaginary people of preadolescent
fantasy may seem to us insubstantial," and the "illusions that transmute his
companions—if they be illusions—may seem to us but certain of an early
end, a disillusionment," yet "whatever his people, real, illusory or frankly
imagined, may be, they are not mean," and "whatever his daydreams with
his chum, whatever his private fantasies, they are not base."[87] As for his
evaluations of others, "here we may take pause and reflect that it may be
we who see 'as through a glass, darkly.'" To be sure, "these young people are
grossly inexperienced," and they "are often misinformed as to the motives
that are prominent in adult life around them," but "I surmise that after the
measure of their experience, they see remarkably clearly. Also, I believe
that for a great majority of our people, preadolescence is the nearest that
they come to untroubled human life—that from then on the stresses of life
distort them to inferior caricatures of what they might have been."[88]

If preadolescence is the stage in life when we are all homosexual,
perhaps the roles of the participants in the project that Pattison and Pattison studied should have been reversed. The rationale for this role reversal
would be that the subjects of the project were more mature, psychologically speaking, than those who were engaged in changing the subjects'
sexual orientation. And, if an adult's tendency to privilege the preadolescent boy who lives inside of him is a sign of psychological immaturity,
Sullivan's suggestion that this preadolescent boy sees more clearly than

---

86. Ibid., 55–56.
87. Ibid., 56.
88. Ibid.

we adults raises serious questions about the assumption that psychological maturity increases with age.

Another concept that those who believe themselves to be thoroughly heterosexual might find instructive is the aspect of Freud's Oedipus complex theory that is rarely mentioned in the literature, namely, that originally the boy's same-sex affections toward his father are as strong, if not stronger than, his other-sex affections for his mother, which leads Freud to conclude that the object-choices and identifications of "any individual will reflect the preponderance in him of one or other of the two sexual dispositions."[89] In effect, the Kinsey scale is designed to measure the preponderance. It is not a therapeutic instrument, much less a crude device to determine whether an individual has experienced a religious conversion, yet it may be a means of enlightenment.

89. Freud, *Ego and the Id*, 23–24. Freud emphasized the constitutional bisexuality of each individual and suggested that initially the boy is affectionately disposed toward his father, an affection based on the fact that they are the same sex. Then, however, the boy develops an object-cathexis for his mother, and for a time these two relationships proceed side by side until the boy's sexual wishes for his mother become more intense and his father is perceived as an obstacle to them—this marks the origination of the Oedipus complex, which is finally resolved when the boy's jealousy of his father is relinquished in favor of an intensified desire to be like his father (see Capps, *Men and Their Religion*, 73–77).

———— 6 ————

God's Gender Confusion and Sexuality in the Church

Introduction

IF I HAVE A belly button, and if Mommy has a belly button, does God have a belly button too? This question, Howard Eilberg-Schwartz notes in *God's Phallus*, is not an uncommon question for children to ask.[1] It is a cute question. It is nonthreatening. But while this question is cute and nonthreatening, the following question that the growing child would likely ask at a later stage of development is not so cute: Does God have a penis, and if so, is he allowed to play with it? This question likely would be offensive to many Jews and Christians and also would be experienced by them as threatening because it would bring attention to certain issues of gender and sexuality in religion. Yet questions about God's body are not at all new. Indeed, Jews and Christians have been asking questions about the nature of God's body, gender, and sexuality—and what this might mean for human beings—for centuries.[2]

1. Eilberg-Schwartz, *God's Phallus*, 80.

2. Brown, *Body and Society*. It is interesting to note that this was an issue for the five-year-old Sergei Pankejeff, the patient of Freud's referred to in chapter 1 and popularly known as "the Wolf-Man." One of the first questions he asked his nurse, who had been assigned the task of teaching him the story of Christ's passion by his mother, was whether Christ had a behind. He also wondered if Christ defecated. He resolved these

In recent decades one of the most eloquent scholars to remind us of the historical debates over God's body is Daniel Boyarin.[3] Boyarin has shown how Jews and Christians, reading the same Scriptures, have conceived of God differently—particularly how Jews have imagined God corporeally and how Christians, conversely, have imagined God incorporeally. One theological upshot from this difference that Boyarin points out is that, for Jews, there is no need for the incarnation—no need for the Word to become flesh (cf. John 1)—because God already has a body (and, as we will see, revealed it from time to time). But Christians, who read the Scriptures allegorically, tend not see God's body and therefore felt the need to give God a body by means of the doctrine of the incarnation.

Just as Jews and Christians have pondered God's body, they also have thought theologically about the human body. In *Carnal Israel: Reading Sex in Talmudic Culture*, Boyarin notes Augustine's infamous charge against "the Jews"—namely, that Jews are "people of the flesh." Ironically, Boyarin, himself Jewish, claims that "Augustine knew what he was talking about."[4] But conceding to Augustine this point enables Boyarin to turn what was once a criticism against Jews into a criticism of Christianity. How? Boyarin argues, "for rabbinic Jews, the human being was defined as a body—animated, to be sure, by a soul—while for Hellenistic Jews (such as Philo) and . . . Christians (such as Paul), the essence of a human being is a soul housed in a body."[5] The importance of this perhaps subtle difference in theological anthropology is that the "notion that the physical is just a sign or a shadow of that which is really real allows for a disavowal of sexuality and procreation, of the importance of filiation and genealogy, and of the concrete, historical sense of Scripture, of, indeed, historical memory itself. The emphasis, on the other hand, on the body as the very

---

questions and doubts by deciding that Christ's behind is simply the continuation of his legs and that if Christ could make wine out of water, so he could make food out of nothing and thereby avoid defecation. Freud suggests that his blasphemous thoughts were thereby repressed and that the result was "a victory for the faith of piety over the rebelliousness of critical research." The result was that young Sergei's "intellectual activity remained seriously impaired" for "he developed no zeal for learning" and "showed no more of the acuteness with which at the tender age of five he had criticized and dissected the doctrines of religion" (Freud, *The History of an Infantile Neurosis*, 70; see also Carlin and Capps, "Freud's Wolf Man").

3. See, e.g., Boyarin, *Carnal Israel*.

4. Ibid., 1.

5. Ibid., 5.

site of human significance allows for no such devaluations."[6] From Boyarin's analysis, one can observe that how religious communities imagine
God's body affects how they understand the human body. Theological
thinking about God's body has implications for human bodies.

Many Christians today are probably unaware of these historical
debates, and, especially for this reason, we believe that there is a pastoral
payoff, especially for men, in reminding ourselves about such questions.
We hope that raising questions about God's body, gender, and sexuality
will help some men to ask questions about their own bodies, genders, and
sexualities, and it is our intention to offer support to men who actually
are confused about their own gender and also to confuse other men who
might be a little too certain and a little too rigid about their own gender
and gender roles. Our argument—which is both serious and not so serious,
and more playful than historical—goes something like this: God is gender
confused and has made some rather poor decisions in the midst of this
confusion, but if God were able to accept a wider range of masculinities,
he would be much better off—as also would men today. Put another way, if
contemporary religious men who relate to the Bible were to become aware
of the problems of gender and sexuality in the Bible, particularly regarding God's body, perhaps this would give them permission to ask questions
about their own bodies, genders, and sexualities. In making this case, we
begin by exploring the work of biblical scholars, proceed by exploring diagnostic issues, and then draw some conclusions regarding the confusions
with which we have been concerned in this chapter.

A Divine Penis

"The title of this book [i.e., *God's Phallus*] is shocking," Eilberg-Schwartz
writes, "because the thought of God having a penis is shocking."[7] He continues: "Most Jews and Christians think of God the [F]ather as lacking a body
and hence as beyond sexuality."[8] But, Eilberg-Schwartz asks, "from where
does the idea of a disembodied God come? What if, historically speaking, it
is discomfort with the idea of God's penis that has generated the idea of an
incorporeal God?"[9] Further, "what if this uneasiness flows from contradic-

6. Ibid., 6.

7. Eilberg-Schwartz, *God's Phallus*, 1.

8. Ibid.

9. Ibid.

tions inherent in men's relationship with a God who is explicitly male?"[10] And so *God's Phallus* "is a book about divine fatherhood and the ways in which the sexual body of a [F]ather God is troubling for the conception of masculinity."[11] Eilberg-Schwartz notes that dozens of feminist works have taken up the problem of how a Father God is problematic for women,[12] but he also points out that few studies have addressed how a Father God is problematic for men and masculinity.[13]

The major problem for Jewish and Christian men's masculinity that Eilberg-Schwartz identifies concerns a paradox around homoeroticism and homophobia. In Jewish and Christian theology, God is depicted overwhelmingly as male, so when men bow down, worship, and mystically unite with this male God, it is hard to deny that this religious structure is homoerotic.[14] This is not to imply, of course, that men who worship a male God are homosexually oriented (though this is sometimes the case in many same-sex religious communities[15]); the point here, rather, is that the traditional or orthodox religious symbolism of Judaism and Christianity is homoerotic and that this homoerotic structure is disguised by means of feminizing men (e.g., imagining Israel as a woman) and veiling God. The central problem with this paradox that Eilberg-Schwartz identifies can be posed as such: For Jewish and Christian men, what are the effects of a monotheistic tradition that encourages a homoerotic religious structure while, at the same time, condemning homosexual practices, largely because of the biblical mandate for men to procreate? Men are being given contradictory messages from their religious traditions and sacred Scriptures in that they are being asked to be fathers by desiring and procreating with women, *and* they are being asked to love one man (God) exclusively. In Christian theology, as Eilberg-Schwartz sees it, this paradox is taken to its logical conclusion with the doctrine of the virgin birth: a father (Joseph) procreates without having sex. Eilberg-Schwartz offers a thoughtful analysis of this paradox by looking at depictions of God's body in the Hebrew Bible, therefore making these problems apparent.

10. Ibid.

11. Ibid.

12. See, for example, Daly, *Beyond God the Father*.

13. See, however, Dittes, *Driven by Hope*; Capps, *Men and Their Religion*.

14. Cf. Kripal, *Roads of Excess, Palaces of Wisdom*.

15. See Jordan, *Silence of Sodom*.

In the Hebrew Bible, Eilberg-Schwartz argues, God's body is hidden rather than nonexistent. Indeed, there is no explicit denial of God having a body in ancient Israelite literature.[16] But a common way of interpreting this language is by reading it metaphorically.[17] Those who argue for metaphorical readings point out that when, for example, God is referred to as a lion (Hosea 11:10), we do not think of God as being an actual animal, so why then should we think of God as having a literal body if we do not think of God as an animal? Yet whether to take these descriptions literally or metaphorically is a long-standing debate in biblical studies, as also is the question as to whether ancient Israelites really believed that God had a body. Eilberg-Schwartz wants to move beyond these debates and to focus our attention on "why, when [the biblical writers] imagined God in human form, that form was so carefully veiled and why it was veiled in the particular way that it was."[18] Eilberg-Schwartz's justification for focusing on the human representations of God rather than on animal representations is that the metaphor of God having a body is a special case, because, *in God sightings*, we do not have God appearing as a lion or bear but instead in human form. This is curious to Eilberg-Schwartz because, in God sightings, God's face is hidden. Eilberg-Schwartz thinks that the hiding of God's face also conceals God's sex and is therefore a diversion away from the genitals; we never see God's penis because the homoerotic structure of monotheism—which, of course, is never recognized—would become apparent.

As we have noted, in order to deny the homoerotic structure of religious language in Judaism, Israel was feminized. In a monotheism that demands the love of men and yet also demands that those men be heterosexual in the sense that their sexuality must lead to procreation through intercourse with a woman, masculinity is inevitably going to be problematic for Jewish men. In place of these problematic dynamics, Eilberg-Schwartz suggests "a reversal of the process of monotheism . . . Instead of feminizing men so they can have an intimate relationship with a male God, we might feminize this God, without always making him into a goddess."[19] He continues: "Indeed, I believe that in many ways the process by which we may now be creating new femininities and masculinities

16. Eilberg-Schwartz, *God's Phallus*, 8–10.

17. Ibid., 64.

18. Ibid., 75.

19. Ibid., 240.

involves redistributing across the genders the traits that previously were thought to inhere in one or the other."[20] Thus, Eilberg-Schwartz does not want to eliminate the traditional masculine imagery for God but instead wants to advocate a "polymorphously perverse theology" in which the images of God may be used by the faithful in a variety of ways—ways as various as our genders and sexualities.[21]

Freud introduced the phrase "polymorphously perverse" in *Three Essays on the Theory of Sexuality*, originally published in 1905.[22] It occurs in his essay on "Infantile Sexuality" in a section titled "Masturbatory Sexual Manifestations." Here he suggests that masturbation is common in early infancy but typically ceases for a couple of years and then tends to return in the child's fourth year. He notes in his discussion of the return of early infantile masturbation in the fourth year that seduction by adults or other children may occur, and this experience, which treats the child as a sexual object prematurely, "teaches him, in highly emotional circumstances, how to obtain satisfaction from his genital zones, a satisfaction which he is then usually obliged to repeat again and again by masturbation."[23] In his following discussion of the "polymorphously perverse disposition," Freud indicates that it is "an instructive fact that under the influence of seduction children can become polymorphously perverse, and can be led into all possible kinds of sexual irregularities. This shows that an aptitude for them is innately present in their disposition."[24] Freud adds, "There is consequently little resistance towards carrying them out, since the mental dams against sexual excesses—shame, disgust, and morality—have either not yet been constructed at all or are only in course of construction, according to the age of the child."[25]

In *An Autobiographical Study*, published in 1925, Freud alludes to his earlier description of children as "polymorphously perverse," and explains, "If I have described children as 'polymorphously perverse,' I was only using a terminology that was generally current; no moral judgment was implied by the phrase."[26] In fact, "psychoanalysis has no concern

---

20. Ibid.
21. Ibid., 242.
22. Freud, *Three Essays on the Theory of Sexuality.*
23. Ibid., 56.
24. Ibid., 57.
25. Ibid.
26. Freud, *Autobiographical Study*, 72.

whatever with such judgments of value."[27] In light of our emphasis in this book on sublimation, it is noteworthy that he goes on to discuss the fact that, for children, "all these affectionate impulses were of a completely sexual nature but have become *inhibited in their aim* or *sublimated*," and, referring to their sublimation, he adds: "The manner in which the sexual instincts can thus be influenced and diverted enables them to be employed for cultural activities of every kind, to which indeed they bring the most important contributions."[28]

This chapter offers beginning steps toward a polymorphously perverse pastoral psychology, one that takes into consideration the liberating effects of religious sublimation, and one that holds religious and psychological truths and findings lightly.[29]

God as Male-Androgyne

In *God's Gym*, Stephen Moore eloquently and subversively presents three distinctive essays that center on a common theme: the relationship between Christianity and the male body. The central thesis of the book is that the God who is portrayed in the Bible is a projection of male narcissism and hypermasculinity, and that this projection still affects contemporary culture. The third essay in his book, titled "Resurrection: Horrible Pain, Glorious Gain," is the essay most relevant to our interests. Here Moore correlates weightlifting with the Christian life, suggesting that "hardcore bodybuilding is a purity system, arguably the most rigorous purity system to be found in contemporary Western culture."[30] And, as a biblical scholar, he suggests that this new purity system "begs comparison" to the purity system in the Pentateuch.

Moore's analysis can shed more light on the nature of God's body. Like Eilberg-Schwartz, Moore realizes that many would not concede that God has an actual body. But Moore simply goes to the Bible and notes

27. Ibid.

28. Ibid. (italics original).

29. It is noteworthy in this connection that Jesus placed a child in the midst of his disciples and declared, "Truly, I tell you, unless you change and become like children, you will never enter the kingdom of heaven" (Matt 18:2–3). We would suggest that the child was four years old and thus in the "play age." See Erikson, *Toys and Reasons*, 98–103, and our reference to the play age in the introduction. The four-year-old child's play marks the confluence of polymorphous perversity and sublimation.

30. Moore, *God's Gym*, 76.

that Yahweh strolls (Gen 3:8), helps shut the door to the ark (Gen 7:16), inhales (Gen 11:5), and so on. Moore writes, "Even the most passionate assertion of Yahweh's unrepresentablity in the Hebrew Bible—that of Second Isaiah (Isa 40:12–26)—is itself riddled with anthropomorphisms."[31] While a complete description of Yahweh's body is not offered in the Bible, Moore thinks we do have enough to "complete the biblical authors' (necessarily) incomplete thoughts on the body of Yahweh, to press the logic of their divine body-talk through to its (possibly unnatural) conclusion."[32]

Moore begins his search for a look at God's body by recalling that the first man (Adam), according to Genesis, was made in the image of God (Gen 1:26–27). So knowing something about Adam's body should tell us something about God's. He also observes that in many biblical passages (see, for example, 1 Kgs 8:27, 2 Chr 2:5–6, 2 Chr 6:18, and Isa 66:1), God is gigantic, which is corroborated with what the Jewish commentaries tell us about Adam (where Adam, too, is imagined as being huge[33]). Also, Moore cites Ezek 28:12ff. to suggest that Adam was perfect in beauty. Thus, God is huge and beautiful.

Moore next turns to an anomaly about the image of God: Why is it that we don't see God's face? We have seen how Eilberg-Schwartz answers this—namely, we do not see God's face because then we would be able to see God's penis and this, in turn, would make apparent the implied homoeroticism of men worshiping a male God. But Moore offers another explanation. Moore notes that the standard answer that biblical scholars give this question (i.e., why don't we see God's face?) is that "face" in Hebrew is a common term for "presence," and to be in the presence of Yahweh is a privilege reserved for very few (such as for the priest who is allowed to enter into the Holy of Holies once a year). Moore is not satisfied with this explanation: "Surely there are other reasons for Yahweh's agonizing shyness in the Hebrew Bible."[34] Moore notes that the "rabbis once again supply the clue, although they fail to follow it through."[35] Adam, in the beginning, had two faces, according to some rabbinic commentary, and Eve, who was created later, is literally taken from Adam, meaning that *Adam was originally a (male) androgyne.* And if Adam the

31. Ibid., 83.
32. Ibid., 86.
33. Ibid., 89.
34. Ibid., 90.
35. Ibid.

androgyne was created in God's image, "it follows that the God of Israel is also androgynous—*physically* androgynous."[36] We do not see God's face, Moore argues, because God is embarrassed about his androgyny.

So God is huge, beautiful, and androgynous. But how, Moore wonders, did Yahweh get so big? In pursuing this question, Moore offers an explanation for God's androgyny. An important clue to note is Yahweh's enormous diet, which is heavily weighted towards red meat (i.e., protein), and another important clue, Moore thinks, is Yahweh's irrational anger in the Hebrew Bible (e.g., Josh 7:25–26). These clues—Yahweh's size, diet, and anger—suggest to Moore that Yahweh's size is the result of nothing other than bodybuilding and steroid use.[37] Moore points out that Ezekiel 23:19–20 intimates that the Egyptian gods were huge, so it is no wonder that Yahweh would be tempted by steroids because he wanted to get big at any cost. And there was a cost, Moore infers, as the excessive use of steroids would explain Yahweh's androgyny: "Certain steroids can produce a condition known as gynecomastia ('bitch tits' in gym vernacular)."[38] Moore thinks that Yahweh developed breasts and also experienced a shrinking of his testicles, which is why we never get a full frontal look at Yahweh.

It is important to keep in mind that Moore believes that Yahweh was not always androgynous; his androgyny was the result of steroid abuse and became a cause for anxiety, evidenced by the fact that he would not let anyone look at him straight on. Yahweh's solution to his own hang-ups around masculinity was to do to Adam as he desired to do to himself: "He would create an androgynous being in his own image and likeness, and he would . . . siphon off its female side and banish it altogether into another body, thereby eradicating it."[39] This "therapy," Moore agues, was partially successful, but throughout the Hebrew Bible we still see both masculine and feminine metaphors for God (more on this below).

Moore next turns his gaze to Jesus. On the basis of John 5:19—"Whatever [the Father] does, the Son does likewise"—Moore reasons that, if Yahweh (God the Father, for Christians) is a bodybuilder, so then must Jesus be. He finds evidence in the Passion narratives, and Jesus's life more broadly, to support this conclusion: Jesus's prayers can be seen as a kind of training; Jesus overturning the tables in the temple (Matt 21:12) can be seen as an

---

36. Ibid., 91 (italics original).

37. Ibid., 96.

38. Ibid., 97.

39. Ibid., 101.

expression of Jesus's 'roid rage; and Jesus and Barabbas appearing before Pilate (John 18:28–38) can be seen as a prejudging bodybuilding contest.[40] While this part of Moore's analysis, though interesting, is not especially relevant for our purposes in this chapter, we would like to point out a question that he neglects: In light of the doctrine of the incarnation, what is the relationship between Jesus and God if God is androgynous? Jesus, Moore notes, becomes the New Adam for Christians (1 Cor 15:45, 47).[41] Since Adam was androgynous (whereas Jesus presumably was not), this raises again the question as to what happened to God's androgyny when it became incarnate in Jesus, assuming that this aspect of God did in fact become incarnate. Moore does not pick up this line of reasoning. If Jesus was not androgynous—and, to our knowledge, we have no historical reason to think that he was—then this aspect of God's being must have been incarnated in some other way. But how? Before we turn to the incarnation, let us first consider the psychological implications of God's androgyny for God, drawing from recent psychological literature.

Diagnostic Issues

Drawing on Moore's analysis, if we were to offer God a psychiatric diagnosis based on his experiences and behaviors, what would it be? We suggest the term *gender confusion*. We are aware that this is not a category in the current *Diagnostic and Statistical Manual of Mental Disorders*. But all such terms and categories are contested and up for debate. For example, in the *Diagnostic and Statistical Manual of Mental Disorders (DSM-IV-TR)*, there is a section on "Gender Identity Disorder," but in the *Diagnostic and Statistical Manual of Mental Disorders (DSM-5)* the term "Gender Dysphoria" is used. The *DSM-5* notes that "*Gender dysphoria* refers to the distress that may accompany the incongruence between one's experienced or expressed gender and one's assigned gender. Although not all individuals will experience distress as a result of such incongruence, many are distressed if the desired physical interventions by means of hormones or surgery, or both, are not available. The current term is more descriptive than the previous *DSM-IV* term *gender identity disorder* and focuses on dysphoria as the clinical problem, not identity per se."[42]

---

40. Ibid., 110–13.

41. Ibid., 116.

42. *DSM-5*, 451.

However, we prefer the term *gender confusion* for our purposes here (and perhaps clinically) for several reasons: (1) While the terms *disorder* and *dysphoria* seem inherently pejorative, the term *confusion* is not necessarily a bad thing; (2) *confusion* seems more accurate for some (but not all) cases because it reflects the distress that one would likely experience in this state of being—the word *disorder*, in contrast, is excessively vague (though the term *dysphoria* does seem to be more descriptive than *disorder*); and (3) the term *gender confusion*, like the term *gender dysphoria*, does not specifically reference identity or social role. While we prefer the term *gender confusion*, we still think, however, that it is useful to use the section on Gender Identity Disorder to diagnose God. We will discuss the diagnostic criteria in the *DSM-IV-TR* and the *DSM-5* and will offer a critique of the criteria in the *DSM-IV-TR*.

Gender Identity Disorder: *DSM-IV-TR*

The section on Gender Identity Disorder in the *DSM-IV-TR* states that "there are two components of Gender Identity Disorder, both of which must be present to make the diagnosis."[43] First there must be "evidence of a strong and persistent cross-gender identification, which is the desire to be, or the insistence that one is, of the other sex."[44] This identification may not be based on "a desire for any perceived cultural advantages of being the other sex" and cannot be made if the person has "a concurrent physical intersex condition."[45] The other component is that there must be "evidence of persistent discomfort about one's assigned sex or a sense of inappropriateness in the gender role of that sex."[46] "To make a diagnosis, there must be evidence of clinically significant distress or impairment in social, occupational, or other important areas of functioning."[47] If Moore is right that God is androgynous—i.e., that what we have in the Bible is a large male deity with female breasts and (probably) shrunken testicles, and that God is distressed enough about this situation that he will not let anyone see his face—then it seems reasonable that we could assume that, in one way or another, God is at least somewhat confused,

43. *DSM-IV-TR*, 576.
44. Ibid.
45. Ibid.
46. Ibid.
47. Ibid.

in a broad and not necessarily pejorative sense, about his own gender, which is not to conflate androgyny with gender confusion but rather to assume a connection between God's androgyny and his behavior (his behavior is confusing to us, as readers, at least). But since God has what might be considered a kind of intersex condition in that God's secondary sexual characteristics (i.e., God's breasts) are female and God's primary sexual characteristics (i.e., God's genitals) are male, this seems like God would disqualify for a diagnosis of Gender Identity Disorder. However, there is also a subcategory titled Gender Identity Disorder Not Otherwise Specified, and it "can be used for individuals who have a gender identity problem with a congruent congenital intersex condition."[48] Yet this diagnosis still does not seem right because it focuses on the primary sexual characteristics. God has the condition of gynecomastia, which can cause significant psychological and social problems.[49]

Pathology and Gender

The psychological community is aware that there are problems around diagnosis and gender. Indeed, in "The Validity of the Diagnosis of Gender Identity Disorder (Child and Adolescent Criteria)" Ian Wilson, Chris Griffin, and Bernadette Wren discuss in some detail many of these problems, and they note that since "the diagnosis of [G]ender [I]dentity [D]isorder was introduced, there has been considerable debate as to whether the cluster of symptoms required for the diagnosis does in fact warrant being described as a psychiatric disorder,"[50] and also note the irony that when homosexuality was removed from *The Diagnostic and Statistical Manual of Mental Disorders*, Gender Identity Disorder was introduced. Wilson, Griffin, and Wren are aware of the fact that gender is constituted and performed differently in various cultures, and that some think that mental disorders per se are social constructions. It is for this reason, the authors suggest, that what is defined as a mental disorder changes over time and is also contested at any given time. They add that in the 1950s and 1960s the terms *gender role* and *gender identity* were introduced—*gender role* referring to the social behaviors expected for

---

48. Ibid., 580–81.

49. Cf. Wiesman et al., "Gynecomastia." *Gynecomastia* refers to the overdevelopment of a male's breasts.

50. Wilson et al., "Validity of the Diagnosis of Gender Identity Disorder," 336.

men and women in a given culture, and *gender identity* referring to one's own sense of maleness or femaleness: "Neither gender role nor gender identity are seen to bear a necessary relation to the sexual body," the authors note, and they continue to explain that Gender Identity Disorders "can be seen as involving an incongruity between sex and gender."[51] The authors note that children who do not conform to society's expectations for them in terms of gender role may be given a diagnosis of Gender Identity Disorder even though developmentally they may be on a normal pathway toward a homosexual orientation. And since most health professionals no longer consider homosexuality to be pathological, and because society is becoming more flexible in terms of gender roles, the authors conclude that the diagnosis of Gender Identity Disorder, when it is "based on gender role expectations should be questioned."[52]

Most of the research to date, Wilson, Griffin, and Wren note, has tended to focus on behavior (i.e., gender *roles*) rather than on gender *identity*. And this is problematic because if, for example, one is clear on one's gender identity but does not conform with his or her socially expected gender roles, the distress that one would experience in this situation would be "qualitatively different" from a situation where one is confused about one's gender identity.[53] The authors report another term that has been suggested—namely, *atypical gender identity organization*—and they advocate the use of this term, because "using the term *atypical gender identity organization* allows the clinician to assess issues around atypical gender role and identity, without the child or adolescent receiving a pathological diagnosis."[54] And this concept as they see it would be able to address the variety of gender identities in ways that the concept Gender Identity Disorder, as presently defined and understood, cannot, mainly because Gender Identity Disorder focuses on gender roles, seems to be heteronormative, and does not account for the fact that gender identities are constituted and experienced differently at various stages of the life cycle.

51. Ibid., 337.
52. Ibid., 346.
53. Ibid.
54. Ibid., 347.

Gender Dysphoria: *DSM-5*

The *DSM-5*, as we noted, has incorporated many of the above critiques, especially those relating to identity, into its new formulation of Gender Dysphoria. If the diagnosis of Gender Identity Disorder did not seem like a right fit for God, the diagnosis of Gender Dysphoria does fit more closely. The *DSM-5* offers two primary diagnostic criteria: (a) a "marked incongruence between one's experienced/expressed gender and assigned gender, of at least 6 months' duration"; and (b) "clinically significant distress or impairment in social, occupational, or other important areas of functioning."[55] With regard to criterion (a), the *DSM-5* provides six sub-criteria, of which a person must present with two to qualify for the diagnosis of Gender Dysphoria. Strikingly, God manifests the first two: (1) "A marked incongruence between one's experienced/expressed gender and primary and/or secondary sex characteristics"; and (2) "A strong desire to be rid of one's primary and/or secondary sex characteristics because of a marked incongruence with one's experienced/expressed gender."[56] God's doing to Adam what he wanted to do to himself—banish his feminine characteristics—seems to indicate both of these criteria. So we believe that it is useful in consulting the *DSM-5* to speculate about the psychological issues that God would likely experience as being gender confused, such as feelings of isolation, low self-esteem, and suicidal ideation. Evidence of such feelings in God might be found in the following questions: *Is God's transcendence a manifestation of his feelings of isolation? Does God demand to be worshipped and exalted because of inner feelings of low self-esteem? And was Jesus's crucifixion a successful suicide attempt by God?* Other possible manifestations of God's psychological distress on account of his gender confusion will be explored below.

Exploring the Evidence

Masculine and Feminine Images for God

Whatever the specific psychological and social problems God would have encountered for having gynecomastia, they would have been exacerbated by the fact that human beings have used both masculine and feminine language for God. Along the same line of reasoning, Moore, as we noted,

55. *DSM-5*, 452–53.
56. Ibid., 452.

suggests that Yahweh was tempted to use steroids because the Egyptian gods were bigger than he was. This very well could be the case. But we also wonder if, once upon a time, human beings primarily imagined God as Creator (and therefore as Mother) so that God subsequently felt the need to prove his masculinity, so much so that he overcompensated by abusing steroids, which, in turn, had the unexpected consequence of gynecomastia. The point here is that God could have been confused by and uncomfortable with human beings using both male and female language for God *prior to* the condition of gynecomastia. Alternatively, maybe God encouraged both male and female language for God—an encouragement that could be representative of God's own gender confusion apart from, and also perhaps prior to, human representations of God; therefore the question arises, to what extent, if at all, was God gender confused before his development of breasts? In any case, the use of masculine and feminine imagery for God is surely significant in understanding the precise nature of God's gender confusion, even if it is not entirely knowable.

God's Sexual Orientation: A Gay God?

With all this discussion about God's gender, one might wonder about God's sexual orientation. We are not sure how much evidence there is in terms of God taking another god—male or female—as a sexual object. Indeed, as Eilberg-Schwartz observes, "The archaeological record suggests that many Israelites may have imagined the goddess Asherah to be a partner of Yahweh, but in the Hebrew Bible, and in the variety of Judaisms that flourished subsequently, Israel imagined God as having no sexual partners."[57] In contemporary America, though, an older man with no known sexual partners is often assumed to be gay. Could God be gay? In any case, in contrast to the absence of discussion of the sexual orientation of God the Father, we *do* have some scholarship on the question as to what kind of objects God the Son may have been attracted, and it is to this evidence that we now turn.[58]

---

57. Eilberg-Schwartz, *God's Phallus*, 4.

58. Based on his study of masculine images of God and their influence on attitudes toward same-sex unions, Andrew L. Whitehead concludes, "Individuals who view God as masculine are signaling a belief in an underlying gendered reality that influences their perceptions of the proper ordering of that reality." Thus, "gay men and lesbians are perceived as violating what many believe are the proper ways in which men and women should express themselves in society. A crucial component of the ordering

Portraits of Jesus's Sexuality:
WWJD—Who Would Jesus Do?[59]

Having referenced two books that deal with God's body and masculinity—one book (*God's Phallus*) being much more serious than the other
(*God's Gym*)—and having taken the less serious book (*God's Gym*) seriously by exploring what the psychological implications for God would
likely be, we are now in a position to turn to theology and to consider
how God's gender confusion became incarnate in Jesus. Moore, as noted,
suggests that God used Adam as a form of "therapy" in that, by splitting
Adam the androgyne in two, he did to Adam what he wanted to do to
himself: cut off his feminine parts. If this so-called therapy were successful, then we would expect that God the Father's gender confusion im-
pacted God the Son (as incarnate in Jesus Christ) in no way whatsoever.
But since, as we noted, masculine and feminine imagery for God's person
is found throughout the Bible—indeed, even Jesus himself used feminine
imagery for himself in the Gospel of Luke (see, e.g., Luke 13:34)—there is
reason to suspect that the "therapy" was not fully successful.

We believe that the primary way that God's gender confusion manifested itself in Jesus was in Jesus's own bisexual confusion. We realize that
many think of Jesus as asexual or beyond sexuality, just like such persons
also often think that God is beyond gender. So it seems likely, then, that
suggesting that Jesus was bisexually confused will be an uphill battle for
many of our readers. Fortunately, however, there has been a significant

---

of reality and the proper roles for men and women appears to be the construction
of family life around marriage and to a lesser extent domestic partnerships. As attitudes toward same-sex unions continue to liberalize in the wider culture, continued
resistance to that liberalization could be found among those who maintain a view that
God is gendered masculine. This would be most important for attitudes toward same-
sex marriage, however. While individuals' masculine image of God influences their
views on same-sex civil unions . . . it exerts a much stronger effect on attitudes toward
same-sex marriage. Masculine images of God may thus prove to be one explanation
as to why religious individuals tend to oppose same-sex marriage much more strongly
compared to same-sex civil unions . . . No longer viewing God as a 'he' would not only
mean a shift in attitudes toward same-sex unions but also in how their own marriages,
society, or religious groups are ordered" (Whitehad, "'Male and Female *He* Created
Them,'" 492). This means, in effect, that "the gendered image of God measure is not
just an additional measure of gender traditionalism or religious belief, it is actually
a measure of the interrelated aspect of the social institutions of religion and gender"
(ibid.). In other words, gender itself is a social institution.

59. We are grateful to Jon Berquist for suggesting this section heading.

amount of scholarship on Jesus's sexuality, which Jeffrey Kripal explores in *The Serpent's Gift*.[60]

In his chapter titled "The Apocryphon of the Beloved," Kripal notes that in "gnostic literature, an *apocryphon* (literally, a 'hiding away' or 'concealing') is a secret teaching usually committed to a trusted disciple by Christ after his resurrection but before he ascends into heaven."[61] By titling his chapter "an apocryphon," Kripal notes that he intends to invoke the meanings of "hidden, secret, personal, revelatory, not quite 'right' or 'straight' (*ortho-dox*), maybe even a bit queer."[62] Kripal adds that what he is offering is not yet another historical Jesus but rather a *heretical* Jesus. About the latter component of his chapter title—"Beloved"—Kripal writes:

> The Gospel of John speaks rather teasingly of "the Beloved disciple whom Jesus loved" . . . But who was this Beloved; that is, what sort of person was the object of Jesus's most intimate and quite public love? The canonical gospels are not at all clear about this; indeed, the Gospel of John, although quite clear that Jesus had a lover, goes out of its way *not* to tell us the identity of the Beloved. This loud silence, as we shall see, is itself highly significant. Bisexual confusion, gender ambiguity, and erotic paradox are themselves a kind of answer to our riddle, to our own Apocryphon of the Beloved.[63]

Since we want to suggest that Jesus was bisexually confused, it is necessary to provide evidence that Jesus had both homoerotic and heteroerotic longings. Kripal provides evidence on both sides.

The Man Jesus Loved

Kripal is well aware of how Christians tend to desexualize love. One common move that we have heard preachers make over the years is that they like to suggest that *agape* in Greek connotes a spiritual and pure love—that is, a nonsexual love—whereas *eros* in Greek is sexual and lustful. But Kripal disabuses Christians of this assumption, declaring it to be "fantastically false," as *agape* in the New Testament is used for both

---

60. Kripal, *Serpent's Gift*.

61. Ibid., 29.

62. Ibid.

63. Ibid., 30.

sexual and spiritual love.[64] This common linguistic mistake alone should be enough to encourage reflection on Jesus's sexuality.

Kripal notes that many have implied or argued that Jesus's Beloved was a man. They include Bernard of Clairvaux, Aelred of Rievaulx, Christopher Marlowe, Jeremy Bentham, Georg Walther Groddeck, Morton Smith, John Boswell, Hugh Montefiore, Robert Goss, Mark Jordan, and Theodore Jennings.[65] So there is a long tradition of homoerotic readings of Jesus's Beloved. The texts most often cited in making this case, Kripal notes, include: Mark 10:17–22, where Jesus gazes at a man lovingly; Mark 14:13 / Luke 22:10, where Jesus instructs his disciples to follow a man carrying water (i.e., a man doing what would have been considered women's work); John 13:1–11, 21–26, where the Beloved lies at Jesus's breast; Matt 8:5–13, where Jesus heals the centurion's slave boy (and likely lover); and John 20:17, where Jesus won't let Mary touch him. There are other passages that have been read homoerotically but these are some of the most cited texts. Kripal realizes that it is unlikely that many traditional believers would be convinced by these interpretations of these Bible citations, and he realizes that these believers would likely continue to think that Jesus was asexual. However, if there is nothing sexual going on between Jesus and the Beloved disciple when they lie down together, then, as Dale Martin[66] asks, would we still be able to say the same thing if the Beloved disciple were a woman?[67] Kripal also "recognize[s] that such a reading must sound, at best, outrageous to the orthodox believer," and adds, "But consider, for a moment, the following thought experiment. Let us begin by imagining that: (1) there were men in first-century Palestine who sexually desired other men; (2) some of these men were Jewish; and (3) a few of these Jewish men were mystically inclined and tried to adapt their Jewish rituals and beliefs to fit their deepest desires."[68] Kripal goes on to ask how might such a man respond to the homoerotic and homophobic tendencies—these tendencies that were so eloquently and convincingly spelled out by Eilberg-Schwartz—within Jewish scriptures and culture? Kripal answers: "Such a first-century Jewish homoerotic mystic might do

64. Ibid., 44.

65. Ibid., 43.

66. See Martin, *Sex and the Single Savior*.

67. Kripal, *Serpent's Gift*, 45.

68. Ibid., 46.

exactly what the gospels have Jesus doing."[69] We would have, then, an explanation for why Jesus reclined and laid with his Beloved, for why he wants to instruct his male disciples naked and at midnight, for why he washes their feet, for why he wants them to eat his flesh—which, many have noted, can be read as fellatio—and for why he so often deconstructs the purity codes of his day. So Kripal gives several reasons as to why one ought to keep an open mind about homoerotic readings of the Beloved: Greek philology, specific readings of certain texts, and thought experiments. But the best reason, he believes, is "the striking realization that, once one adopts a homoerotic hermeneutic, *the pieces fit* . . . It is not, then, this or that piece of the hermeneutical puzzle, but rather *the whole picture* the puzzle forms when the pieces are put together with a coherent theory and set of disciplined readings."[70]

The Woman Jesus Loved

But could the Beloved of Jesus be a woman? One noncanonical text suggests that the Beloved was Mary Magdalene. In the canonical gospels, she is the first to witness Christ's resurrection and their interaction, Kripal notes, has an erotic charge.[71] The extracanonical literature, Kripal adds, consistently presents "this Mary as an inspired visionary, as a potent spiritual guide, as Jesus's intimate companion, even as the interpreter of his teaching."[72] And in the *Gospel of Philip* Jesus kisses Mary to make her capable of bearing offspring, which Kripal reads as displaced cunnilingus. In later writings—e.g., in the medieval Catharists and Albigensians—Mary is identified as Jesus's concubine and, Kripal notes, Martin Luther assumed a sexual relationship between Jesus and Mary![73]

"Given all this," Kripal writes, "can we say anything about the specific loves of the historical Jesus?"[74] Kripal suggests that it is more fruitful to say what we *cannot* say; that is, we don't know what the precise nature of Jesus's sexuality was, and we can't know if Jesus was attracted to men, to women, to both, or to neither. But what *is* certain is that early Christian

69. Ibid., 47.

70. Ibid., 45.

71. Ibid., 51; cf. John 20.

72. Ibid., 52.

73. Ibid., 52–53.

74. Ibid., 57.

communities imagined Jesus and his Beloved in different ways, and that they all fought for their own particular story. Peter won these battles, as it turned out, and so we have been given a Jesus stripped of his sexuality. Kripal writes, "Our beliefs, for better or for worse (often for worse, I think), thus follow closely on the heels of those who shouted down, threatened away, or simply destroyed the historical memories, sometimes even the bodies and persons, of the rest of us."[75]

Conclusions Concerning the Confusions: What a Friend We Have in Jesus

Jeffrey Kripal was clear that he was not offering another historical Jesus. But what if we did take the evidence that Kripal offered as an accurate portrait of Jesus? What if, in other words, many of the early traditions—taken together—could be considered accurate in that they are confused about Jesus's sexuality because Jesus himself was confused? This might explain why Jesus never said anything about heterosexual or homosexual practices; Jesus himself had not sorted out and deeply reflected upon his own variety of sexual longings. This would seem to make a kind of theological sense. Indeed, if God were gender confused, shouldn't we expect that Jesus had a variety of sexual longings, because, as the *DSM-IV-TR* states about Gender Identity Disorder, "for sexually mature individuals, the following specifiers may be noted on the individual's sexual orientation: Sexually Attracted to Males, Sexually Attracted to Females, Sexually Attracted to Both, and Sexually Attracted to Neither"?[76] It is significant to note that "Males with Gender Identity Disorder include substantial proportions with all four specifiers,"[77] because these are *exactly* the possibilities that Kripal raised with regard to Jesus's sexuality. The *DSM-IV-TR* also notes that "some males with Gender Identity Disorder resort to self-treatment with hormones and may very rarely perform their own castration or penectomy."[78] This may shed light on the fact that Jesus encouraged his disciples to become eunuchs for the kingdom of God (Matt 19:12) and also raises the question as to whether Jesus himself became a eunuch. The *DSM-IV-TR* further suggests that some men with Gender

75. Ibid., 50–51.
76. *DSM-IV-TR*, 578.
77. Ibid.
78. Ibid.

Identity Disorder engage in prostitution. Could this be one reason Jesus allegedly hung around prostitutes?[79] Was Jesus a male prostitute?

Thus far we have neglected another important theological possibility in light of the doctrine of the incarnation. If Jesus is God incarnate, and if the church is the body of Christ, what is the relationship between the church and God's gender confusion? We think the answer is obvious: God's own gender confusion is reflected in the current debates over sexuality in the church. Historically, it seems that the church has tried to suppress its own homosexual longings and, given the ongoing scandals in the church relating to sexuality in recent decades, this strategy has had its costs. Also, splitting the church is reminiscent of how God separated Eve from Adam, thereby institutionalizing patriarchy, which, we have come to see, was another form of bad therapy. If only God and the church could accept their own gender and sexual confusions, if only we could celebrate the variety of expressions of gender and sexuality, then maybe we could all be a little more healthy, a little more sane, a little more sexual, and a little more human. And here we are entirely serious. While much of our argument has been playful, we do think that the current debates over sexuality in the church are a manifestation of God's gender confusion, which we take to be a projection of our own confusions about gender and sexuality. Because we have made God in our own image, in accepting God's gender confusion we accept our own.

Perhaps we don't have enough biblical evidence to conclude that God is gender confused, and perhaps we have little reason to listen to Moore, despite the fact that we do have texts that suggest Adam was a male androgyne, and despite the fact that a theological argument could have been grounded in these sources and with the tools of a historian via Peter Brown[80] or Daniel Boyarin[81] rather than via Moore's inventive methods, which we have favored. Or we could have reported on Diana Swancutt's essay that shows how contemporary exegetes—Richard Hays and Robert Gagnon—have anachronistically read the modern medical assumption of two genetic sexes into Paul, and how Paul, when he says that there is no longer male or female but that all are one in Christ, is advocating a one-sex, one-body, multigender model in Christ, who is the new androgynous Adam.[82] We have chosen to play with some books over others, perhaps arbitrarily.

79. See Schaberg, *Resurrection of Mary Magdalene.*

80. Brown, *Body and Society.*

81. Boyarin, *Carnal Israel.*

82. Swancutt, "Sexing the Pauline Body of Christ."

In any case, if it is true that God has been confused about gender, maybe we can then feel free to give up our own certainty around gender and won't have, therefore, any need to regulate it. And if it is true that God attempted to deal with his own gender confusion by doing to Adam what he wanted to do to himself, then maybe we can learn from God's mistakes and be wary of any justifications, no matter how sacred to religious or psychological communities, for banishing the feminine. In their own way, this is precisely what Eilberg-Schwartz, Moore, and Kripal are arguing: that the Judeo-Christian orthodoxies of gender and sexuality have been and are still problematic for women and men, and that this is so for men has only come to the attention of religious studies scholars in recent years. A lesson that we hope boys and men could take from this scholarship is that they might learn to be comfortable in their own bodies. And if they become comfortable enough, there won't be any temptation to use steroids as Yahweh did. And if the Egyptian gods are bigger, so be it, because boys and men in the church would be so comfortable in their own gender confusions and in their varieties of sexualities that they could teach God a thing or two; or, if they are able to empathize with God and his own gender confusion, maybe then men who are gender confused and men who need to be confused about gender would find out just what a friend we do have in Jesus, the most special of all friends.[83]

And so we come back, full circle, to a central theme in chapter 1, namely, that friendship may itself be a form of sublimation. And perhaps there is no better way to conclude this study of the gift of sublimation than by observing that the friend we have in Jesus is especially noteworthy for his faithfulness. As the hymn "What a Friend We Have in Jesus" asks: "Can we find a friend so faithful, / Who will all our sorrows share?" The answer, of course, is no. In fact, he is the one to whom we may turn when other friends "despise" and "forsake" us, for in such times of betrayal, "In his arms he'll take and shield thee, / Thou wilt find a solace there."[84] And with this, we conclude our study of the gift of sublimation.

83. Cf. Dykstra, "Subversive Friendship"; Dykstra et al., *Faith and Friendships of Teenage Boys*, ch. 3.

84. Scriven, "Pray Without Ceasing." Joseph Scriven was born in Ireland. He wrote this poem in 1869, which was set to music a few years later by Charles C. Converse, an American lawyer and composer. Scriven's fiancée drowned the night before they were to be married. He immigrated to Canada shortly thereafter, in 1844. In Canada, he fell in love again. He was planning to get married, but his fiancée suddenly fell ill of tuberculosis. He himself drowned at the age of sixty-seven, when he became critically ill and, in a delirious state, got out of bed, went outdoors, and fell into a creek. See Christian Music, "What a Friend We Have in Jesus." Also see Capps, *Striking Out*, 81.

Bibliography

Agnes, Michael, ed. *Webster's New World College Dictionary*. 4th ed. Foster City, CA: IDG, 2001.

American Psychiatric Association. *Diagnostic and Statistical Manual of Mental Disorders*. 4th ed. Text revision. Washington DC: American Psychiatric Association, 2000.

———. *Diagnostic and Statistical Manual of Mental Disorders*. 5th ed. Arlington, VA: American Psychiatric Association, 2013.

Bakan, David. *Disease, Pain & Sacrifice: Toward a Psychology of Suffering*. Chicago: University of Chicago Press, 1968.

———. *The Duality of Human Existence: Isolation and Communion in Western Man*. Chicago: Rand McNally, 1966.

Barker-Benfield, G. J. *The Horrors of the Half-Known Life: Male Attitudes toward Women and Sexuality in Nineteenth-Century America*. New York: Harper & Row, 1976.

Bell, Alan P., and Martin S. Weinberg. *Homosexualities: A Study of Diversity among Men and Women*. New York: Simon & Schuster, 1978.

Bergeron, David M. *King James & Letters of Homoerotic Desire*. Iowa City: University of Iowa Press, 1999.

———. *Royal Family, Royal Lovers: King James of England and Scotland*. Columbia: University of Missouri Press, 1991.

Bettelheim, Bruno. *Symbolic Wounds: Puberty Rites and the Envious Male*. New rev. ed. New York: Collier, 1962.

Bigham, Thomas J. "Pastoral and Ethical Notes on Problems of Masturbation." *Pastoral Psychology* 11 (1960) 19–23.

Boucier, Elisabeth, ed. *The Diary of Sir Simonds D'Ewes (1622–1624)*. Publications de la Sorbonne. Littératures 5. Paris: Didier, 1974.

Boyarin, Daniel. *Carnal Israel: Reading Sex in Talmudic Culture*. Berkeley: University of California Press, 1993.

Breuer, Josef, and Sigmund Freud. *Studies on Hysteria*. Translated and edited by James Strachey. New York: Basic Books, 1957.

Brown, Peter. *The Body and Society: Men, Women, and Sexual Renunciation in Early Christianity*. Lectures on the History of Religions, new series 13. New York: Columbia University Press, 1988.

Capps, Donald. *Deadly Sins and Saving Virtues*. 1987. Reprinted, Eugene, OR: Wipf & Stock, 2000.

———. *Giving Counsel: A Minister's Guidebook*. St. Louis: Chalice, 2001.

———. *Jesus: A Psychological Biography*. 2000. Reprinted, Eugene, OR: Wipf & Stock, 2010.

———. *Men and Their Religion: Honor, Hope, and Humor*. Harrisburg, PA: Trinity, 2002.

———. *Striking Out: The Religious Journey of Teenage Boys*. Eugene, OR: Cascade Books, 2011.

———. "Teenage Girls in Rural New York: A Case of Conversion Disorder." *Pastoral Psychology* 64 (2015) 1–19.

Capps, Donald, and Nathan Carlin. *Living in Limbo: Life in the Midst of Uncertainty*. Eugene, OR: Cascade Books, 2010.

———. "Sublimation and Symbolization: The Case of Dental Anxiety and the Symbolic Meaning of Teeth." *Pastoral Psychology* 60 (2011) 773–89.

Carlin, Nathan. "From Grace *Alone* to *Grace* Alone: Male Body Image and Intimacy at Princeton Seminary." *Pastoral Psychology* 56 (2008) 269–93.

Carlin, Nathan, and Donald Capps. "Freud's Wolf Man: A Case of Successful Sublimation." *Pastoral Psychology* 60 (2011) 149–66.

———. *100 Years of Happiness: Insights and Findings from the Experts*. Psychology, Religion, and Spirituality. Santa Barbara, CA: Praeger, 2012.

Chaucer, Geoffrey. *Canterbury Tales*. Translated by Nevill Coghill. London: Penguin, 2003.

Christian Music. "What a Friend We Have in Jesus." http://christianmusic.suite101.com/article.cfm/what_a_friend_we_have_in_jesus/.

Cohen, Ed. *Talk on the Wilde Side: Towards a Genealogy of a Discourse on Male Sexualities*. New York: Routledge, 1993.

Cole, Thomas R. *The Journey of Life: A Cultural History of Aging in America*. Cambridge: Cambridge University Press, 1992.

Cole, Thomas R., and Mary G. Winkler, eds. *The Oxford Book of Aging: Reflections on the Journey of Life*. New York: Oxford University Press, 1994.

Coleman, Daniel. "Some Therapists Say a Single Session May Be Enough." Health. *New York Times*, May 2, 1991. http://www.nytimes.com/1991/05/02/health/therapists-say-a-single-session-may-be-enough.html/.

Cominos, Peter. "Late-Victorian Sexual Respectability and the Social System." *International Review of Social History* 8 (1963) 18–48, 216–50.

Connell, R. W. *Masculinities*. 2nd ed. Berkeley: University of California Press, 2005.

Coriat, Isador H. *Repressed Emotions*. New York: Brentano's, 1920.

———. *What Is Psychoanalysis?* New York: Moffat, Yard, 1917.

Coston, Stephen A. *King James the VI of Scotland & the I of England: Unjustly Accused*. St. Petersburg, FL: KonigsWort, 1996.

Culbertson, Philip L. *Counseling Men*. Creative Pastoral Care and Counseling Series. Minneapolis: Fortress, 1994.

Daly, Mary. *Beyond God the Father: Toward a Philosophy of Women's Liberation*. Boston: Beacon, 1973.

Dittes, James E. *Driven by Hope: Men and Meaning.* Louisville: Westminster John Knox, 1996.

Dykstra, Robert. "Subversive Friendship." *Pastoral Psychology* 58 (2009) 579–601.

Dykstra, Robert et al. *The Faith and Friendships of Teenage Boys.* Louisville: Westminster John Knox, 2012.

Eilberg-Schwartz, Howard. *God's Phallus and Other Problems for Men and Monotheism.* Boston: Beacon, 1994.

Engelhardt, H., Tristram, Jr. "The Disease of Masturbation: Values and the Concept of Disease." *Bulletin of the History of Medicine* 48 (1974) 234–48.

Erikson, Erik H. *Identity: Youth and Crisis.* New York: Norton, 1968.

———. *Toys and Reasons: Stages in the Ritualization of Experience.* New York: Norton, 1977.

———. *Young Man Luther: A Study in Psychoanalysis and History.* New York: Norton, 1958.

Fairlie, Henry. *The Seven Deadly Sins Today.* Notre Dame, IN: University of Notre Dame Press, 1979.

Fausto-Sterling, Anne. "The Five Sexes: Why Male and Female Are Not Enough." *The Sciences* (April 1993) 20–24.

Festinger, Leon, and Daniel Katz. *Research Methods in the Behavioral Sciences.* New York: Dryden, 1953.

Freud, Sigmund. *An Autobiographical Study.* Edited and translated by James Strachey. New York: Norton, 1952.

———. *Civilization and Its Discontents.* Edited and translated by James Strachey. New York: Norton, 1961.

———. *The Ego and the Id.* Translated by Joan Riviere. New York: Norton, 1962.

———. *Five Lectures on Psycho-Analysis.* Edited and translated by James Strachey. New York: Norton, 1989.

———. *Group Psychology and the Analysis of the Ego.* Edited and translated by James Strachey. A Bantam Classic. New York: Bantam, 1960.

———. *The History of an Infantile Neurosis, and Other Works*, 1–123, edited by James Strachey and Anna Freud. The Standard Edition of the Complete Psychological Works of Sigmund Freud 17. London: Vintage, 2001.

———. *The Interpretation of Dreams.* Edited and translated by James Strachey. Discus Books. New York: Avon, 1965.

———. *Introductory Lectures on Psycho-Analysis.* Edited and translated by James Strachey. New York: Norton, 1966.

———. *Leonardo da Vinci: A Study in Psychosexuality.* Translated by Abraham A. Brill. New York: Random House, 1947.

———. *Moses and Monotheism.* Translated by Katherine Jones. New York: Vintage, 1939.

———. "The Moses of Michelangelo." In *Totem and Taboo, and Other Works*, 209–38, edited by James Strachey. The Standard Edition of the Complete Psychological Works of Sigmund Freud 13. London: Vintage, 2001.

———. *New Introductory Lectures on Psycho-analysis.* Translated and edited by James Strachey. The Standard Edition of the Complete Psychological Works of Sigmund Freud 22. New York: Norton, 1989.

———. "Thoughts for the Times upon War and Death." In *On Creativity and the Unconscious*, selected, with an introduction and annotations by Benjamin Nelson, 206–35. Harper Torchbooks. New York: Harper, 1958.

———. *Three Essays on the Theory of Sexuality*. Translated and edited by James Strachey. New York: Basic, 2000.

Gay, Peter. *Freud: A Life for Our Time*. New York: Norton, 1988.

Gay, Volney P. *Freud on Sublimation: Reconsiderations*. SUNY Series in Religious Studies. Albany: State University of New York Press, 1992.

Glesne, David N. *Understanding Homosexuality: Perspectives for the Local Church*. Minneapolis: Kirk House, 2004.

Graham, Wendy. *Henry James's Thwarted Love*. Stanford: Stanford University Press, 1999.

Green, Michael et al. *The Church and Homosexuality*. London: Hodder & Stoughton, 1980.

Hale, Nathan G., Jr. *Freud and the Americans: The Beginnings of Psychoanalysis in the United States*. Vol. 1, *The Beginning of Psychoanalysis in the United States, 1876–1917*. New York: Oxford University Press, 1971.

———. *James Jackson Putnam and Psychoanalysis: Letters between Putnam and Sigmund Freud, Ernest Jones, William James, Sandor Ferenczi, and Morton Prince, 1877–1917*. Cambridge: Harvard University Press, 1971.

Hall, G. Stanley. *Adolescence: Its Psychology and Its Relations to Physiology, Anthropology, Sociology, Sex, Crime, Religion, and Education*. 2 vols. New York: Appleton, 1904.

———. *Jesus, the Christ, in the Light of Psychology*. 2 vols. New York: Doubleday, Page, 1917.

———. "Some Fundamental Principles of Sunday School and Bible Teaching." *Pedagogical Seminary* 8 (1901) 439–68.

———. "The Moral and Religious Training of Children." *The Princeton Review* 9 (1882) 26–48.

———. "The Religious Content of the Child-Mind." In *Principles of Religious Education*, edited by N. M. Butler et al., 161–89. New York: Longmans, Green, 1900.

Hare, E. H. "Masturbatory Insanity: The History of an Idea." *Journal of Mental Science* 108 (1962) 1–25.

Haynes, Timothy. "Surgical Treatment of Hopeless Cases of Masturbation and Nocturnal Emissions." *Boston Medical and Surgical Journal* 109 (1883) 130.

The Holy Bible. (King James Version). New York: American Bible Society, 1978.

The Holy Bible (Revised Standard Version). New York: Nelson, 1952.

Hood, Ralph W. "When the Spirit Maims and Kills: Social Psychological Considerations of the History of Serpent Handling Sects and the Narrative of Handlers." *International Journal for the Psychology of Religion* 8/2 (1998) 71–96.

James, William. "A Suggestion about Mysticism." *Journal of Philosophy, Psychology, and Scientific Method* 7 (1910) 85–92.

———. *The Varieties of Religious Experience*. Mineola, NY: Dover, 2002.

Jordan, Mark D. *The Silence of Sodom: Homosexuality in Modern Catholicism*. Chicago: University of Chicago Press, 2000.

Kant, Immanuel. *Lectures on Ethics*. Translated by Louis Infield. The Library of Religion and Culture. Harper Torchbooks. New York: Harper & Row, 1963.

Kaplan, Abraham. *The Conduct of Inquiry: Methodology for Behavioral Science*. Chandler Publications in Anthropology and Sociology. San Francisco: Chandler, 1964.

Kinsey, Alfred Charles et al. *Sexual Behavior in the Human Male*. Philadelphia: Saunders, 1948.

Klasen, Stephan, and Claudia Wink. "'Missing Women': Revisiting the Debate." *Feminist Economics* 9 (2003) 263–99.

Kripal, Jeffrey J. *Roads of Excess, Palaces of Wisdom: Eroticism & Reflexivity in the Study of Mysticism*. Chicago: University of Chicago Press, 2001.

———. *The Serpent's Gift: Gnostic Reflections on the Study of Religion*. Chicago: University of Chicago Press, 2007.

Le Bourg, Eric et al. "Reproductive Life of French-Canadians in the 17th-18th Centuries: A Search for a Trade-off Between Early Fecundity and Longevity." *Experimental Gerontology* 28 (1993) 217–32.

Lewis, R. W. B. *The Jameses: A Family Narrative*. New York: Farrar, Straus & Giroux, 1991.

Loder, James E. *The Logic of the Spirit: Human Development in Theological Perspective*. San Francisco: Jossey-Bass, 1998.

Lyman, Stanford M. *The Seven Deadly Sins: Society and Evil*. New York: St. Martin's, 1978.

Martin, Dale B. *Sex and the Single Savior: Gender and Sexuality in Biblical Interpretation*. Louisville: Westminster John Knox, 2006.

Masters, William H., and Virginia E. Johnson. *Human Sexual Inadequacy*. Boston: Little, Brown, 1970.

Masters, William H., and Virginia E. Johnson, in collaboration with the Reproductive Biology Research Foundation. *Human Sexual Response*. Boston: Little, Brown, 1966.

McElwee, William. *The Wisest Fool in Christendom: The Reign of King James I and VI*. New York: Harcourt Brace, 1958.

McGrath, Alister. *In the Beginning: The Story of the King James Bible and How It Changed a Nation*. New York: Anchor, 2001.

Menninger, Karl. *Man against Himself*. New York: Harcourt Brace, 1938.

———. *Whatever Became of Sin?* New York: Hawthorn, 1973.

Meyer, Monroe A. Review of Ernest Jones, *Papers on Psychoanalysis*, 3rd. ed., *Mental Hygiene* 8 (January 1924) 266–67.

Moore, Stephen D. *God's Gym: Divine Male Bodies of the Bible*. New York: Routledge, 1996.

Müller, Hans-Georg et al. "Fertility and Life Span: Late Children Enhance Female Longevity." *Journal of Gerontology: Biomedical Sciences* 57A/3 (2002) B202–B206.

Olshansky, S. Jay et al. "In Search of Methuselah: Estimating the Upper Limits of Human Longevity." *Science* 250 (1990) 634–40.

Osherson, Samuel. *Finding Our Fathers: How a Man's Life is Shaped by His Relationship with His Father*. New York: Fawcett Columbine, 1986.

Otto, Rudolf. *The Idea of the Holy: An Inquiry into the Non-rational Factor in the Idea of the Divine and Its Relation to the Rational*. Translated by John W. Harvey. London: Oxford University Press, 1923.

Pattison, E. Mansell. "Confusing Concepts about the Concept of Homosexuality." *Psychiatry* 37 (1974) 340–49.

Pattison, E. Mansell, and Myrna Lloyd Pattison. "'Ex-gays': Religiously Mediated Change in Homosexuals." *American Journal of Psychiatry* 137 (1980) 1553–62.

Perry, Ralph Barton. *The Thought and Character of William James.* 2 vols. Boston: Little, Brown, 1935.

Pfister, Oskar. *Christianity and Fear: A Study in History and in the Psychology and Hygiene of Religion.* Translated by W. H. Johnston. London: Allen & Unwin, 1948.

Pittman, Frank S. *Man Enough: Fathers, Sons, and the Search for Masculinity.* New York: Berkeley, 1993.

Pollack, William. *Real Boys: Rescuing Our Sons from the Myths of Boyhood.* New York: Random House, 1998.

Pope, B. A. "Opium as a Tonic and Alterative; With Remarks upon the Hypodermic Use of the Sulphate of Morphia, and Its Use in the Debility and Amorosis Consequent upon Onanism." *New Orleans Medical and Surgical Journal* 6 (1879) 724–25.

Prochnik, George. *Putnam Camp: Sigmund Freud, James Jackson Putnam, and the Purpose of American Psychology.* New York: Other Press, 2006.

Putnam, James Jackson. *Human Motives.* Mind and Health Series. New York: Little, Brown, 1915.

Rank, Otto. *Der Künstler, Ansätze zu einer Sexual-Psychologie.* Vienna: Internationaler Psychoanalytischer Verlag, 1907.

Rennison, Nick. *Freud & Psychoanalysis.* Pocket Essential. Hapenden, UK: Pocket Essentials, 2001.

Rocke, Michael. *Forbidden Friendships: Homosexuality and Male Culture in Renaissance Florence.* Studies in the History of Sexuality. New York: Oxford University Press, 1996.

Rosenberg, Charles. "Sexuality, Class and Role in 19th-Century America." *American Quarterly* 25 (1973) 131–53.

Rosenzweig, Saul. *The Historic Expedition to America (1909): Freud, Jung, and Hall the King-maker.* 2nd rev. ed. St. Louis: Rana House, 1994.

Saghir, Marcel T., and Eli Robins. *Male and Female Homosexuality: A Complete Investigation.* Baltimore: Williams & Wilkins, 1973.

Saraglou, Vassilis, and Jean-Marie Jaspard. "Does Religion Affect Humor Creation? An Experimental Study." *Mental Health, Religion & Culture* 4/1 (2001) 33–46.

Schaberg, Jane. *The Resurrection of Mary Magdalene: Legends, Apocrypha, and the Christian Testament.* New York: Continuum, 2004.

Sen, Amartya. "More Than 100 Million Women are Missing." *New York Review of Books* 37 (1990) 1–12. http://www.nybooks.com/articles/archives/1990/dec/20/more-than-100-million-women-are-missing/.

Simon, Linda. *Genuine Reality: A Life of William James.* New York: Harcourt Brace, 1998.

Snow, Vernon F. *Essex the Rebel: The Life of Robert Devereux, the Third Earl of Essex 1591–1646.* Lincoln: University of Nebraska Press, 1970.

Stapleton, Ruth Carter. "God Gave Man a Variety of 'Gifts.'" *Atlanta Journal*, January 23, 1979, 9.

Strout, Cushing. "William James and the Twice-Born Sick-Soul." In *Philosophers and Kings: Studies in Leadership,* edited by Dankwart A. Rustow, 1062–81. The Daedalus Library. New York: Braziller, 1970.

Sullivan, Andrew. "Log Cabin Republican: How Gay Was Lincoln?" *The New Republic*, January 10, 2005.

———. *Love Undetectable: Notes on Friendship, Sex, and Survival.* New York: Vintage, 1999.

Sullivan, Harry Stack. *Conceptions of Modern Psychiatry*. William Alanson White Memorial Lectures 1. New York: Norton, 1953.

Swancutt, Diana M. "Sexing the Pauline Body of Christ: Scriptural Sex in the Context of American Culture War." In *Toward a Theology of Eros: Transfiguring Passion at the Limits of Discipline*, edited by Virginia Burris and Catherine Keller, 65–98. Transdisciplinary Theological Colloquia. New York: Fordham University Press, 2006.

Szasz, Thomas. "Remembering Masturbatory Insanity." *Ideas on Liberty* 50 (May 2000) 35–36.

———. *The Therapeutic State: Psychiatry in the Mirror of Current Events*. Buffalo: Prometheus, 1984.

Tissot, Samuel. *A Treatise on the Diseases Produced by Onanism*. New York: Collins & Hannay, 1832. https://archive.org/details/57110430R.nlm.nih.gov/.

Townsend, Kim. *Manhood at Harvard: William James and Others*. New York: Norton, 1996.

Tripp, C. A. *The Intimate World of Abraham Lincoln*. Edited by Lewis Gannett. New York: Free Press, 2005.

Troiden, Richard R. "Becoming Homosexual: A Model of Gay Identity Acquisition." *Psychiatry* 42 (1979) 362–73.

Van Aarde, Andries G. "Social Identity, Status Envy, and Jesus' Abba." *Pastoral Psychology* 45 (1997) 451–72.

Waehler, Charles A. *Bachelors: The Psychology of Men Who Haven't Married*. Westport, CT: Praeger, 1996.

Weatherhead, Leslie D. *The Mastery of Sex through Psychology and Religion*. New York: Macmillan, 1947.

West, D. J. *Homosexuality Re-examined*. 4th ed. London: Duckworth, 1977.

Whitehead, Andrew L. "Male and Female He Created Them: Gender Traditionalism, Masculine Images of God, and Attitudes toward Same-Sex Unions." *Journal for the Scientific Study of Religion* 53 (2014) 479–96.

Wieland, Carl. "Living for 900 Years." *Creation* 20 (1998) 10–19. http://creation.com/living-for-900-years/.

Wiesman, Irvin M. et al. "Gynecomastia: An Outcome Analysis." *Annals of Plastic Surgery* 53 (2004) 97–101.

Wikipedia. "Joseph M. Scriven." http://en.wikipedia.org/wiki/Joseph_M._Scriven/.

Wilson, Ian et al. "The Validity of the Diagnosis of Gender Identity Disorder (Childhood and Adolescent Criteria)." *Clinical Child Psychology and Psychiatry* 7 (2002) 335–51.

Winnicott, D. W. *Home Is Where We Start From: Essays by a Psychoanalyst*. Edited by Clare Winnicott et al. New York: Norton, 1986.

———. *Playing and Reality*. London: Tavistock, 1971.

Wood, Robert W. *Christ and the Homosexual: Some Observations*. New York: Vantage, 1960.

Worchester, Elwood et al. *Religion and Medicine: The Moral Control of Nervous Disorders*. New York: Moffat, Yard, 1908.

Young, Michael B. *King James and the History of Homosexuality*. New York: New York University Press, 2000.

Index

www.ingramcontent.com/pod-product-compliance
Lightning Source LLC
Chambersburg PA
CBHW030829270326
41928CB00007B/972

9 781498 203012